S0-BQX-403

The Blue Guides

Prague

Michael Jacobs

BLUE GUIDE

A&C Black • London
WW Norton • New York

1st edition © Michael Jacobs, 1999
Published by A & C Black (Publishers) Limited
35 Bedford Row, London WC1R 4JH

Maps and plans drawn by Robert Smith, RJS Associates, © A&C Black

Illustrations © Jim Urquhart

A CIP catalogue record of this book is available from the British Library.

ISBN 0–7136–4428–1

Published in the United States of America by
WW Norton and Company Inc.
500 Fifth Avenue, New York, NY 10110

Published simultaneously in Canada by
Penguin Books Canada Limited
10 Alcorn Avenue, Toronto
Ontario M4V 3B2

ISBN 0–393–31933–4 USA

Cover photograph: detail of Mucha's windows in Prague cathedral.
Title page: view of Our Lady Before Týn.

Michael Jacobs studied at the Courtauld Institute of Art, where he received a Ph.D in 1982 for his researches into eighteenth-century Italian art. A full-time author and translator of Spanish and Latin American drama, he has written numerous books on art and travel, including *The Phaidon Companion to Art and Artists in the British Isles* (1980, with Malcolm Warner), *The Good and Simple Life: Artist Colonies in Europe and America* (1991), *A Guide to Provence* (1990). *Santiago de Compostela* (1991), *Between Hopes and Memories : A Spanish Journey* (1994), *The Painted Voyage: Art Travel And Exploration, 1564-1875* (1995), *Madrid Observed* (1997), *Andalucia* (1990; revised 1998) and *Budapest: A Cultural Guide* (1998). He is currently senior honorary research fellow in the Hispanics department at Glasgow University. He is also the author of the *Blue Guide Barcelona* and *Blue Guide Czech and Slovak Republics*.

Printed and bound in England by Butler & Tanner Ltd., Frome and London.

Preface

The dramatic opening up of Prague after the fall of communism in 1989 has helped to emphasise that this is not simply a city of haunting and mysterious beauty but also a place whose cultural complexity is virtually unrivalled for somewhere of its size. Visiting Prague as an impressionable schoolboy in the sad aftermath to 1968, it was easy for me to perceive the city essentially in terms of Kafka, magic, dark medieval alleys, shrieking gables and blackened gothic spires with crow-like turrets. Coming here instead today, the visitor is more likely to be confronted with images of colour, light and *fin-de-siècle* elegance. Garish wide-spread restoration, the renewal of grand turn-of-the-century hotels and cafés, and promotional campaigns stressing Prague as the city of Mozart and Mucha, may have cheapened the city's appeal, and turned much of it into a pastel-coloured Disneyland; but they have shown as well how this city so rich in fantastical medieval and Renaissance monuments is also a place that has contributed enormously to the flowering of the Baroque, Rococo and Art Nouveau. In recent years there also been a growing awareness of Prague's major role in the history of early 20th century modernism: the city's 'Cubist' buildings, together with the idiosyncratic structures of Jože Plečník, have come to aquire a cult following, while the recent re-opening of the Trade Fair Palace as a museum of modern art has done much to highlight both the sheer originality of Czech art between the wars and the stunning beauty of Functionalist architecture in its pioneering phase.

Ten years ago, when I first began visiting Prague on a more regular basis, there was hardly a single guide-book in English on the place; since then more guide-books have appeared on Prague than on almost any other European city, including Paris and Barcelona (no fewer than twenty-three were on sale in 1998 in London's Traveller's Bookshop). The excuse for this present one, the first to Prague in the Blue Guide series, is the continuing lack of a book that is both a comprehensive guide to the city's sights as well as a cultural companion to a place whose artistic, architectural and literary history remains comparatively little known outside the Czech Republic, despite the thousands of new visitors. Apart from renewing my thanks to all those who assisted me in Prague when I was researching what has now now become the *Blue Guide to the Czech and Slovak Republics*, I would like to acknowledge the pleasure I have had when visiting the city in the company of Julia Borbély, John and Kathy Elgin, Cyril and Mary Iles, Jana Kieli, Jim Urquhart, Tony Worcester, and, above all, Jackie Rae. Suzana Dancak from London's Czech Tourist Centre has been unfailingly helpful, while Adam Yamey provided detailed notes that were invaluable to me while preparing the essay on Music in Prague. My thanks also to my agent David Godwin, to Silvie Reková and Martin Tomášek of Tom's Travel, to Michal Kodicek of the Czechbook Agency, and, of course, to the staff at A&C Black, in particular my patient editors Gemma Davies and Judy Tither.

Contents

Prague ~ The Guide

Maps and plans

Practical information

by Clare de Vries

Planning your trip

When to go

Prague's climate is typically continental, with warm summers and cold winters, and the best time to visit is either in spring or autumn. Spring can sometimes not show at all, but is the best season when it does. Average temperatures in March are between 1 and 7°C and in April and May between 9 and 15°C. Summer, when the average temperature is between 14 and 24°C, sees Prague abandoned to tourists and very crowded. Autumn is a close contender with spring for prettiness, with crisp air, clear skies and an average temperature between 6 and 15°C. Winter is long, cold and grey, and many shops and restaurants are shut, but the romance of Christmas helps break it up. When it snows, Prague is charming, but the smog from coal heating is often bad. Average winter temperatures are between -4 and 3°C.

Passports and formalities

Visitors from the US, the EC and most other European countries do not need a visa to enter the Czech Republic but do need a valid passport, with eight months to spare by the end of the visit. Canadians and New Zealanders no longer require a visa, but Australians do, although now it costs nothing. Visitors from elsewhere need a visa from their local Czech embassy. Visas are also obtainable at three border crossings, at Waidhaus–Rosvadov, Wullowitz–Dolní Dvořiště and Klein Haugsdorf–Hatě, and at Prague's Ruzyně airport. For visa information once in Prague, ☎ (02) 61 44 11 19.

British, Canadian and Slovakian nationals can stay for up to 180 days; New Zealanders, Irish, and other EC nationals for up to 90 days; and Americans for up to 30 days. If you wish to stay longer than your visa or visa-free period allows, you will need an extension which can be obtained from the Foreigners' Police Headquarters (Úřadovna cizinecké policie) at Olšanská 2, Žižkov, Prague 3, ☎ (02) 614 412 20. These visas are very difficult to obtain unless you have a job lined up. Many people avoid the issue by leaving the country for a few days. If you do this, make sure you get your passport stamped.

Technically you are meant to register with the local police within 30 days of arrival in Prague—hotels will do this for you—but many visitors do not bother.

National Tourist Boards

UK. Czech Tourist Authority, 95 Great Portland St, London W1N 5RA. ☎ (0171) 291 9920, fax: (0171) 436 8300. Open Mon–Fri 10.00–18.00. The Authority will send out free of charge tourist brochures on all regions in the Czech Republic, national accommodation details, road maps and advice for motorists, lists of campsites, listings of cultural events in Prague and other regions and information on tour operators and travel agents from the UK to the Czech Republic (send a stamped and self-addressed envelope).

Czech and Slovak Tourist Centre, 16 Frognal Parade, Finchley Road,

London NW3 5HG. ☎ (0171) 794 3263/3264, fax: (0171) 794 3265; free call: 0800 026 7943; website: www.czech-slovak-tourist.co.uk; email: cztc@cztc.demon.co.uk. This is a tour operator for the whole Czech Republic, with information on everything except timetables for trains, which change constantly. It can help you with many enquiries, whether it be printing opera tickets or organising your wedding ceremony.

US. Czech Cultural Centre, 1109 Madison Avenue, New York, NY 10028. ☎ (212) 288 0830, fax: (212) 772 0586 or 3200 Linnean Ave NW, Washington DC 20008. ☎ (202) 363 6315. Open Tues–Fri 09.00–17.00. The Centre has information on all subjects.

Canada. Czech Tourist Authority, 130 King St W, Suite 715, Exchange Tower, Box 198, Toronto, Ontario, M5X 1A6. ☎ (416) 367 3432, fax: (416) 367 3492.

When planning your trip, the following **websites** have plenty of information on every aspect of life in Prague:

The Czech Tourism Pages, www.infotec-travel.com/CZGENERA.html
The Czech Info Centre, www.muselik.com/czech/
Czech Days, www.netlink.co.uk/users/webman/czech/
Czech Republic, www.czech.cz/

Tour operators and travel agents

UK. Martin Randall Travel, 10 Barley Mow Passage, London W4 4PH. ☎ (0181) 742 3355, fax: 0181 742 7766. Upmarket art and architecture tours.
Bohemian Promotions, 61 Mere Road, Erdington, Birmingham B23 7LL. ☎ and fax: (0121) 373 9107.
Czechbook Agency, Jopes Mill, Trebrownbridge, near Liskeard, Cornwall PL14 3PX. ☎ and fax: (01503) 240 629.
Czech and Slovak Tourist Centre Ltd, 16 Frognal Parade, London NW3 5GH. ☎ (0171) 794 3263, fax: (0171) 794 3265.
Czech Travel Ltd, 1 Trinity Square, South Woodham Ferrers, Essex CM3 5JX. ☎ (01245) 328 647, fax: (01245) 322 407.
Čedok Travel Ltd, 53–54 Haymarket, London SW1Y 4RP. ☎ (0171) 839 4414, fax: (0171) 839 0204.
  Ireland. Thomas Cook, 11 Donegall Place, Belfast BT1 5AJ. ☎ (01232) 554 455, fax (01232) 550 029.
Thomas Cook, 118 Grafton St, Dublin. ☎ (1) 677 1721, fax (1) 677 1258. Website: www.thmoascook.co.uk
Joe Walsh Tours, 8–11 Baggot St, Dublin. ☎ (1) 676 8915, fax (1) 676 6572.
Budget Travel, 134 Lower Baggot St, Dublin. ☎ (1) 661 1866, fax (1) 662 9388.
  US. Abercrombie & Kent, 1520 Kensington Road, Suite 212, Oak Brook, IL 60521-2141.☎ (630) 954 2944/800 323 7308, fax: (630) 954 3324, website: www.abercrombiekent.com. Deluxe tours.
Czech and Slovak Travel Service, 7033 Sunset Boulevard, Suite 210, LA, CA 90028. ☎ (213) 389 2157.
Travcoa, Box 2630, 2350 SE Bristol St, Newport Beach, CA 92660. ☎ (714) 476 2800/800 992 2003, fax: (714) 476 2538.
Maupintour, Box 807, 1515 St Andrews Drive, Lawrence, KS 66047. ☎ (785) 843 1211/800 255 4266, fax: (785) 843 8351.

ČEDOK, 10 East 40th St, Suite 3601, New York, NY 10016. ☎ (212) 689 9720, fax: (212) 213 4461, email: viktul@aol.com. Open Mon–Fri 09.00–17.00. **Fugazy International**, 770 US-1 North Brunswick, NJ 08902. ☎ (800)828 4488.

Getting to Prague

By air

Several airlines fly to Prague **from the UK** at least once a day. **British Airways**, ☎ (0345) 222 111, website: www.british-airways.com and **British Midland**, ☎ (0345) 554 554, website: www.iflybritishmidland.com depart from Heathrow twice daily. **Czech Airlines** (České aerolinie or ČSA), 72-73 Margaret St, London W1N 8HA, ☎ (0171) 255 1898, website: www.csa.cz departs from Heathrow twice daily and also from Stansted (daily except Sat) and Manchester (daily except Sun). Flights take 2 hours. A return flight by British Midland currently costs £185 for travel during the week and £205 at the weekends. British Airways costs £205 mid-week and £16 extra at weekends. Czech Airlines costs £195 in the low season and £310 in the high season.

Details of discount flights are available from the Sunday papers and from specialist agents: **Campus Travel**, 52 Grosvenor Gardens, London SW1W 0AG. ☎ (0171) 730 3402. **STA Travel**, 86 Old Brompton Road, London SW7 3LQ. ☎ (0171) 581 4132.

There are no direct flights to Prague from **Ireland**. Flying via London is the easiest way, and **Aer Lingus**, ☎ (0645) 737 747 (Dublin ☎ (1) 844 4777), **Ryanair**, ☎ (1) 844 4777 (Dublin ☎ (1) 677 4422) and British Midland fly to London daily. Return flights to Luton or Stansted with Ryanair cost IR£60. Flights with Aer Lingus and British Midland are a little more expensive at IR£75, but fly direct to Heathrow, saving you time. Flights from Belfast to London on British Airways cost £95. Good deals and packages are available from several travel agents (see above).

To those travelling **from the US**, all the major airlines offer plenty of flights from plenty of airports, but **ČSA** (Czech Airlines), ☎ (212) 765 6022/6545, website: www.csa.cz, is the only non-stop carrier from the States, departing from New York and Chicago. All others make stopovers in Europe. Flights from New York take 9–10 hours and from Los Angeles 16 hours.

The cheapest flights can be bought from specialist agents, but these allow little flexibility, and the same applies to charter flights. Fares always depend on the season—the high season is the summer and around Christmas and Easter, and weekend flights cost about $50 more than those in mid-week. The cheapest flights are Apex tickets, but must be booked 21 days before your departure, and you must spend at least seven days abroad. Super Apex tickets limit your stay to between 7 and 21 days. Most cheap fares require you to spend a Saturday in the Czech Republic.

Other operators include: **Continental**, ☎ (800) 231 0856, website: www.flycontinental.com; **Delta**, ☎ (800) 221 1212, website: www.delta-air.com; **American Airlines**, ☎ (800) 433 7300, website: www.aa.com; **United Airlines**, ☎ (800) 538 2929, website: www.ual.com; **KLM**, ☎ (800) 3 747 747, website: www.klm.nl; **Air France**, ☎ (212) 247 0100, website: www.air-france.com

ČSA also flies direct to Prague **from Canada**, with daily flights from Montreal and Toronto in the summer.

Prague's airport, Ruzyně, was built by British Aerospace and is small but brand new. The airport is about 20km northwest of the centr of Prague, and is only served by buses, although some hotels will collect you if you book ahead. The **express airport bus** is quick and cheap. Two buses run into town: Touristic Praha goes to náměstí Republiky every half hour between 08.30 and 19.00 and costs 75Kč; Cedaz goes to náměstí Republiky (90Kč) and to Dejvická metro station (60Kč), the last station on the green line A, and runs every hour from 05.00–10.00.

Other useful numbers include: **arrival and departure information**, ☎ (02) 20 11 33 14; **other information**, ☎ (02) 20 11 40 33; **Cedaz**, ☎ (02) 231 7598; **Touristic Praha**, ☎ (02) 29 06 40.

Three **local buses** go from the airport to metro stations every 20mins between 05.00 and 24.00. The cheapest but slowest is bus No. 179, which goes to Metro Nové Butovice (yellow line B). Bus No. 108 goes to Metro Hradcanská (green line A) and bus No. 119 goes to Metro Dejvická (green line A). It costs 6Kč.

Special airport **taxis**—usually white limousines—also operate a service. Normal taxis are not allowed to park at the airport. The airport taxi will cost 400Kč if your hotel is in the centre of Prague, and about 600Kč if it is on the further side of town.

By rail

From London's Victoria station the train journey takes 24 hours. Trains leave at 08.00 and run via Ostend, Brussels, Cologne, Frankfurt and Nuremberg before entering the Czech Republic by the Schirnding/Cheb border crossing. The train arrives at Praha Hlavní Nádraží, off Wenceslas Square, Wilsonova 2, which is the city's main international railway station.

With Eurotrain, a standard return ticket from London costs £264. You can shorten your journey by taking the Eurostar to Brussels, which costs £79 return (as long as you are away over a Saturday night), plus £185 for a return ticket from Brussels to Prague; couchettes cost an extra £10 each.

Students and those under 26 can get better deals, £160 to Prague (via Ostend). An InterRail ticket costs £209 a month if you are under 26 and over 65, £279 for others. This covers two zones of the European rail network.

Useful numbers include: **Eurostar**, Waterloo Station, London SE1, ☎ (0345) 881 881. **Le Shuttle**, information and ticket sales, ☎ (0990) 353 535. **British Rail European Travel Centre**, Victoria Station, London SW1, ☎ (0990) 848 848. **Eurotrain**, Campus Travel, 52 Grosvenor Gardens, London SW1, ☎ (0171) 730 3402.

By bus

This is the cheapest and most uncomfortable way of getting to Prague. Do not forget to take a small amount of German and Belgian money to buy snacks. **Eurolines** departs from Victoria Coach Station, London every day at 09.30 and arrives at 09.00 the next day. Tickets cost £58 single and £89 return. Students pay £52 single and £84 return. **Kingscourt Express** leaves on Tues, Weds, Sat and Sun at 19.00 and arrives 18 hours later in Prague. Tickets are £50 single and £85 return. Under 26s pay £45 single and £79 return. During the high season (June to September) there are six departures a week (every day except Mon). All buses arrive at Florenc station, except for Eurolines buses which arrive at Želivského bus station.

Other useful numbers include: **Eurolines**, National Express, 164 Buckingham Palace Road, London SW1. ☎ (0990) 808 080 or (0345) 303 030. **Kingscourt Express**, 15 Balham High Road, London SW12. ☎ 0181 673 7500.

By car

The drive from the UK to Prague takes at least 20 hours, without an overnight stop. Paris to Prague is 1078km (670 miles), Brussels to Prague is 925km (575 miles) and Geneva to Prague is 950km (590 miles).

It is best to use the **Channel Tunnel** at Folkestone, and take **Le Shuttle** (for address, see above) to Calais. Return fares cost £160–£220 per vehicle between April and September. There are discounts in the low season. At peak times, crossings leave every 15 minutes and every hour during the night. Throughout the continent, you have to pay motorway tolls. Prices vary from country to country, but make sure you have some money in the currency of each country you will be passing through.

From Calais/Dunkirk, follow signs to Lille, Brussels, Cologne, Frankfurt and Nuremberg. You can enter the Czech Republic at the Waidhaus–Rozadov border crossing. The other border crossing is the Reitzanhain–Pohraniční which you reach by following signs to Lille, Brussels, Cologne, Hessen via Erfurt and Chemnitz.

Arriving in Prague

The tourist offices (informační centrum) in Prague give out maps and pamphlets on local sights and can help with accommodation The **Prague Information Service** (Pražká informační služba or PIS) provides free information, maps and general help: **Prague Information Service**, Na příkopě 20, Prague 1, ☎ (02) 264 022/general info ☎ 187/544 444. Metro Můstek or náměstí Republiky. Open Mon–Fri 09.00–19.00, Sat, Sun 09.00–17.00.

Tour operators in Prague include: **Tom's Travel Ltd**, Ostrovní 7, 11008-Prague 1; ☎ (02) 229 39 72 or (02) 229 93 49, fax (20) 229 18 66, are extremely helpful organisation which can organise every aspect of your visit to Prague.

ČEDOK, Na příkopě 18, Nové Město, Prague 1. ☎ (02) 419 72 03, fax: (02) 24 19 72 34. Metro Můstek or náměstí Republiky. Open Mon–Fri 09.00–17.00, Sat 09.00–13.00.

Martin Tour, Štěpánská 16, Prague 1. ☎ and fax: (02) 24 21 24 73. Open Mon–Fri 09.00–16.30. Guided tours for groups and individuals.

PIS, Staroměstské nám 1, Prague 1. ☎ (02) 24 18 25 69 or (02) 24 48 23 80. Guided tours for groups and individuals.

Where to stay

Finding a room used to be quite a challenge in Prague. Hotels were poor compared to those in the West—you could easily find yourself in a high rise—and expensive. Service and accommodation have vastly improved now that entrepreneurs have finished their renovation schemes, and a law has been passed that prohibits charging foreigners more than locals. That said, accommodation is still over-priced and will be the most expensive part of your stay.

Hotels should always be booked ahead, as most places are full months in advance during the high season. ČEDOK offices abroad will arrange accommodation for you, but will only contact the more expensive hotels. If you speak German, it is a good idea to phone the hotel of your choice directly. Rooms can still be very expensive, especially in the high season (April–September) although tour groups receive discounts. If you are staying a while, say two weeks, you can get better deals. Most hotels have bars and restaurants and breakfast is included in the price of the room. **Pensions** are generally cheaper and often friendlier than hotels.

Choosing **private accommodation**, a room in someone's house, is a good way of paying less and feeling more of a local, but be sure you are not stuck in the outskirts. Check which facilities you will have to share with the owners, and what your proximity to them will be. It is probably best to stay one night and then decide if you want to stay longer. Private rooms can be booked through foreign-based agencies such as the Czech Agency (see p 8) and local tourist offices and accommodation agencies such as AVE (☎ (02) 24 22 35 21; this has offices at the airport and at both international railway stations) and the City of Prague Accommodation Service (Haštalské náměsti 3; ☎ 231 02 02). It is obviously cheaper to arrange such accommodation directly with the owners. Look out for signs saying *Zimmer frei* or *pokoje*. Breakfast is not always included in the price of the room.

Youth hostels do not exist: the Youth Travel Agency (Cestovní kancelář mládeže or CKM) is affiliated to Hostelling International but is not much of a bargain. Unofficial youth hostels charge very little, for which you get very little in return, and are best avoided.

Hotels and pensions
Expensive: over 4500Kč (£90); Moderate: 200Kč–4500Kč (£50–£90); Cheap: 1500Kč–2500Kč (£30–£50).

Malá Strana and Hradčany
Expensive
Café Dvorak, Na Kampé 3, 118 00 Praha; ☎ (02) 530078. Three stylish rooms above the beautiful pedestrianised main square of the Kampa Island.
The Charles, Josefská 1, 100 00 Praha 1; ☎ (02) 5731 5491/4; fax (02) 5731 1318. Newly opened luxury hotel in elegantly restored 17C building, intimate in atmosphere, and with painted wooden beam ceilings in bedrooms (Room 109 is especially impressive).
Pod Věží, Mostecká 2, 118 00, Praha 1; tel (02) 533 710; fax (02) 531 859. Soberly decorated bedrooms in pale grey in a wonderfully situated Baroque palace overlooking the Charles Bridge.
Savoy, Keplerova 6, 110 00, Praha 1; ☎ (02) 243 02430; fax (02) 243 021 28. Only the façade remains from the grand turn-of-the-century building that has now been artlessly and pretentiously transformed into one of the city's most luxurious hotels; a salon has been adorned with mock 19C bookcases, while the plush redbar and draped dining-room are worthy of some high-class brothel.

U Krále Karla, Úvoz 4, 118 00 Praha 1; ☎ 53 88 05; fax (02) 53 88 11. Warmly restored Baroque palace of 1639, with grandly decorated rooms featuring murals, stained glass, wooden beam ceilings and elaborate wooden furniture.
U Páva, U Lužického semináře 32, 118 00 Prague 1; ☎ (02) 245 10 922; fax (02) 53 33 79. In the same ownership as the U Krále Karla (see above), this similarly appointed and tastefully restored 17C palace on the northern half of the Kampa Island has a number of rooms with outstanding views up to Prague Castle.
U Raka, Cernínská 10, 118 00 Praha 1; ☎ (02) 205 111 00; fax (02) 205 105 11). This tiny former pension in a cottage-like building with a wooden log exterior, is located at the bottom of the quiet, toy-like district of the Novy Svét; it now forms part of the Romantik Hotels and Restaurants chain.
U Tří Pštrosů, Dražického nám. 12, 118 00, Praha 1; ☎ (02) 57320565; fax (02) 57320611. Occupying a famous building at the foot of the Charles Bridge, this was once Prague's most endearing hotel but is now slightly lack-lustre in character; at least the riverside views remain as enchanting as ever.

Moderate
Pension Dientzenhofer, Nosticova 2, 118 00, Praha 1; ☎ (02) 53 16 72; fax (02) 57 32. Hidden away in a quiet and attractive corner of the southern half of the Malá Strana, this is a simple and friendly pension occupying the birthplace of the architect Killián Ignac Dientzenhofer.
Kampa Hotel, Všehrdova 16, 118 00 Praha 1; ☎ (02) 5732 0508; fax (02) 5732 0262. Drably furnished and impersonal, but well situated.
Sax, Jánsky Vršek 328/3, 118 00 Praha 1; ☎/fax (02) 53 84 22. A bland modern conversion of an elegant early 19C building.
Hotel U Křízé, Újezd 20, 118 01 Praha 1; ☎ (02) 53 33 26; fax (02) 53 34 43. On a busy street next to the Petrín Park.

Cheap
Penzion U Kiliana, Všehredova 13, 118 00 Praha 1; ☎ (02) 561 81 40; (02) fax 73 41 10. A couple of rooms above popular eatery, directly in front of Kampa Hotel.

Staré Mesto and Josefov
Expensive
Casa Marcello, Řásnovka 783, 110 00 Praha 1; ☎ (02) 231 0260; fax (02) 231 1230. Hotel of character housed in a building of 13C origin once used as a dormitory by nuns of the adjoining St. Agnes Convent.
Maximilian, Haštalská 14, 110 00 Praha 1. Situated in an increasingly fashionable part of the Josefov, this is a smartly modernized hotel created out of a turn-of-the-century building.
Grand Hotel Bohemia, Královdorká 4, 110 00 Praha 1; ☎ (02) 24 804 111; fax (02) 232 95 45. Not nearly as stylish as the nearby Paríz (see below), but with spectacular neo-Rococo ball-room in basement.
Intercontinental, Námeští Curieovych 43/5. 110 00 Praha 1; ☎ (02) 248 811 18; fax (02) 248 100 71. Rightly described as a blight on the Prague skyline, and generally packed with tour groups, this has none the less an unsurpassed location at the very centre of the city.
Paříž, U Obecního domu 1, 110 00 Praha 1; ☎ (02) 22 195 195; fax (02) 24 225 475. Turn-of-the-century elegance reinterpreted for the modern age.

Ungelt, Malá Stupartská 1, 110 00 Praha 1; ☎ (02) 248 11 330; fax (02) 231 95 05. Ten apartments sleeping up to four people in what looks like a modernised version of a grand country inn; just behind the Tyn Church.

Moderate

Betlem Club, Betlémské námestí 9, 110 00 Praha 1; ☎ (02) 242 168 72; fax (02) 242 180 54. The 13C cellar bar is the most appealing interior feature of this tackily furnished if well situated hotel.

U Klenotníka, Rystířská 3, 110 00 Praha 1; ☎ (02) 242 116 99; fax (02) 261 782. Distinguished by its offbeat decor and Surrealist works of art.

U Zlatého Stromu, Karlova 6, 110 00 Praha; ☎ (02) 242 213 85; fax (02) 242 213 85. Miniscule rooms behind attractive gabled facade on the 'Royal Way'.

Cheap

U Krále Jiřího, Liliová 10, 110 00 Praha 1; ☎/fax (02) 242 219 83. Basic but clean and excellently located bed and breakfast.

Penzion Unitas, Bartolomějská 9; ☎ (02) 232 77 00; fax (02) 232 77 09. Cheap white-washed cells with iron doors in former monastery once used for putting up detainees of the secret police, including Václav Havel (he stayed in the now much saught-after Room P6). This is now run by the Sisters of Mercy, who show little mercy to those who smoke, drink or stay up later than one o'clock at night.

Nové Mesto

Expensive

Adria, Václavské námeští 26, 110 00 Praha 1; ☎ (02) 210 81 111; fax (02) 210 81 300. A restaurant dripping with stalactites is about the most imaginative feature of this otherwise unadventurously transformed late 18C building. However this is comfortable, efficiently run, and rather less sleazy than the other hotels on Wenceslas Square.

Ambassador Zlata Husa, Václavské námeští 26 110 00 Praha 1; ☎ (02) 241 93 111; fax (02) 242 23 563. Luxury at its most vulgar and depressing.

Esplanade, Washingtova 19, 110 00 Praha 1; ☎ (02) 2421 1715; fax (02) 2422 9306. Despite the major renovation programme carried out over the last few years, this newly re-opened hotel retains the same marbled, chandeliered magnificence of the original 1920s structure. Imposing yet friendly and intimate, this is in many ways the most appealing of Prague's grand hotels.

Palace, Panská 12, 111 21 Praha 1; ☎ (02) 2409 3111; fax (02) 24422 1240. Characterless recreation of a grand turn-of-the-century establishment.

Moderate

Atlantic, Na Poříčí 9, 110 00 Praha 1; ☎ (02) 2481 1084; fax (02) 2481 2378. Grim modern refurbishment of famous old hotel.

Europa, Václávské námeští 25, 110 00 Praha; ☎ (02) 242 281 17; fax (02) 242 245 44. Art nouveau splendour gone somewhat to seed, this will appeal to those who prefer architecture and atmosphere over comfort and cheerfulness.

Julius, Václavské námeští 22, 110 00 Praha; ☎ (02) 24 21 70; fax ()2) 24 21 8545. Functionalism that has become lacklustre, but with more pleasant bedrooms than the entrance lobby would suggest.

Getting around Prague

Public transport

Walking is the best way to see the centre of the city. Not only is it faster than public transport, but it allows you to see the large squares, winding alleys and hidden arcades that you might otherwise miss. The rest of Prague is covered by a cheap and efficient public transport system which runs 24 hours. The daytime service runs from 05.00 to 24.00 and the night service from 00.00 to 05.00.

Information on the system is obtainable at the **Prague Public Transit Company Information Offices** (Informacní strediska Dopravního podníku Hl, M Prahy), Metro Můstek. ☎ (24) 22 51 35. Open daily 07.00–21.00. The staff here will help you find your way around. They speak some English and German and sell tickets, maps, tram and bus schedules.

Travel **tickets** can be used on any form of transport, bus, tram and metro. A 15min ride above ground (no transfers) or one ride on the metro (no more than four stops) costs 8Kč. Unlimited travel on all forms of transport, with transfers,

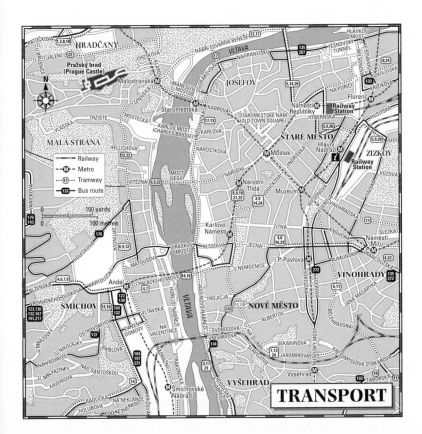

TRANSPORT

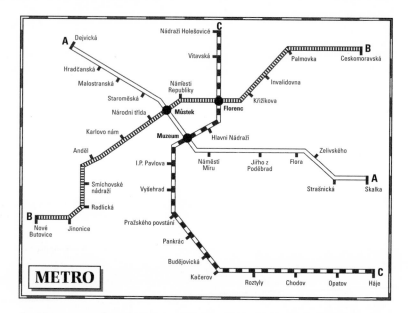

for 60mins at peak times and 90mins at slow times, costs 12Kč. Children under 6 go free, children under 15 are half-price.

You can also buy the following passes: **One Day Pass**, 70kč; **Three Day Pass**, 80Kč; **Seven Day Pass**, 170Kč; **15 Day Pass**, 280KčOne Month Pass, 380 Kč; **Three Month Pass**, 1000Kč; **One Year Pass**, 3400Kč.

Tickets can be bought at PIS offices, tobacconists at the counter marked DP at most metro stations, and anywhere displaying a red-and-yellow sticker in the window. Once on board a bus or tram you must stamp your ticket in a machine. If you do not have a valid ticket, you could be fined up to 200Kč on the spot.

The **metro** is extremely efficient and runs from 05.00 to 24.00. Trains are clean and frequent. There are three lines, green line A (Skalka–Dejvická), yellow line B (Ceskomoravská–Zlicín) and red line C (Nádraží Holešovice–Háje). A fourth line is scheduled to be built sometime after the millennium. There are only three transfer stations: Muzeum (where A and C connect), Florenc (where B and C connect) and Můstek (where A and B connect).

There are 23 **tram lines** running during the day, from 04.30 to 24.00, and eight at night. Trams run every 7mins at peak times and every 15mins at other times. Remarkably, they respect almost to the second the time-tables posted at each tram stop. A good way to see the city is to ride on tram 22 or 91—the historical tram. This runs from April to October and takes 40mins for the journey from Vystavište through Malostranská and Wenceslas Square to náměstí Republiky. Tickets cost 10Kč for adults and 5Kč for children.

Buses run from 05.00 to 24.00, every 10mins at peak times and 20mins at other times. There are 196 daytime bus lines and 10 night bus lines. For bus information, ☎ (24) 21 10 60.

Prague has plenty of **taxis**, but these can be very expensive. Prague's taxi drivers are notoriously dishonest and, in spite of recent regulations, you are almost bound to be overcharged. Avoid taking taxis near tourist locations. Agree your fare before you get in, or make sure that the meter is on. When you get in the taxi, the fare should read 10Kč. The meter rate should be set at 1—that is, no more than 18Kč per kilometre. Ask for a receipt at the end of your trip. It should have all the details of your journey, including the name of the taxi company and the driver. Only ever use an authorised taxi. One reliable service is **ProfiTaxi**, ☎ (42) 02 22 13 55 55.

Cars and bicycles

Cycling in Prague is not easy. There are no bike lanes, drivers take no notice of you and even pedestrians are hostile if you go anywhere near the pavement.

Driving in Prague is an even worse idea. The narrow streets are difficult to negotiate, and you have to deal with trams and the possibility of theft. To drive your own car in Prague, you need a driver's licence but no longer require an international insurance green card. You must carry your vehicle's registration documents with you. The wearing of seatbelts is compulsory and you must never drink and drive. You should carry a red warning triangle, replacement bulbs and a first aid kit. Children under 12 must always sit in the back.

The **speed limit** is 55mph/90kph on main roads, 35mph/60kph in towns and 70mph/110kph on motorways. Drive on the right-hand side of the road. A yellow diamond sign means you have right of way, a black line through it means you do not have right of way. Give way to pedestrians at lights if turning left or right. Do not drive on tram lines; trams always have right of way.

You must have an authorisation sticker (*dálniční známka*) to drive on any **motorway**. This costs around 880Kč (valid for up to one year) and is available from petrol stations, post offices and border crossings. Failure to display the disk results in heavy fines.

There are three types of **petrol**: 96 octane (*super*), 90 octane (*special*) and lead-free (*natural*). Many petrol stations close after 18.00. They do not accept credit cards, only Czech currency. Petrol currently costs 18Kč a litre (£0.40/$0.60).

To **rent a car**, you must be over 21 and have a driver's licence. Insurance is arranged by the rental agency. If you hire from abroad, a small car for a week will cost £130/$200. The well-known car hire companies charge much more than local Czech ones.

Car hire companies in the **UK** include **Avis** ☎ (0990) 900 500; **Budget** ☎ (0800) 181 181; **Europcar** ☎ (0345) 222 525; **Hertz** ☎ (0990) 996 699; **Holiday Autos** ☎ (0990) 300 400.

In the **US**: **Avis** ☎ (800) 331 1212; **Budget** ☎ (212) 641 5700; **Hertz** ☎ (800) 654 3131; **Holiday Autos** ☎ (800) 422 7737.

Car hire in **Prague**: **Alamo**, Prague Airport, ☎ (02) 20 11 35 34; **Budget**, náměstí Curieových 5/43 (Hotel Intercontinental), Prague 1. ☎ (02) 24 88 99 95; **Rent Car**, Wenzigova 5, Prague 2. ☎ (02) 24 26 21 31; **Rent A Car**, Palace of Culture, 5 května 65, Prague 4, 5. ☎ (42 02) 61 22 20 79.

General information

Calendar

March: Prague City of Music Festival.

May: Prague Spring Music Festival. ☎ (02) 53 34 73. Prague Marathon. Prague Writers' Festival. International Children's Film Festival.

June: Prague International Film Festival. Smetana National Opera Festival.

July: Prague Summer Culture Festival. Karlovy Vary Film Festival.

October: Prague Festival of 20th Century Music. ☎ (02) 23 21 086.

December: Christmas fairs take place in the city.

Communications

Post offices can be confusing because each window has a different service, and you may find yourself queuing up unnecessarily unless you are careful. The main post office in Prague is at Jindřišská 14, Prague 1, where you can buy stamps, send faxes and change money. You can also receive letters (at position 28) if they are addressed c/o Poste Restante Jindřišská 14. Stamps for postcards to the UK cost 6Kč, to the US 8Kč. Sending letters to the UK costs 9Kč and to the US 12Kč. Stamps can also be bought at newsstands and tobacconists. Mail boxes are orange. Post takes up to five working days to reach the UK, and between seven and ten days to the US.

Most **public telephones** now run on cards which can be bought from post offices, train stations, metro stations, kiosks, large department stores, hotels and anywhere displaying a blue-and-yellow Telecom sticker. They come in 50 units, 100 units and 150 units. Units cost 2Kč and for local calls last three minutes from 07.00 to 16.00 on weekdays, six minutes from 16.00–07.00 weekdays and all day weekends and Sundays. You need a more expensive card for international calls. In telephones which take cash, local calls cost 3Kč. Numbers consist of five, six, seven or eight digits.

It can sometimes be a challenge calling AT&T, Sprint and other card companies. Persevere, because some hotel operators may refuse to make the connection and when they do, will charge you premium rate. If you have problems, call the international operator, ☎ 0135; if you want to make a collect call, dial 0132, and say 'na účet volaného London/New York/etc'. Most operators understand English.

Dialling codes are as follows (leave out the zero for local codes if dialling from outside the Czech Republic).

Czech Republic: 420

Prague: 02

International calls from Prague: dial 00 first.

Calling Prague from the UK: 00 42 02.

Calling Prague from the US: 011 42 02.

Calling the UK from Prague: 00 44.

Calling the US and Canada from Prague: dial 00 1.

Calling Ireland from Prague: 00 353.

Calling Australia from Prague: 00 61.

Crime
Petty crime such as pickpocketing is more likely to affect you than anything more serious. Be sensible: make photocopies of your passport and note down the numbers of your travellers' cheques and credit cards. Carry your valuables in a money belt or leave them in the hotel safe. Report anything stolen to the municipal police, as you will need documentation for your insurance company. *Byl jsem okraden* means 'I've been robbed.'

Currency
The Czech crown (*koruna čescá* or Kč) is made up of 100 haléřů (h). Coins come in 10h, 20h, 50h, 1Kč, 2Kč, 5Kč, 10Kč, 20Kč and 50 Kč. Notes come in 20, 50, 100, 500, 1000, 2000 and 5000Kč denominations. There are about 48.8Kč to the £1 sterling and 32Kč to the US dollar (November 1998).

Customs
Visitors over the age of 18 can take 250 cigarettes or 100 cigars, 1 litre of spirits, 1 litre of wine and up to 3000Kč worth of consumer goods into the Czech Republic. On leaving the country you can take 250 cigarettes, 2 litres of wine, 1 litre of spirits and up to 500Kč worth of consumer goods. These limits are liable to change so check before you go. You are not allowed to export antiques. To find out if your chosen object is an antique or not, contact the curator at the National Museum in Prague: ☎ (02) 24 49 71 11. Visitors entering the country must be able to prove access to at least 6000Kčs (£150/$225); this rule is unlikely to be enforced unless you look like a tramp. Note also that there is a 5000Kč limit on the import and export of Czech currency.

Disabled travellers
Prague is not the best place for disabled travellers, and very few allowances are made for them. Buses and trams are inaccessible for wheelchairs; trains are a little better, as some have been designed to take wheelchairs, and several metro stations have lifts. There are no hand-control cars at all available from car rental companies.

Museums are also impossible to get into, but the National Theatre now has some chairs for disabled people. It is best to travel with a non-disabled partner. For more information, travellers could try the following organisations. **UK Holiday Care Service**, 2nd floor, Imperial Building, Victoria Road, Horley, Surrey RH6 9HW. ☎ (01293) 774 535. **RADAR**, 12 City Forum, 250 City Road, London EC1V 8AS. ☎ (0171) 250 3222.

In the **US: Society for Advancement of Travel for the Handicapped**, 347 5th Ave, New York, NY 10016. ☎ (212) 447 7284; **Mobility International USA**, Box 10767, Eugene, OR 97440. ☎ (541) 343 1284 or fax: (541) 343 6812.

In **Europe: Mobility International**, at 18 Boulevard Baoudouin, B-1000 Brussels, Belgium. ☎ (32 2) 201 5608, fax: (32 2) 201 5763.

Electricity
Electricity in Prague is standard Continental 220 volts AC. Visitors from Britain and the United States will need adaptors for European-style two-pin round plugs for hairdryers, razors and other appliances. Americans will also need a transformer.

Embassies

Foreign embassies in Prague

American Embassy, Tržiště 15, Malá Strana, Prague 1. ☎ (02) 57 32 06 63, fax: (02) 57 32 09 20. Metro Malostranská. Open Mon–Fri 09.00–12.00 and 14.00–15.30.

Australian Trade Commission and Honorary Consulate, Na Ořechovce 38, Prague 6. ☎ (02) 24 31 07 43/(02) 24 31 00 71. Metro Dejvická. Open Mon–Thur 09.00–17.00, Fri 09.00–14.00.

British Embassy, Thunovská 14, Malá Strana, Prague 1. ☎ (02) 57 32 03 55, fax: (02) 57 32 10 23. Metro Malostranská. Open Mon–Fri 09.00–12.00.

Canadian Embassy, Mickiewiczova 6, Prague 6. ☎ (02) 24 31 11 08, fax: (02) 24 31 02 94. Metro Hradčanská. Open Mon–Fri 09.00–12.00 and 14.00–16.00.

Czech embassies abroad

Australia 169 Military Road, Dover Heights, Sydney, NSW 2030. ☎ (02) 371 8878.

Canada, 541 Sussex Drive, Ottawa, Ontario K1N 6Z6. ☎ (613) 562 3875.

Ireland, Confederation House, Kildare St, Dublin 2. ☎ (1) 671 4981.

New Zealand (consulate) 48 Hair Street, PO Box 43035, Wainuiomata, Wellington. ☎ (04) 564 6001.

UK, 26 Kensington Palace Gardens, London W8 4QY. ☎ (0171) 243 1115, fax: (0171) 727 9654. visa hotline: (0891) 171 267, email: london@embassy.mzv.cz

US, 3900 Spring of Freedom St, NW Washington DC 20008. ☎ (202) 274 9100, fax: (202) 966 8540. email: washington@embassy.mzv.cz, website: www.czech.cz/washington

English language bookshops

Most bookshops in Central Prague have a section devoted to books in English, including the excellent translations from Czech produced by the locally-based Twisted Spoon Press. However, the main specialist English language bookshop in the city is the *Big Ben Bookshop*, which has branches at Malá Stupartská 5, 110 00 Praha 1 (☎ 24 82 65 65) and Národní 10, 125 01 Praha 1 (☎ 325 783). Another alternative in *The Globe Coffee House and Bookstore* (Janovského 14, Praha 7), which has slightly shop-soiled products and is based on San Francisco's celebrated *City Lights* shops.

Health

Health care in Prague is not quite up to Western standards, but is improving all the time. There are no major health problems in Prague and no vaccinations are needed. The tap water is safe to drink, but does not taste great.

Pharmacies (*lékárna*) are open until about 18.30. Pharmacies that are open 24 hours a day are listed in the front of the Yellow Pages under 'Lékárny s nepřetržitou pohotovostní službou'. A central **pharmacy** in Prague, open 24 hours, is at Belgická 37, Prague 2, ☎ (02) 24 23 72 07 and another is at Lékárna U Anděla, Štefánikova 6, Prague 5, ☎ 53 70 39. First Aid Palackého 5, Prague 1, ☎ (02) 24 22 25 20, is open Mon–Fri 07.00–19.00 and 24 hours Sat–Sun.

The **emergency medical service** for foreigners is at U Nemocnice 2, Prague 2, ☎ (02) 24 96 11 11/24 96 30 56. American citizens will have to pay for this,

British citizens do not. **Medical insurance** is a good idea wherever you have come from; do not forget to ask for proof of any expenses.

Other useful numbers include **Canadian Medical Center**, Veleslavínská 30/1. ☎ (02) 31 65 519; **Dental Emergencies**, Vladislavova 22, ☎ (02) 24 22 76 63; **Na Homolce Hospital for Foreigners**, Roentgenova 2, Motol, Prague 5. ☎ (02) 52 92 21 46.

Money

It is now much easier to use credit cards such as Visa, Mastercard and Amex in restaurants and shops, but you should carry travellers' cheques in sterling, US dollars or Deutschmarks—Thomas Cook and American Express are the best known. Eurocheques are not a good option. You can withdraw cash from cashpoints, but do not rely on this alone.

The Czech crown is fully convertible. Commission at banks (2%) is less than at the exchange bureaux (up to 6%), but the queues are longer and the opening times less flexible. It is always a good idea to change some money before you arrive to avoid delays at the airport exchange counter.

Accommodation will take the largest chunk out of your money, but otherwise everything is still very cheap, though prices are creeping up. You should expect to spend about £30/$45 a day. This assumes you want to eat well and are not roughing it. You can easily double this if splashing out.

Newspapers

British readers can find international editions of the *Financial Times* and the *Guardian* (which are printed in Frankfurt) in Prague. They arrive at the newsstands around noon. The normal editions of the British broadsheets tend to be a day old. The *European*, *International Herald Tribune* and *USA Today* are also available.

Prague Post, a weekly newspaper in English, appears on Wednesdays. *Prognosis*, which has details of what's going on in Prague as well as club, pub and bar listings, is also in English and appears fortnightly on Fridays.

Opening hours

Banks are open Mon–Fri 08.00–17.00 with a break at lunch.
Government offices are open Mon–Fri 08.30–17.00.
Post offices are open Mon–Fri 08.00–17.00 and Sat 08.00–12.00.
Restaurants generally open for lunch around 11.00 and stay open until 22.00 or 23.00; they are usually open on Sundays.
Shops open Mon–Fri 08.00 or 09.00 to 17.00 or 18.00. Many shops are open until 12.00 Sat. Some close for lunch and many close in August. 24-hour shops are called *vecerka*.
For museum opening times, see **Tourist sites**, below.

Public holidays

January 1 (New Year's Day)
Easter Sunday and Monday
May 1 (Labour Day)
May 8 (VE Day)

July 5 (Cyril and Methodius Day)
July 6 (Jan Hus Day)
October 28 (Independence Day)
December 24–26 (Christmas)

Time

Prague is one hour ahead of the UK and six hours ahead of US Eastern time. Times go forward one hour in the summer (usually April/May) and back one hour in the winter (usually September).

Tipping

In restaurants, round your bill up to a few crowns above the total (VAT at 23% is included in the price of your food): this may have been done for you already, so check. Don't leave the tip on the table, but pay it with the bill.

It is normal to tip 10% in all the places you would tip in the West—taxis, hotels, and so on.

Toilets

Public conveniences are few and far between. Those that do exist are clean and have attendants, whom you pay for sheets of toilet paper (2Kč). If desperate you can always use the toilets in a restaurant or hotel.

Tourist sites

Some tourist attractions are only open in the summer. Many **museums** are closed from the end of October until Easter Monday. Opening hours tend to be Tues–Sun 09.00–16.00 or later, closed Mon. Ticket prices are very low and students can gain admission for half price.

Most museums only have Czech labelling although they may provide English pamphlets. Among the museums that certainly should not be missed are the **Jewish Museum** (which includes several synagogues as well as the **Old Jewish Cemetery**), the **Museum of Decorative Arts**, and the various buildings of the **National Gallery**, most notably the **Collection of Czech Gothic and Baroque Art** in the St George's Convent, the **Collection of Pre-modern European Art** at the Sternberk Palace, and the **Collection of Modern Art** in the Trade Fair Palace. There are a number enjoyable single artist/musician museums, above all the **Mozart Museum** (Bertramka), the **Antonin Dvorak Museum**, the **Bilek Villa**, and the newly opened **Mucha Museum**. The history of science and transport in the Czech Republic is entertainingly recorded in the **National Technical Museum**, while natural history is the principal subject of the huge but disappointing **National Museum**, which is of interest largely for its architecture.

A welcome feature of Prague is that the most interesting of its palace interiors—for instance, those of the **Old Royal Palace** and the **Troja Château**—can be visited without the obligatory and generally tedious guided tour characteristic of so many of the palaces and castles outside the city.

Large **churches** sometimes charge an entry fee to their cloisters or crypts. Most of the churches outside Prague are open only a couple of hours a day, probably just before or after a service. If you find the priest (*kněz*), however, he will be happy to show you around.

Useful addresses and telephone numbers
Information

Directory enquiries (Prague), ☎ 120.

Directory enquiries (rest of country), ☎ 121.

Directory enquiries (international), ☎ 149.
Operator, ☎ 120.
Speaking clock, ☎ 112.

Emergency numbers
Police, ☎ 158.
Ambulance, ☎ 155.
Fire, ☎ 150.
Emergency medical service,
☎ (02) 496 11 11.
Dental emergencies, ☎ (02) 24 22 76 63.
Emergency road service, ☎ 154.

Travel
Prague airport, ☎ (02) 20 11 33 14.

Prague main railway station,
☎ (02) 24 22 42 00.
Air France, ☎ (02) 24 22 71 64.
Austrian Airlines, ☎ (02) 20 11 43 24.
British Airways, ☎ (02) 22 11 44 44
Czech Airlines, ☎ (02) 36 70 760
Delta, ☎ (02) 20 11 43 84
KLM, ☎ (02) 20 11 43 22
Lufthansa, ☎ (02) 20 11 44 56
Sabena, ☎ (02) 20 11 43 23
Swissair, ☎ (02) 20 11 43 24

Money
American Express, Václavské nám 56, Prague 1.
Eurocard/Mastercard, Na příkopě 14, Prague 1.

Food and drink

by Michael Jacobs

'Morning and evening, I endured the atrocious, nauseating cummin-flavoured food. I consequently walked around all day with a constant desire to vomit,' recalled Albert Camus of his rather unsatisfactory visit to Prague made in 1935 (see p 68). Nearly one and a half centuries earlier Dr Johnson's friend Hester Lynch Piozzi found instead that the 'eating here is incomparable ... I never saw such poultry even in London or Bath, and there is plenty of game that amazes one; no inn so wretched but you have a pheasant for your supper, and often partridge soup.' Although in the international Prague of today there is food to satisfy all palates, the typical Czech cuisine is one likely to inspire a response somewhere in between Camus' and Piozzi's. It is filling and slightly monotonous food, best appreciated on a cold winter's evening, and washed down with copious quantities of the outstanding local beer.

Dumplings

Bacon and above all caraway seed (rather than cumin, as Camus thought) are the ubiquitous flavourings of Czech food and, as in Russian and Hungarian cooking, soured cream is an accompaniment to numerous dishes. The first thought which comes to mind at the very mention of Czech food, however, is of dumplings (*knedlíky*), which have the same role in Bohemia and Moravia as chips do in other countries. There are several types of dumpling, including potato dumplings (*Bramborové knedlíky*), plum dumplings (*Švestkové knedlíky*) and, most common of all, a type of dumpling known as *Houskové knedlíky*, which is made in the shape of a Swiss roll from a mixture of flour, eggs and cubes of white bread, and is served in slices that are invariably, though unintentionally, stale; some of the better restaurants will even provide you with a separate tray piled high with a selection of all of these.

Starters

Shortly after you sit down in some of the fancier restaurants here you are likely to be offered aperitifs from a trolley followed by a tray of unappealing canapés, for which you will be charged individually; the canapés, of glazed, artificial appearance, invariably feature cream or cream cheese, one of the more popular ones being a ham roll filled with cream cheese and gherkin slices; others are coated with hard lumps of jelly, and should be avoided at all costs. A normal Czech meal, however, begins with a soup; two common varieties are potato soup (*Bramborová polévka*) and a thick white soup known as *Kmínová polévka*, both of which are heavily flavoured with caraway seed; a popular clear soup is *Polévka s játrovými knedlíčky*, which is beef broth with little dumplings made from liver, garlic, lemon rind, eggs and breadcrumbs.

Main courses

Main courses on restaurant menus are usually divided between *Minutky* and *Hotová jí dla*, the former being dishes that are cooked to order, the latter being ready cooked ones in heavy sauces. The most typical main dish you can eat in Bohemia and Moravia is pork or Frankfurter-style sausage accompanied by dumplings and sauerkraut. Meat is consumed in vast quantities all over the Czech Republic, and tends to be tough and overcooked. Pork is often served with eggs and ham on top and, like veal, is frequently dipped in a mixture of flour, bread-crumbs and eggs to form an escalope or *řízek*; a tastier dish is *Vepřová pečeně*, or pork roasted with caraway seeds. Thick fillets of beef piled high with cream and cranberries can be found in the more pretentious establishments, but beef is more commonly served as braised slices in a brown onion sauce (*Dušená roštěnka*) or else as boiled slices in a delicious dill-flavoured white sauce known as *Koprová omáčka*. There are far fewer poultry than meat dishes in the Czech Republic: the most usual one is roast chicken (*Pečené kuře*); goose is becoming less common but is traditionally served roast with sauerkraut (*Pečená husa se zelím*).

Fish dishes are few, despite the impression to the contrary given by Hester Piozzi, who recorded how barrows roamed the streets of Prague carrying 'round bathing-tubs ... full of the most pellucid water, in which the carp, tench, and eels, are all leaping alive, to a size and perfection I am ashamed to relate.' Carp is by far the most popular fish in the Czech Republic, but even so tends to be eaten mainly as a traditional Christmas Eve dish, when it is served with a near indi-gestible black sauce made from fish stock, raspberry juice, beer, lemon rind, sugar, honey cake, raisins and almonds (*Kapr na černo*).

The great joy of the Czech cuisine, if such an extreme term can be used, is its game, which is sometimes roasted over a wood fire and flavoured with juniper berries. The best place to eat it in Prague is the wonderful *Myslivna Restaurant* in the Vinohrady district (see p 186).

'A smaller selection is usually possible when it comes to fresh vegetables (ster-ilised ones are often served even in summer)', wrote one of the authors of a government-sponsored guide to Czechoslovakia published in 1989. Fresh fruit and vegetables are now far more widely available than before, but for some reason are still only rarely found in restaurants, where tinned fruit (often served as a mixed compote known as a *Míchaný ovocný kompot*), sauerkraut (*zelí*) and pickled vegetable salads such as cucumber salad (*Okurkový salát*) predominate. Cheese tends to be processed and served in dried-out slices.

Puddings are of the hearty kind, such as plum jam cake (*Povidlový koláč*) or, more commonly, *palačinky*, pancakes that are usually heaped with mountains of cream and chocolate sauce, and occasionally flambéd. The legacy of Austria is fortunately still apparent in the delectable range of cakes and pastries to be found in the country's cafés and bakeries. The coffee itself, however, is mainly Turkish (*turecká káva*), while the so-called espresso—regarded by many as a more refined alternative—is more often than not tepid instant coffee of insipid flavour.

Spirits, wine and beer

Spirits and liquors tend to be drunk neat as an aperitif or as a beer chaser, one of the most famous being the greenish, herb-flavoured liquor known as *becherovka*, a speciality of the Bohemian spa town of Karlovy Vary (Carlsbad) and reputedly far more beneficial to the health than the town's waters. Most spirits, however, come from Moravia and Slovakia and include plum brandy (*slivovice*, one of the more renowned brands being *Jelínec*), and a juniper-flavoured gin known as *borovička*, a particular speciality of the Slovak town of Trenčín: according to popular tradition a glass of *borovička* drunk half an hour before eating is a considerable aid to the digestion, though its potential beneficial effects are sometimes lost as a result of the hors-d'oeuvres that often come with it. Since 1991 absinthe has been served in some of the more fashionable Prague bars, thus making this city the only place in Europe apart from Barcelona where this generally outlawed and potentially lethal drink can openly be found.

The finest Czech wines are from Southern Moravia, with excellent Ruländer, Sauvignon, Traminer and Spätburgunder wines being made in places such as Velké Pavlovice, Mikulov, Musov and Znojmo; Bohemia's small number of wines are grown mainly around Mělník, an area which was planted with Burgundy grapes during the reign of Charles IV. Wine is less commonly drunk in the Czech Republic than beer, which is by far the most popular local drink, and the usual accompaniment to meals. When it comes to discussing Czech beer, superlatives can at last be used with complete honesty, for it is generally agreed to be the best in the world, and has a reputation going back to the Middle Ages. Beer is made throughout the country, and dark as well as light beer can be found here, as can a number of small breweries, some of which are attached to their own pubs. However the general consensus of opinion is that the finest beers are the light and creamy ones from the Bohemian towns of České Budějovice (the original Budweiser) and, above all, Plzeň, where the Prazdroj or Urquell brew served as the prototype for Pils-style beers throughout the world. Prague's own beers (slightly more bitter than the ones above) include Staropramen, Braník and Smíchov. The most widely available dark beer is Purkmistr, while slightly treacly home brews are served at two of Prague's most tourist-loved beer halls—*U Fleků* and *U zlatého tygra*.

Eating out in Prague

A few words should now be said about the actual places where you can eat and drink in Prague. The smartest of the restaurants, bars and nightclubs here generally prefer their clients to be formally dressed, and all of them have cloakrooms where you are obliged to leave your coats immediately on entering; booking is now essential in Prague throughout the year, sometimes up to one week in advance.

The wine-bars or *vinárna* are smart establishments generally situated in historic cellars, and always provide food, though they will never serve you with beer. The modest restaurants, pubs and beer-cellars are invariably the liveliest and friendliest of all the eating and drinking establishments here, and their smoke-filled atmosphere, dirty walls and floors, and portly waiters or wait-resses—who will slam a large glass of beer on to your table often without your asking for it—are an intrinsic part of their charm; food is served at most of the pubs and beer-cellars and is usually no worse, and certainly far cheaper, than in the more pretentious establishments. In such places you will often find yourself sharing a table with others; though your privacy will be respected, it is customary to wish each other 'bon appetit' ('*dobrou chut*') when the food arrives.

The hurried tourist could snatch a bite at a *bufet*, a self-service establishment where you are generally obliged to eat standing up; an *automat* is the same but with cold rather than hot food. Even more time could be saved at one of the many outdoor kiosks, which specialise in *bramborák* (a type of potato pancake) and *klobása*s (Frankfurter-style sausage), the latter served on a paper plate together with a mountain of mustard. A *cukrárna*, which is only open during the day-time, is a café specialising in cakes and pastries.

Many readers of this book will now be wondering about specific places where they might go to savour the city's restaurant, café and bar life. Listed below are a number of the city's more long-standing establishments, together with several of the more fashionable places of the moment, some of which—in the rapidly changing Prague of today—might well have closed down or been radically altered by the time you visit them. The best way of obtaining up-to-date recom-mendations is to buy a copy either of the weekly *Prague Post* or else of the annu-ally up-dated *Gurmán Choice of Prague Restaurants* (printed locally), which gives points to food, service and atmosphere.

As a general rule, the restaurants specialising in Czech cuisine differ compar-atively little in terms of the actual quality of the food, and should be chosen prin-cipally for their atmosphere and architectural setting. Of the ubiquitous roman-tically lit 'cellar-style' restaurants, four of the most renowned are *U Zlaté Hrušky* (Nový svět 3; ☎ 205 14778), *U Maltézských rytířů* (Prokopská 10/297; ☎ 536357), *U Mecenáse* (Malostránské nám. 10; ☎ 533881), and *U Modré Kachničky* (Nebovidská 6; ☎ 57 32 03 08), all of which are situated in beau-tiful old houses in the Malá Strana. Good to variable food combined with excel-lent views of the city are to be found at *Nebozízek*—which is the half-way stop on the funicular line up the Petrín hill (Petřínské sady 411; ☎ 537 905)—and at the superb art nouveau *Hanavsky Pavilon* (Letenské sady 173; ☎ 325 792). Also wonderfully located are the riverside restaurants *Kampa Park* (Na Kampě 83; ☎ 57313493/4) and *Parnas* (Smetanovo nábřeží 2; ☎ 24211901), and the *Lví dvůr*, which is situated in the Renaissance Belvedere of the Hradčany (U Prašného mostu 6; ☎ 2431022). But in terms of sheer atmosphere, no restau-rant can compete with the *Pálffy Palác* (Valdštejnská 14; ☎ 57320570), an entirely candle-lit Baroque hall with creaking parquet floors and the odd snatches of violin music coming from the adjoining conservatoire.

Among the few Czech restaurants worth visiting for the food alone is the unappealingly decorated *Myslivna* (Jagellonská 21; ☎ 62 70 209), which for many years has been virtually unrivalled for its game dishes. Those satiated by the over-abundance of meat in Czech cuisine might find relief in such fish restaurants as **Na Rybárně**—a place once frequented by Havel (Gorazdova 17, ☎ 29 99 795)—and the modest and friendly **Rybářský Klub** (U Sovorých mlýnů 1; ☎ 53 02 23), which has tench delivered daily from a fish farm in South Bohemia. The gastronomically adventurous and dietary conscious enthusiast of Czech food should try the excellent *U Lípy II* (Kodaňská 29a; ☎ 73 32 52), which counts among its specialities the microscopic snail liver.

Significantly, most of the best regarded Prague restaurants of today (no fewer

Menu

Polévky	**Soups**	*Pstruh*	Trout
Boršč	Beetroot soup	*Zavináč*	Herring
Bramborová	Potato soup		
Čočkov	Lentil soup	**Zelenina**	**Vegetables**
Fazolová	Bean soup	*Brambory*	Potatoes
Hovězí	Beef soup	*Hranolky*	Chips
Hrachová	Pea soup	*Cibule*	Onion
Slepičí	Chicken soup	*Česnek*	Garlic
Rajská	Tomato soup	*Houby*	Mushrooms
Zeleninová	Vegetable soup	*Hrášek*	Peas
		Květák	Cauliflower
Chléb	Bread	*Kyselé zelí*	Sauerkraut
Máslo	Butter	*Lečo*	Ratatouille
Vejce	Eggs	*Mrkev*	Carrot
Niva	Soft blue cheese	*Rajče*	Tomato
Oštiepok	Smoked curd	*Špenát*	Spinach
	cheese	*Zelí*	Cabbage
Pivný sýr	Beer-flavoured	*Žampiony*	Champignons
	cheese		
Tvaroh	Curd cheese	**Ovoce**	**Fruit**
		Banán	Banana
Maso	**Meat**	*Broskev*	Peach
Čevapčici	Spiced meatballs	*Citren*	Lemon
Hove̊zí	Beef	*Víno*	Grapes
Játra	Liver	*Hruška*	Pear
Kachna	Duck	*Jablko*	Apple
Klobásy	Sausages	*Meruňk*	Apricot
Kuře	Chicken	*Pomeranč*	Orange
Salám	Salami	*Třešně*	Cherry
Sekaná	Meatloaf		
Slanina	Bacon	**Nápoje**	**Drinks**
Šunka	Ham	*Čaj*	Tea
Telecí	Veal	*Káva*	Coffee
Vepřové	Pork	*Koňak*	Brandy
		Minerální voda	Mineral water
Ryby	**Fish**	*Mléko*	Milk
Kapr	Carp	*Pivo*	Beer
Makrela	Mackerel	*Víno*	Wine

than seventeen of Gurmán's top twenty 'winners in meals') are those serving international food. Good to excellent French food is served in such splendid settings as the sumptous *Esplanade Hotel* (Washingtova 19; ☎ 24 21 36 96), the Baroque cellar of *U Malířů* (Maltézské nám. 11; ☎ 57 32 03 17), Frank Gehry's 'Fred and Ginger' building (*La Perle de Prague*, Rašínovo nábřeží 80; ☎ 21 98 41 60),and the art nouveau *Villa Voyta Hotel* (K Novému dvoru 124; ☎ 47 22 711) and *Obecní Dům* (náměstí Republiky 5; ☎ 22 00 27 77); the French chef of the *Circle Line* (Malostranské nám.12; ☎ 53 0308) prepares some of the most exquisite fish and sea-food dishes in town. Refined Italian cuisine is cooked by the Tuscan chef Davide Cannela at the newly opened and superbly situated *Restaurant Ostroff* (Strelecky Ostrov 336; ☎ 24919235), and there are a host of good and popular pizzerias, including *Pizza Coloseum* (Vodičkova 32; ☎ 24 21 491 4) and *Pizzeria Grosseto* (Jugosl. partyzánu 8; ☎ 31 22 694). Outstanding Indian cuisine in a regal setting can be had at the successful *Jewel of India* (Parízská 20; ☎ 24 81 10 10), while a curious and delicious mixture of Czech and Japanese cuisine is to be found at *Miyabi* (Navrátilova 10; ☎ 29 53 76), which is run by a Czech woman who lived a long time in Japan. Fish freshly flown in from Iceland is the speciality of *Reykjavic* (Karlova 20; ☎ 24 22 92 51), which has a good if amorphously cosmopolitan cuisine. What is still lacking in Prague is a truly sophisticated vegetarian restaurant: for the most part vegetarians will have to make do with the worthy and often stodgy food served in such foreign-run establishments as *The Globe* (Janovského 14; ☎ 66 71 26 10) and the *Radost FX Cafe* (Bělehradská 120; ☎ 25 12 10).

Note: although most of the restaurants mentioned in this section are expensive by Czech standards, they have an average price of around £12 per head and rarely exceed £20.

Cafés, drinking and nightlife

Café life is still thriving in Prague, and, in recent years, a number of the celebrated cafes or *kavárny* of old have been reconstructed or smartly refurbished. Traditionalists will enjoy the *Kavárna Slavia* (Národní 1), the *Café Louvre* (Národní tr. 20), the *Café Savoy* (Vítězná 1), the *Café Europa* in the Obecní dum (náměstí Republicky 5) and the cafes of the *Hotel Europa* (Václavské náměstí 25) and the *Hotel Paříž* (U Obecního domu 1); a passable pastiche of the sort of café Kafka might have frequented is the *Café Milena* (Staroměstské nám.22), which is run by the Franz Kafka Society, and is named after Kafka's great love and translator, the journalist Milena Jesenská. Literary cafés are also back in vogue, and there are a number of places filled with newspapers, books, and young would-be writers trying to look glumly intellectual: among these cafés are the *Literární Kavárna* (Betlémská 14), the newly opened *Týnská Literární Kavárna* (Tynská 6) and *The Globe Bookstore and Coffeehouse* (Janovského 14), a perennial foreigner's favourite that was founded in 1993 by a Beat Generation enthusiast from San Francisco, Scott Rogers.

Tourist groups have now come to dominate most of the city's more famous beer haunts, among which are *U Schnellu* (Tomášská 2), *U Svatého Tomáse* (Letenská 12), *U Kocoura* (Nerudova 2), *U Zltého Tygra* (Husova 17), *U Fleků* (Kremencova 11), and the *Novoměstsky Pivovar* (Vodičkova 20), which has tables arranged around the vats of the micro-brewery to which it is attached. Popular bars of more recent foundation include the Canadian-run *Jo's*

Bar (Malostranské nám.7; a backpackers' favourite), the adjoining *Rubín* (a smoky small cellar bar with adjoining fringe theatre), the *Konvikt Klub* (Konviktská 22; usually crowded with students), the *Whisky Bar* (Dlouhá 31; boasting one of the original tables from the Slavia), the serious, bookshelf-lined *Blatouch* (Vězeňská 4) and the delightful Irish-run *Molly Malone's* (U Obecního dvora 4), which has an endearingly rambling interior and a friendly Irish staff. Up-market posers and the self-consciously beautiful crowd gather at places such as *Barock* (Pařížská 24; decorated with baroque kitsch), the more tastefully appointed *Alexander's* (Rýbná 29; its visiting card is marked 'restaurant-bar-lifestyle') and the narrow and lively *Bugsy's Bar* (Pařížská 10), which specialises in elaborate cocktails acrobatically shaken by handsome tall blondes. For an ultra-sophisticated experience you should visit the *Ostroff Brasserie* (Střelecký Ostrov 336), where you can sit on stainless steel chairs sipping such exotically-named cocktails as 'Sex on the Beach', and enjoying superlative views of the floodlit National Theatre.

Despite the relatively cheap prices of the drinks, and the high expectations of so many visitors to this city, Prague's night-life is remarkably restrained and parocchial in comparison to that of many other European capitals. Some of the best-known nocturnal venues are the city's jazz clubs, including the Clinton-favoured *Reduta* (Národní tr. 20; see page) and the rather more appealing *AghaRTA Jazz Centrum* (Krakovská 5). The American-run *Radost* (Bělehradská 120) remains the most popular dance club.

Language

by Elizabeth Brimelow

Czech **grammar** is complex, in the manner of other highly inflected Indo-European languages: nouns and adjectives decline in seven cases; adjectives agree with nouns in number, case and gender; verb forms reflect both tense and aspect. No one will expect a visitor using a phrase-book, however, to have got to grips with all this.

Czech uses the Latin alphabet. The orthography, reformed by Jan Hus at the start of the 15C, provides admirable consistency in **spelling and pronunciation**. To English eyes it appears dense and prickly, but it is not as difficult as it looks. The following is a simplified guide. Approximate transliterations of Czech words are given in square brackets.

Vowels

a   Southern English 'u' as in 'cup', or Northern English short 'a' as in 'grass'

        eg. *ano* [u-no], yes

á   'a' as in 'half'

        eg. *dáma* [dah-ma], lady

e   'e' as in 'mend'

        eg. *den* [den], day

é   no real equivalent in English: roughly like the first part of the vowel sound in 'there' or 'pear' eg. *léto* [leh-to], summer

ě   'ye' as in 'yet'

eg. *pět* [pyet], five

i   'i' as in 'pit'

eg. *pivo* [pi-vo], beer

í   'ee' as in 'need'

eg. *víno* [vee-no], wine

o   'o' as in 'not'

eg. *okno* [ok-no], window

ó   'aw' as in 'claw'

eg. *móda* [maw-da], fashion

u   southern English 'u' as in 'put' or 'oo' as in 'book'

eg. *ruka* [ru-ka], hand

ů or ú   'oo' as in 'school'

eg. *dům* [doom], house

eg. *údolí* [oo-do-lee], valley

y, ý   exactly the same as i, í

The letters l and r can do duty as vowels and form a syllable when standing between two other consonants:

eg. Brno [Br-no], the chief city of Moravia

eg. *vlk* [vlk], wolf (cf. American pronunciation of 'missile' or 'turn')

Diphthongs

Unlike in English, both letters of a diphthong are pronounced equally clearly.

au   'ow' as in 'now'

eg. *auto* [ow-to], car

ou   'o' as in a Northern English 'oh'

eg. *houska* [hoh-ska], bread roll

eu   does not occur in any single English word; rather like the vowels in Northern English 'Eh up'

eg. *pneumatika* [pneoo-ma-ti-ka], tyre

Consonants

Generally the same or nearly the same as in English, but there are exceptions:

c   'ts' as in 'oats'

eg. *co* [tso], what

č   'ch' as in 'child'

eg. *český* [che-skee], Czech

g   always hard as in 'get', never soft as in 'general'

eg. *guma* [goo-mah], rubber

j   'y' as in 'you'

eg. *jak* [yak], how

eg. *kraj* [krai], region (rhymes with 'try')

eg. *olej* [o-lei], oil (rhymes with 'pray')

ch   Scottish 'ch' as in 'loch'

eg. *chléb* [khlehb], bread

r   rolled Scottish 'r' as in 'red'

eg. *ryba* [ri-ba], fish

ř   no equivalent in English; combines a rolled Scottish 'r' with the 'zh' sound as in 'pleasure'

eg. *řeka* [rzhe-ka], river

š   'sh' as in 'she'

eg. *šest* [shest], six

ž   the 'zh' sound in 'pleasure'

eg. *žena* [zhe-na], woman

d, t, and n, if followed by i or í, are softened, ie, pronounced as though there was an (English) 'y' after the consonant:

eg. *divadlo* [dyi-va-dlo], theatre

eg. *titulek* [tyi-tu-lek], headline, caption

eg. *není* [ne-nyee], it isn't, there isn't

These consonants may also occasionally be softened other than when followed by i or í; this is indicated by an apostrophe after the consonant or, for the letter n, a háček above it

eg. *loď*, boat

eg. *zbraň*, weapon

Stress and intonation. The main stress in Czech always falls on the first syllable of the word. Stressed syllables can be either long or short. So can unstressed ones. The idea of unstressed long syllables may seem odd, but they occur in English too: try saying 'always', or 'for his part' with the stress on 'his'. Unstressed syllables don't get reduced and distorted as they do in English; eg, in the word *matka* [mat-ka] ('mother') the second letter 'a' is pronounced in exactly the same way as the first. The word is not pronounced 'maht-ker' as it probably would be in English.

Intonation is roughly like English: down at the end of a sentence for a statement, up at the end for a question.

Useful phrases

Mluvíte anglicky? [mloo-vee-te ang-glits-ki] Do you speak English?

Nerozumím česky. [ne-ro-zoo-meem che-ski] I don't understand Czech.

Rozumíte? [ro-zoo-mee-te] Do you understand?

Jsem Angličan(ka). [Y-sem An-gli-chan(ka)] I am English (the 'ka' ending is used if the speaker is a woman).

Ano [a-no], Yes

Ne [ne], No

Prosím [pro-seem], Please

Děkuji (mockrát) [dye-koo-yi mots-kraht], Thank you (very much)

Díky [dyee-kil], Thanks

Dobrý den [do-bree den], How do you do (lit. 'good day', general purpose greeting)

Na shledanou [na-skhle-da-noh], Goodbye, au revoir

Dobrou noc [dob-roh nots], Goodnight

Kdy? v kolik hodin? [gdi? fko-lik ho-dyin?], When? At what time?

Jak dlouho? [yak dloh-ho], How long? (i.e. time)

Kde? [gde], Where?

Kde mohu koupit...? [gde mo-hu koh-pit], Where can I buy...?

Co? [tso], What?

Jak? [yak], How?

Jak se dostanu k...? [yak se do-sta-nu k], How do I get to...?
Smím...? [smeem], May I...?
Máte...? [mah-te], Have you got...?
Chtěl bych (chtěla bych)... [khytyel bikh/khtye-la bikh], I would like... (the 'a' on the end is used if the speaker is a woman)
Kolik (stojí...)? [ko-lik sto-yee], How much (does it cost)?
Prosím napište... [pro-seem na-pish-te], Please write (may be helpful if you are getting an answer in Czech which is an address, a number, a date or time of day)
Promiňte [pro-min-te], Excuse me. (As in English, this can be used either when accosting or interrupting someone, or as a mild apology.)
Je mi (velice) líto [ye mi ve-li-tse lee-to], I'm (very) sorry
Není zač [ne-nyee zatch], Not at all (lit. 'there is nothing for which', a polite response to thanks or apologies)
Máte lístek v angličtině? (mah-te lees-tek van glitch-ti-nye]. Have you got a menu in English?
Prosím, platit [pro-seem pla-tyit], The bill please (lit. 'please, to pay')
Pane, Paní, Slečno [pa-ne, pa-nyee, sletch-no] Mr, Mrs, Miss (Like 'Monsieur' or 'Madame' in French, they can be used with or without a proper name following. They are given here in the vocative case, which is used when you are talking *to* someone rather than about them.)
Intermediate numbers work like English, or, more precisely, like American English: 127 is said as 'one hundred twenty-seven', *sto dvacet sedm* (there is no 'and'). Czechs may, however, reverse the order of tens and units when saying or writing the words, eg. 'seven-and-twenty', *sedmadvacet* (the same words in reverse order, with an 'a' in the middle) as this avoids some grammatical complications. You may therefore hear '*sto sedmadvacet*' for 127. If in doubt, ask for the number to be written down.

For menu terms, see **Food and drink** (p 27).

Signs and notices

Pozor, Attention, warning, mind out for...
Vchod, Entrance
Východ, Exit
Otevřeno, Open
Zavřeno, Closed
Zakázán, Forbidden
Vstup zakázán, No admittance
Kouření zakázáno, No smoking
Nešlapte (nevstupujte) po trávě, Keep off the grass
Vlevo, Left, to the left
Vpravo, Right, to the right
Záchod, WC
Muži, Men
Páni, Gentlemen
Ženy, Women

Dámy, Ladies
Informace, Information
Zvoňte, Ring
Volný, Free (ie. vacant, not taken)
Obsazeno, Reserved (table), full up (bus), taken (seat)
Pitná voda, Drinking water
Pokladna, Cash desk, booking office
Platte u pokladny, Pay at the desk
Samoobsluha, Self-service
Šatna, Cloakroom
Objížďka, Diversion
Silnice v opravě (se opravuje), Roadworks, Road up
Letiště, Airport
Nádraží, Railway station
Nástupiště, Platform

Odjezd, Departure
Příjezd, Arrival

Občerstvení, Refreshments, snack-bar
Čekárna, Waiting room

Tourist glossary

Ulice, Street
Ulička, Alley
Náměstí, Square
Třída, Avenue
Silnice, Road
Cesta, Path
Kostel, Church
Chrám/katedrála, Cathedral
Kaple, Chapel
Klášter, Monastery
Svatý, Saint
Most, Bridge
Křižovatka, Cross-roads
Nábřeží, Embankment
Trh, Market
Tržiště, Market-place
Kašna, Fountain
Hrad, Castle
Zámek, Château
Palác, Palace
Věž, Tower
Radnice, Town hall
Město, Town
Vesnice, Village
Staré město, Old town
(Historická) čtvrtˇ, (Historic) quarter
Památky, Monuments, historic buildings
Hřbitov, Cemetery
Zahrada, Garden
Sad, Garden
Muzeum, Museum
Galerie, Gallery
Výstava, Exhibition
Národní, National

Knihovna, Library
Divadlo, Theatre
Opera, Opera
Socha, Statue
Obrazy, Pictures
Lesy, Woods, forest
Hory, Mountains
Kopec, Hill
Vrch, Hill
Důl, Mine
Řeka, River
Pramen, Spring
Mlýn, Mill
Jezero, Lake
Ostrov, Island
Rybník, Man-made lake, fish-pond
Přístaviště, Landing-stage
Loďˇ, Boat
Průvodce, Guide (either a person or a
  guidebook)
Kavárna, Café
Restaurace, Restaurant
Hospoda, Inn, tavern
Pošta, Post office
Známky, Stamps
Noviny, Newspapers
Koruna, Crown (Czechoslovak
  currency)
Haléř, one-hundredth of a Crown
Porucha, Breakdown
Nehoda, Accident
Lékář, Doctor
Policie, Police
Pas, Passport

Numbers

0 *nula* [nu-la]
1 *jeden* [ye-den]
2 *dva* [dva]
3 *tři* [trzhi]
4 *čtyři* [chti-rzhi]
5 *pět* [pyet]
6 *šest* [shest]
7 *sedm* [se-dum]
8 *osm* [o-sum]

9 *devět* [de-vyet]
10 *deset* [de-set]
11 *jedenáct* [ye-de-nahtst]
12 *dvanáct* [dva-nahtst]
13 *třináct* [trzhi-nahtst]
14 *čtrnáct* [chtr-nahtst]
15 *patnáct* [pat-nahtst]
16 *šestnáct* [shest-nahtst]
17 *sedmnáct* [se-dum-nahtst]

18 *osmnáct* [o-sum-nahtst]
19 *devatenáct* [de-va-te-nahtst]
20 *dvacet* [dva-tset]
30 *třicet* [trzhi-tset]
40 *čtyřicet* [chti-rzhi-tset]
50 *padesát* [pa-de-saht]

60 *šedesát* [she-de-saht]
70 *sedmdesát* [se-dum-de-saht]
80 *osmdesát* [o-sum-de-saht]
90 *devadesát* [de-va-de-saht]
100 *sto* [sto]
1000 *tisíc* [tyi-seets]

Days and months
Sunday, *neděle* [ne-dye-le]
Monday, *pondělí* [pon-dye-lee]
Tuesday, *úterý* [oo-te-ree]
Wednesday, *středa* [strzhe-da]
Thursday, *čtvrtek* [chtvr-tek]
Friday, *pátek* [pah-tek]
Saturday, *sobota* [so-bo-ta]

January, *leden* [le-den]
February, *únor* [oo-nor]
March, *březen* [brzhe-zen]

April, *duben* [du-ben]
May, *květen* [kvye-ten]
June, *červen* [cher-ven]
July, *červenec* [cher-ve-nets]
August, *srpen* [sr-pen]
September, *září* [zah-rzhee]
October, *říjen* [rzhee-yen]
November, *listopad* [lis-to-pad]
December, *prosinec* [pro-si-nets]
Note that days and months do not
have capital letters in Czech.

Background information

The history of Prague
Appropriately for a city of such fairy-tale appearance, there is a legend connected with the founding of Prague. In around AD 800, Countess Libuse, a woman with great powers of divination, sent her henchmen into the forest with instructions to found a town at the spot where they saw a ploughman (*přemysl*) constructing the threshold (*práh*) of a house. She married the ploughman (thus establishing the Přemyslid dynasty) and from her palace at Vršhrad, situated on a rocky outcrop above the right bank of the Vltava, predicted that the new town, later to be called Praha or Prague, would have a future so glorious that its fame would reach the stars.

The Přemyslids
The real origins of Prague are rather more prosaic and are connected with Slavic settlers occupying the left bank of the Vltava (to the north of Vyšehrad) about the beginning of the 6C AD. The citadel which was established here at the end of the 9C by the first documented member of the Přemyslid family, Count Borivoj, became the first seat of the Přemysl dynasty, and not Vyšehrad, as legend would have us believe. Prague was made a bishopric in 973, during the reign of Boleslav II, the Pious. In the course of the same century, numerous Jewish, German, Italian and French merchants settled on the right bank of the Vltava, at the meeting-place of several trade routes, and directly opposite the Slavic settlement on the left bank; the two areas were connected by a wooden bridge at the end of the century. The first known traveller's description of Prague dates from c 965, when the town was visited by Ibrahim ibn Ya'qub, an erudite Spanish Jew who had been sent by the Cordoban Caliph al-Hakam II as a member of a diplomatic mission to Emperor Otto I in Merseburg. He described in detail the lively international mercantile life of Prague, a town which belied its relative smallness by seeming to him to have been made 'richer by commerce' than all the other places he visited in Central Europe.

Prince Vratislav II (from 1085 King Vradislav I) transferred his residence to Vyšehrad, which was to remain the seat of the Czech rulers until 1140, when the seat was moved back to its original location. The importance of Vyšehrad Castle greatly declined thereafter, but the area of the right bank to the north of it, where the merchants had settled, became an increasingly bustling commercial centre, particularly from the 1170s onwards, when the wooden bridge across the Vltava was replaced by a stone one—the so-called Judith's Bridge— and special privileges were granted by Prince Sobéslav II to encourage more Germans to stay here. This commercial settlement, featuring a walled merchant's court known as the Týn, formed a separate township which was granted a municipal charter in around 1230 and is called today the Staré Město or Old Town; the extensive Jewish community was contained from the early 13C within their own walled ghetto attached to the northern side of this settlement. Meanwhile on the left bank of the Vltava, in the sparsely populated outer bailey of the castle, King Přemysl Otakar II founded in 1257 the township later to be called the Malá Strana or Little Quarter, the population of which was originally made up largely of German colonists summoned by the king. In the early 13C the district of Hradčany was founded just to the west of the castle, and Prague emerged as one of the most important and densely populated cities in Europe.

The 'Golden Age'

The highpoint of Prague's medieval development was to be reached during the reign of Charles IV (1344–78), who was to turn the city in 1355 into the capital of the Holy Roman Empire. Under Charles IV Prague became the 'Rome of the North', attracting scholars and artists from all over Europe, including the Italian poet Petrarch. Elevated to archbishopric in 1344, Prague became in 1348 the seat of the first university in Central Europe, an institution which bears to this day the name of Charles University. In that same year Charles greatly increased the size of Prague by founding yet another township, the Nové Město or New Town, which incorporated the former horse and cattle markets (respectively today the Wenceslas and Charles Squares) and came eventually to extend from Vyšehrad all the way to the northeastern corner of the Old Town. Numerous churches and other monuments were founded by Charles, most notably the Gothic cathedral of St Vitus, on which there worked one of the outstanding medieval architects of Europe, Peter Parler, who was summoned to Prague by Charles in 1353. In 1357, to replace the Judith's Bridge, another of Prague's great landmarks was created, the Charles Bridge.

With the succession of Wenceslas IV to the throne in 1348, social and religious tensions led to a period of cultural and economic decline. Urged by the religious reformer Jan Hus, Wenceslas curtailed the rights of the Germans at the Charles University, thus leading to the exodus of 2000 students and many professors. The peculiarly Czech tradition of throwing people to their deaths from high places—initiated by Wenceslas with the ejection of the prelate Jan Nepomucky from the Charles Bridge in 1379—continued in 1419 with the shoving of two Catholic councillors out of the window of the New Town Hall, an event which sparked off the Hussite Wars and was later dignified with the absurd and pompous name of First Defenestration. Renewed stability and building activity set in with the reign of George of Poděbrady (1458–71), but Prague's importance as a trading centre continued to decline. George's successor, Vladislav II Jagiello (1471–1516), brought the Renaissance to Prague by inviting here the outstandingly original architect Benedikt Ried, whose idiosyncratic Vladislav Hall in Prague Castle is the earliest example in Bohemia of the influence of contemporary Italian architecture. Vladislav also consolidated the political decline of Prague, however, by transferring his court in 1490 to the Hungarian capital of Buda.

The Habsburgs and decline

Through most of the period of Habsburg rule, which began in 1526, Prague continued to play a secondary role in European politics, the city being now subservient to Vienna. It experienced a brief political and cultural revival during the rule of the Emperor Rudolph II (1576–1612), who established his court at Prague, and indulged here his passions for collecting, lavish festivities, astronomy and the occult. He attracted to Prague artists associated with the so-called Mannerist style (most notably Bartolomaeus Spranger, Adriaen de Vries and Giuseppe Arcimboldo), as well as such leading and controversial European scientists as the astronomers Tycho Brahe and Johannes Kepler, the alchemist Edward Kelley, the surgeon Jan Jesenius (who conducted the first public dissection in Prague) and the mathematician Jost Bürgi, the inventor of logarithms. In 1612 he was forced to abdicate in favour of his brother Matthias, who brought the court back to Vienna in 1617. On 23 May 1618, over 100 members of the Bohemian nobility rose up in revolt against the Habsburgs and made their way to Prague Castle, where they perpetrated the Second Defenestration, an incident giving rise to the Thirty Years War. After the defeat of the Protestants at the Battle of the White Mountain in 1620—which took place on the western outskirts of Prague, near the star-shaped hunting lodge of Hvezda—27 of the Protestant leaders were executed on the Old Town Square. Occupied by Saxons in 1631–32, Prague was later besieged by the Swedes, who managed to take possession of the Little Quarter just before peace was declared in 1648.

As with the rest of Bohemia, Prague was left in a state of devastation at the end of the Thirty Years War. Yet the process of rebuilding the city (beginning with the reconstruction from 1630 onwards of the Little Quarter), together with the spectacular reassertion of the Catholic Church following years of religious strife, led to the transformation of Prague into one of the great Baroque centres of Europe. The highpoint of the city's Baroque development was reached during the early 18C, during the period of architectural supremacy of the prolific Kilian Ignaz Dientzenhofer, who was responsible for the vast Clementinum and countless palaces and churches, most notably that of St Nicholas in the Little Quarter, which is comparable to Longhena's Church of the Salute in Venice in dominating the skyline of the city. This same century saw the burgeoning of palace gardens in the Little Quarter, the creation of the wooded parks of Letná, Troja and Petřín, and the extension, between 1753 and 1775 of Prague Castle into the complex of buildings and courtyards that is to be seen today. In place of the medieval fortifications around the Old Town there was laid out between 1760 and 1781 Prague's first boulevard, comprising Ná Prikope and its continuation, Národní třída. Prague's development into a bustling modern city was consolidated in 1784 with the bringing together into a single administrative unit of the four hitherto separate townships of the Old Town, New Town, Little Quarter and Hradčany.

The 19th century, Czech nationalism and the arts

The rapid industrialisation of Prague in the 19C, and the increase in the city's population from 80,000 to well over 200,000, went hand-in-hand with a mood of growing Czech nationalism, and ever greater tensions between the Czechs and Germans in the city. In 1848 a Czech national uprising centred on Prague was crushed, but in that same year there also took place here the first Panslavic Congress. Germans lost their majority in the Prague Municipal Parliament for the first time in 1861, and in 1882 the Charles University was divided up according to nationality. In the latter years of the century the city's skyline was enriched by two massive neo-Renaissance buildings that expressed the aspirations of the Czech people: one was the National Theatre at the western end of Národní třída, the other was the National Museum, situated above what was now emerging as the new focal point of Prague life, the Wenceslas Square. Other major urban changes occurring in Prague at this time included the demolition of the city's remaining ramparts in 1874–76, and the destruction of the Jewish quarter through the creation in the 1890s of a long street named after the city of Paris and lined, as its name would suggest, with pompous apartment blocks and fashionable shops. An important Industrial Exhibition held in Prague in 1891 confirmed the city's position as one of the main industrial and commercial centres of the Habsburg Empire.

By the early years of the 20C, Prague was already becoming a leading European centre of the avant-garde, and the visionary achievements of a writer such as Kafka were matched by the construction of exceptionally original 'Cubist' buildings by the likes of Gočár and Chochol. However, it was the establishment of the Czech Republic in 1918 which led to one of the richest and liveliest periods in the cultural history of Prague. Pioneering poets, painters, designers, photographers and architects were all brought together by the Prague-based group Devětsil, which was closely associated with the city's developing reputation as the European centre of Constructivism and Functionalism. Uncompromising structures in concrete and glass grew up in the very centre of the city, while suburbs such as Podbaba and Barrandov became showpieces of modernist architecture.

Communism and democratic future

The German occupation of 1939–45, followed by the repressive years of Communism, drove the city's cultural life underground, but by no means extinguished it, as became evident in the great burst of literary, cinematic and theatrical talent in the 1960s, culminating in the 'Prague Spring' of 1968. World attention was drawn once again to Prague, but admiration turned to horror in August of that year, when television cameras showed Soviet tanks entering Prague's Old Town Square. On 16 January 1969, at a spot near the Wenceslas Square, the student Jan Palach set fire to himself in protest against the Soviet invasion. The subsequent years, up to the signing in 1977 of Charter '77, were among the greyest in the city's history, though they were also ones of rapid urban growth: in 1974 the city's underground railway system was opened, and the city boundaries were greatly increased by the incorporation within them of 74 outlying communities, bringing the total population of Prague up to 1,200,000 inhabitants. The new architecture was generally drab and mediocre, reducing the exciting Functionalism of the 1920s to unimaginative uniformity; a lively literary culture, however, continued to exist in the city, thanks principally to *samizdat* publishing, typewritten articles and books that circulated from hand to hand within a wide illicit network. Leading dissident meeting-places included jazz clubs, the *Café Slavia* (opposite the National Theatre), and the back-rooms of the Magic Lantern theatre, the latter coming to play a vital role in the 'Velvet Revolution' of November 1989, a revolution which had begun on 17 November with a large student demonstration making its way from the Vltava down Národní třída and eventually settling in the Wenceslas Square. Among the first acts of the Civic Forum Government led by the playwright president Václav Havel was, in January 1990, to rename Red Army Square after Jan Palach. The renaming of numerous other squares and streets in Prague gathered momentum in the course of 1990, and in November of that year the remains of Jan Palach were brought back to the Olšany Cemetery in the Prague district of Vinohrady.

The problems of popularity

With the return of democracy Prague has had to face the inevitable physical consequences of the sudden onslaught of capitalism and mass tourism. President Havel, though coming himself from a family of architects and developers, has frequently expressed his concern that the foreign investors now swarming into Prague will over-crowd the city with crass office-blocks, hotels, conference centres and shopping malls: in 1995 he praised as 'the first victory for common sense' the City Council's decision to call off an architectural competition for the design of a 180-room hotel to be built near the Charles Bridge. But a problem even more worrying than new development is the way in which so much of old Prague is being turned through insensitive and haphazard renovation into a Disneyland designed to please tourists. Façades that had been left to crumble during the Communist period are now being covered in garish colours that are often not only historically inaccurate but also potentially destructive as a result of the wrong types of paint being used: some modern gloss paints are impossible to remove without damaging the building, and can also trap moisture that might lead to further deterioration. In 1997 the director of the city's Centre for the Preservation of Architecture successfully petitioned the New York-based World Monument Fund to include the city's historical centre on its list of the 100 most endangered sites in the world. Without financial assistance, he claimed, few of Prague's original façades and roofs would soon be left, and the whole city would be turned into a characterless reconstruction like Nuremberg.

A chronology of Czech rulers

Czech State
The Přemyslids (870–1306)
Princes

Bořivoj	870–894?
Spytihněv	894–905?
Vratislav	905–21?
Wenceslas (Saint)	921?–935
Boleslav I	935–972
Boleslav II	973–999
Břetislav I	1034–55
Spytihněv II	1055–61
Vratislav II	1061–92 (in 1085 acquired the title of king for himself)
Vladislav I	1120–25
Soběslav I	1125–40
Vladislav II	1140–72 (in 1158 acquired the hereditary title of king)
Soběslav II	1173–78

Kings

Přemysl I	1197–1230
Wenceslas I	1230–53
Přemysl II Otakar	1253–78
Wenceslas II	1278–1305
Wenceslas III	1305–6

The Luxembourgs (1310–1419)

John	1310–46
Charles IV	1346–78 (Holy Roman Emperor from 1355)
Wenceslas IV, Emperor	1378–1419
George of Poděbrady, King	1458–71

Jagiello Dynasty (1471–1526)

Vladislav II Jagiello, King	1471–1516
Louis Jagiello, King 1516–26	

The Habsburgs (1516–1918)

Ferdinand I	1526–64
Ferdinand II	1620–37
Ferdinand III	1637–57
Leopold I	1657–1705
Joseph I	1705–11
Charles VI	1711–40
Maria Theresa, Queen	1740–80
Joseph II	1780–90
Francis II	1792–1835
Ferdinand V	1835–48
Francis Joseph I	1848–1916
Charles I	1916–18

Czechoslovak Republic
Presidents

T.G. Masaryk	1918–35
E. Beneš	1935–38
E. Hácha	1938–45
E. Beneš	1945–48
K. Gottwald	1948–53
A. Zápotocký	1953–57
A. Novotný	1957–68
L. Svoboda	1968–75
G. Husák	1975–1989
V .Havel	1989–1992

Czech Republic
Presidents

V.Havel	1993–

Art and architecture

Few Westerners coming to Prague for the first time are likely to be familiar with the names of most of the great artists and architects whose works make this one of the European cities with the richest concentration of monuments. Understandably for a city at the confluence of so many cultures, Prague is a place of exceptional stylistic diversity where you need only walk the shortest of distances to be confronted in turn by Gothic arches, Renaissance gables, Baroque statuary, Art Nouveau canopies, Cubist columns, and pioneering sheets of plane glass. But it is also a place where influences from France, Italy, Austria and Germany have often been distorted to strange and fantastical effect, as in the richly decorated gables crowning the toy-like houses, the exhilaratingly inventive vaulting of Peter Parler and Benedikt Ried, the swollen-formed Cubist buildings of Gočár and Chocol, and the near uncategorisable anti-Modernist structures of Jože Plečník. Prague, in short, is a city that will constantly excite the curious, open-minded visitor in search of novel cultural experiences.

From Romanesque to Gothic

Among the earliest and most distinctive survivals of Czech architecture are a number of **rotundas** ranging in date from c 900 to c 1225, the oldest being probably that of Levý Hradec near Prague, which appears to have been founded by Count Bořivoj, the first of the Přemyslid counts to be converted to Christianity. Of slightly later date is St Vitus's Rotunda in Prague, the foundations of which were discovered between 1911 and 1925 in the course of excavations below the Wenceslas Chapel in St Vitus's Cathedral: built by Prince Wenceslas (who was buried in its southern apse) this 13-metre wide structure soon came to attract so many pilgrims on St Wenceslas's Day that in the mid-11C Prince Spytihněv I was forced to build a large new basilica to contain them all. There are three other, heavily restored Romanesque rotundas in Prague, the earliest of these being St Martin's Rotunda at Vyšehrad, which is the only intact survival of the palace founded there in the late 11C by Prince Vratislav II, the future first King of Bohemia; the second of the rotundas is that of the Holy Cross (in the middle of the Old Town, at the intersection of Karolina Svetlá and Konvikstká), while the third is the late 11C St Longinus Rotunda, which adjoins the Church of St Stephen in the New Town. But the most interesting and extensive Romanesque survival in Prague is the early 12C **Basilica of St George**, which is the second largest church within Prague Castle: containing rare remains of Czech Romanesque painting, this building is in the shape of a Roman basilica but with heavy walls and small openings that suggest the influence of Ottonian Germany.

A **French style** of art and architecture was introduced into Bohemia and Moravia with the arrival in the early 13C of the Cistercians, whose influence first became apparent in the St Agnes Convent, the oldest early Gothic complex in Prague. A comparable Cistercian-Burgundian style can also be found in the magnificent Old-New Synagogue, which—given the law forbidding Jews from becoming architects—was probably built by the same Franciscans who had worked at St Agnes. In the meantime important advances were being made in Bohemian **town planning**, with Prague acquiring the first of its pre-planned quarters—the Havelské Město, and the areas around the Ovocný trh, the Uhelný trh, and the Rytířská streets. As with Bohemia's many towns of 13C foundation that were laid out on a regular ground-plan, Prague came to acquire as its central feature a large market-place (today's Old Town Square) lined with arcaded houses.

But it was during the reign of **Charles IV** that Prague was to experience the first great flowering of its art and architecture. Charles had been brought up in France, and it was thus not surprising that for the first major commission of his rule—the rebuilding of St Vitus's Cathedral in Prague—he should have called in a French architect, Matthew of Arras (?–1352). Matthew, who had previously worked at Avignon under Charles's friend Clement VI, produced a plan with radiating chapels in the ambulatory which was closely based on the French cathedral at Narbonne. However, Matthew died only eight years after work had begun on the building, and in 1352 Charles summoned to Prague an architect of a very different background, **Peter Parléř** (1330–1405/6).

Parléř, one of the outstanding builders of the Middle Ages, had been born to a family of architects in Cologne in 1330, and had probably received most of his training in the Rhineland. Within the limits imposed by Matthew of Arras's plan, Parléř introduced into St Vitus's Cathedral elements that look ahead to the German Sondergotik or Late Gothic. Among his achievements here was the creation of a bold, openwork staircase which was to be copied in the cathedrals at Ulm and Strasbourg; but his principal contribution was his exceptionally inventive vaulting, which included a dazzling star-shaped formation and a system of free-standing ribs spread out like a fan.

The age of Charles IV saw the development of an important local school of painting, to which much impetus was given by Charles's large collection of French and Italian illuminated manuscripts, and by the numerous foreign artists who were attracted to his court, such as the Italian painter Tommaso di Modena. Italian and in particular Sienese influence can be felt in the work of many of the early Bohemian artists, for instance, the Master of Vyšší Brod and in the anonymous painter of the *Votive Panel of Jan Očko of Vlašim*, a work which shows the Virgin and Child flanked by the donor and Charles IV in a way which recalls an Italian *sacra conversazione*. The leading and most idiosyncratic painter in Charles's circle was **Master Theodoric**, who is best known for a series of 129 panels painted between 1357 and 1365 for the Holy Rood Chapel at Karlštejn Castle: his solid but softly modelled figures are set here against a background studded with semi-precious stones, an unusual feature—also to be found in the Wenceslas Chapel in St Vitus's Cathedral—which reflects Charles's passionate love of jewellery. At the end of the century, during the reign of Charles's successor Wenceslas IV, the dominant Bohemian painter came to be the **Master of the Třeboň Altarpiece**, whose art, with its strong sense of colour and feeling for linear rhythm, turned not to the south but to the west, and has strong affinities with contemporary Burgundian artists such as Melchior Broederlam.

The intense period of building and cultural activity which Charles IV had initiated was cut short in 1420 with the outbreak of the Hussite Wars, and was not to be renewed until the end of the century, when the kingdoms of Bohemia, Hungary and Poland were united under the rule of Vladislav Jagiello I. Vladislav's rule saw some of the more spectacular achievements of the late Gothic style, as well as a budding influence from Renaissance Italy. Exuberant late Gothic ornamentation can be seen in the fantastical Royal Oratory in St Vitus's Cathedral and in the structures associated with Matěj Rejsek (c 1450–1506), for instance, the public fountain at Kutná Hora and the Powder Gate in Prague.

The Renaissance period

Later in his life Vladislav was to move his court to Buda and surround himself with Italian artists and architects, but before doing so he invited to Prague in around 1480 a German architect of extraordinary originality, **Benedikt Ried** (c 1454–1534). Ried, who came probably from South Germany and soon was to supersede all other architects in Bohemia, was given the monumental task of extending the fortifications of Prague Castle and rebuilding the Royal Palace there. For the latter he constructed in 1493 the vast Vladislav Hall, in which Renaissance features (in the doors and windows) are to be found in Bohemia for the first time, but combined eccentrically with late Gothic vaulting of a fantasy and complexity virtually unparalleled in the rest of Europe. Similarly elaborate vaulting was created by him in St Barbora's Cathedral at Kutná Hora, which he took over in 1515 from Matěj Rejsek, whose own vaulting here, though complex, lacks the flowing energy of Ried's.

The main painter at Vladislav's court in Prague was the **Master of the Litoměřice Altarpiece**, who is sometimes identified with the German artist Hans Elfelder; he was at any rate someone who had been brought up in South Germany and might also have had a first-hand knowledge of North Italian art. The altarpiece from which he derives his name was painted around 1500 for the chapel adjoining the Vladislav Hall, and is characterised by its lively and detailed realism. Artists from his workshop are often said to have been responsible for the frescoes of c 1509 on the upper walls of the Wenceslas Chapel, which reveal an Italianate sense of composition and perspective, as do the slightly earlier frescoes in the Smíšek chapel at Kutná Hora.

With the coming to power of the Habsburgs in 1526, the art and architecture of Bohemia and Moravia came to be dominated by Italians, most of whom were from the Como region. From the time of Benedikt Ried, Classical detailing had sometimes been applied to Gothic structures, but it was not until the 1530s that work was begun in Prague on a truly Italianate building. This, the so-called Belvedere in the Hradčany, was commissioned by Ferdinand I from Paolo della Stella, and is surrounded by a most elegant arcaded loggia decorated with exquisitely carved mythological and Classical scenes. The only feature which singles the building out as a work executed outside Italy is its bizarre copper roof in the form of the upturned hull of a ship, an addition of the mid-16C by the Bohemian court architect **Bonifác Wohlmut** (?–1579). Wohlmut's architecture represents a curious synthesis of Italian and Czech elements, and indeed he created for the same Belvedere an upper floor inspired by Bramante's Tempietto in Rome; another work of his is the organ loft in St Vitus's Cathedral, which seems at first wholly in the spirit of the High Renaissance and yet conceals Gothic vaulting behind its Classical arches. Such a synthesis was to typify the spirit of the Czech Renaissance, and even the many Italian architects and craftsmen who were to come to Bohemia in the wake of Paolo della Stella were to adapt to local building traditions.

Dormer windows, as well as fantastical parapets and stepped gables of every conceivable shape and size, are among the main distinguishing characteristics of the Czech Renaissance, as is the tendency to cover the exteriors of buildings with what are known as **sgraffito** decorations: the latter, created by incising into the plaster, are generally of scenes from Classical history and mythology, but are sometimes wholly ornamental. This style of architecture was applied as much to grand palaces such as the magnificent Šternberk Palace in Prague's Hradčany as to modest burghers' dwellings, and was to be current in Bohemia right up to the late 17C.

The last great period of court patronage in Bohemia took place under **Rudolph II**, at the turn of the 16C. Rudolph's mania for art, and his habit in later life of shutting himself up in his *Schatzkammer* to contemplate obsessively the accumulated treasures therein, gave him much in common with his Spanish cousin Philip II, with whom he also shared a taste for the bizarre and the erotic. However, unlike Philip II, the artists whom Rudolph admired tended to be precious and ultra-refined, the eroticism of Correggio's *Io*, for instance, being apparently preferred to the more full-blooded sensuality characteristic of Titian's mythologies. His favourite sculptor was the Flemish-born Italian Mannerist Giambologna, in whom he showed an interest which was one-sided and hardly subtle: after amassing almost all this artist's statuettes of Venus he wrote to him to ask for 'another naked female figure of the same size'. Rudolph tried unsuccessfully to lure Giambologna to Prague, but succeeded instead in attracting here from Italy the latter's pupil Adriaen de Vries (1546–1626), as well as two other Flemish-born artists, the painters Hans van Aachen (1552–1615) and Bartolomaeus Spranger (1546–1611), both of whom could combine precious eroticism with the sort of allegorical subject-matter that appealed to Rudolph's love of the esoteric.

As for Rudolph's taste for the bizarre, this was amply satisfied by the Milanese artist, **Giuseppe Arcimboldo** (1527–93), who had been first summoned to Prague in 1566 by Ferdinand I, and who was so admired by Rudolph that in 1592 he was given the title of Count Palatine. Arcimboldo, who worked at Prague not only as a painter but also as an organiser of lavish festivities, developed a speciality in 'visual punning' which was dismissed after his death as a mere curiosity but was to be greatly appreciated in the 20C by the Surrealists: he portrayed members of the court with appropriate still-life objects, thus turning the royal gardener into a composite of flowers, or the court historiographer Wolfgang Lazius into an accumulation of books. In comparison to Rudolph's patronage of the visual arts, relatively little has been written about the architectural commissions associated with him, though these were in fact considerable. Mention, above all, should be made of the Italian Chapel in Prague's Clementinum, which was designed in 1590 by Ottaviano Mascharino and was the first church in Bohemia with an oval ground-plan, a form which was to be much used by Bohemian architects of the Baroque period.

Bohemian Baroque

It is ironical that a country with such strong Hussite and Protestant traditions as Bohemia should have ended up as one of the great Baroque centres of Europe. The devastation caused by the Thirty Years War led to a rebuilding campaign on a vast scale, and most of Bohemia's old towns, in particular Prague, today have a predominantly 17C and 18C look. A vital role in the artistic and architectural renewal of the country was played by the **Jesuits**, who were determined to create resplendent buildings and works of art that would embody the spirit of the triumphant Catholic Church. In many ways their propaganda was quite subtle, for in their attempts to give a fresh image to the country, they turned to Bohemia's past and formed out of this a new national mythology which they hoped would counteract the Protestant one. A particular stroke of genius was to have discovered an obscure prelate called John of Nepomuk who had fallen foul of Wenceslas IV in 1393 and been thrown into the river Vltava. In the course of the 17C legends began circulating about him—that he had refused to betray the queen's secrets in the confessional, that a constellation of stars had hovered above his floating body—and eventually in 1693 he was canonised as St Jan Nepomucký, thus inspiring the consecration of many new churches and providing the subject of much of the religious statuary to be seen around the Czech Republic.

A truly Baroque style of architecture was slow to develop in Bohemia, and was not in fact to emerge until the arrival of the Dientzenhofers towards the end of the 17C. The majority of 17C architects continued to be from the Como region, and were for the most part deeply conservative. Shortly after the Catholic victory at the Battle of the White Mountain, a former Lutheran church in Prague's Lesser Quarter was transformed into Our Lady of Victory, which was little more than a gloomy, impoverished version of the Mannerist Jesuit Church in Rome. During the same decade the Duke of Wallenstein commissioned for himself a building misleadingly referred to as Prague's 'first baroque palace', though it is actually a structure wholly in the spirit of the Florentine High Renaissance.

The two leading Como architects of the middle and late years of the century were Carlo Lurago (1615–84) and Francesco Caratti (?–1677/9), both of whom achieved their effects of splendour largely through the unsubtle means of repeating the same elements over enormously long façades, the masterpiece in this style being Caratti's façade of the Černín Palace in Prague (1679–88). The main architect to break the Comasque hegemony at this time was **Jean-Baptiste Mathey** (c 1630–c 1695), a Burgundian by birth who had trained in Rome not as an architect but as a painter. The elegance and low relief of much of the detailing of his work are very French, and at the Troja Château on the outskirts of Prague he broke away from the block-like or quadrangular Italian villa through the introduction of a French pavilion system and projecting wings. An admirer of Mathey was the outstanding Viennese architect **Johann Bernard Fischer von Erlach**, whose own work was none the less essentially Italian in inspiration. Though active mainly in Austria, he executed one of Prague's most magnificent palaces, the Clam-Gallas Palace (1713), which reveals the influence of Palladio while at the same time accommodating statuary by the most dynamic of Bohemia's Baroque sculptors, Matthias Braun.

The major architects of the Bohemian Baroque were virtually all of foreign origin, and it seems possible that nationalist tensions within Bohemia led to difficulties being put in the way of indigenous Czech architects, whether Czech- or German-speaking. Significantly, the greatest of these indigenous architects, Balthasar Neumann (who was born in 1687 in the Bohemian town of Cheb) worked entirely in Germany, while the foremost German architects active in Bohemia, **Christoph and Kilian Ignaz Dientzenhofer**, originated from Bavaria. Remarkably little is known about Christoph Dientzenhofer

(1655–1722), other than that he settled in Prague at some time in the late 1670s, married there in 1685 and died there at the age of 67; there is also a document of 1689 which refers to him as someone who 'understood his art very well ... despite an inability either to read or write'. It is not always easy to distinguish his works from those of his extraordinarily prolific son, Kilian Ignaz (1689–1751), but it is generally agreed that he was the more brilliant and innovative of the two. The two architects can at any rate claim together to have popularised in Bohemia a dynamic architectural style indebted to the work of both Francesco Borromini and, above all, Guarino Guarini, who himself had produced a design in 1692 for Prague's Theatine Church of Our Lady of Perpetual Succour. The hallmarks of the Dientzenhofer style include undulating façades and interiors, plans based on intersecting ovals, a rich play of convex and concave surfaces, piers that project diagonally into the nave, and Gothic-inspired cross-vaulting such as Guarini had advocated. The supreme expression of this style is the Church of St Nicholas in Prague's Lower Quarter (1703–55), the most dominant landmark in this city after the castle, and as such a particularly eloquent assertion of resurgent Catholicism.

Though Guarini and in turn the Dientzenhofers had revived the use of a Gothic system of vaulting, it was left to Bohemia's most original Baroque architect, **Johann Santini-Aichel** (1677–1723), to devise a new style of church architecture which was later christened as 'Baroque Gothic'. Born in Prague, Santini was the crippled grandson of an immigrant mason from Como, whose family later added the name Aichel. As with Mathey, under whom his father had worked, Santini's training was as a painter, and he seems to have had no building to his credit when in 1702 he was chosen to replace the architect P.I. Bayer in the rebuilding of the Cistercian abbey church at Sedlec (now a suburb of Kutná Hora). Santini's adoption of a Gothic style for this and the later Bohemian monasteries that he was to rebuild can be linked to the same motifs which had led the Jesuits to create the cult of St Jan Nepomucký. Sedlec had been burnt down by the Hussites, and by reconstructing it in a medieval manner Santini was looking back to a past as yet uncontaminated by Utraquism and later heresies. The brilliance of Santini's work at Sedlec lies above all in the vaulting, which was certainly inspired by that of Benedikt Ried at Kutná Hora and combines the latter's elegance and complexity with Baroque dynamism. To appreciate the full originality of Santini's later architecture, one has to travel beyond Central Bohemia, notably to the Benedictine abbey of Kladruby in Western Bohemia (where, in the words of the abbot, he evolved 'a hitherto unseen Gothic style') and to the town of Žd'ár in Eastern Bohemia, where a bizarre climax to his art was reached in a symbolically formed pilgrimage chapel commemorating the rediscovery of the undecayed tongue of St Jan Nepomucký. Santini, a prolific architect, displayed a more conventional if none the less lively Baroque manner in his various works in Prague, for instance the neighbouring Thun and Morzin Palaces (which are particularly striking for their sculptural decorations by Braun and Brokoff respectively) and the recently restored Lederburg Gardens—one of a number of Baroque terraced gardens that give the Little Quarter so much of its charm.

The great surge of building activity in Bohemia from the late 17C onwards was accompanied by a renascence of the local schools of painting and sculpture. Few artists of interest were active in the first half of the century, with the exception of **Karel Škréta** (1610–74) who, though not the genius that is often claimed by Czech art historians, was a painter of great energy and versatility, who led an intriguing early life. Born to a Protestant family in Záborice in 1610, he and his mother fled to Freiburg in Saxony in 1628. From there he went to Italy, and spent time in Venice and Bologna before completing an artistic training in Rome, where he met and made a portrait of the French painter Nicolas Poussin in 1634. Whether out of genuine conviction or a longing to return to his native Bohemia, he converted to Catholicism shortly after leaving Italy, and eventually settled in Prague, becoming there a prolific painter of altarpieces. As a painter he owes nothing to Poussin but embraces a whole spectrum of Italian Baroque artists from Caravaggio to Guercino and Annibale Carracci. His dark and dramatic canvases sometimes display an impressive realism, which is particularly evident in his portraits, of which the most famous is a lively and informal group portrait of the gem-cutter Dionisio Miseroni and his family. Two painters of a slightly later generation are Michael Willman (1630–1706) and the latter's stepson and pupil Jan Liška (c 1650–1712), the former working in a strongly Rubens-inspired manner, the latter evolving a loosely handled and vividly coloured style which is sometimes described as proto-Rococo.

The leading painter active in Bohemia at the beginning of the 18C was **Peter Brandl** (1686–1735), who, like the sculptor Matthias Braun, enjoyed the patronage of the eccentric and visionary Count Sporck. Brandl was an artist as varied in his style and subject-matter as Škréta, painting portraits in an heroic French manner one moment and the next dark, religious canvases in which the paint is handled with an agitation reminiscent of the sculptural effects of Braun. A contemporary of Brandl was the portraitist **Jan Kupecký** (1667–1740), in many ways the greatest of all Bohemian painters, but who neither studied nor worked in his native Bohemia. An active member of the Moravian Brethren, he was born in Prague but was forced to emigrate with his Protestant parents to Pezinok, in western Slovakia. When he was 15 he ran away from home to avoid being apprenticed to a weaver, and entered a painter's workshop in Vienna before going on to Italy. After suffering years of hardship he was finally able to establish a workshop in Rome and stayed there until 1729, when he accepted an invitation from Prince Adam von Liechtenstein to settle in Vienna. His friend the portraitist Johann Caspar Füssli (the father of the Swiss-born English painter Henry Fuseli) described Kupecký's portraits as combining 'the power of Rubens, the delicacy and spirituality of Van Dyck, the sombreness and magic of Rembrandt'. Another contemporary, Anton Graff, gave a better idea of Kupecký's pictures when he wrote that you found in them 'true nature, life itself'. The realism of his portraits is certainly remarkable and gave much inspiration to the Bohemian artists at the end of the century who were trying to get away from the pleasing but shallow Rococo manner of painters such as Norbert Grund (1717–60).

The great specialists in large-scale **decorative painting** in Europe were the Italians, but relatively few of these worked in Bohemia. At the end of the 17C two obscure Italians, Francesco and Giovanni Marchetti, were invited to decorate the Troja Château near Prague but suffered the humiliation of being replaced there by the Dutch artist Abraham Godyn, who covered its main hall with one of the most spectacular examples of Italian-inspired illusionistic painting to be seen in this country. One of the main Italian exponents of this heavily architectural style of decorative painting was Padre Pozzo, who moved in later life to Vienna, where he influenced a number of Bohemia's artists, among them Johann Hiebel (1681–?) and the prolific V.V. Reiner (1689–1743). A more painterly and colourful style of ceiling painting was practised by the great Austrian decorators, all of whom were active at some stage in Bohemia and Moravia, including Johann Michal Rottmayr, Paul Troger and, above all, Franz Anton Maulbertsch, whose ceiling in the Philosophical Hall at Prague's Strahov Monastery (1796) is one of the culminating works of the Bohemian Baroque. Among the indigenous decorators to be influenced by the Austrians were Franz Xavier Karl Palko (1727–67) and Johann Lucas Kracker (1717–79), the latter being responsible for the masterly ceiling paintings in the Church of St Nicholas in Prague's Little Quarter.

Few countries in Europe have such a wealth of **public statuary** as Bohemia, and much of this was the creation of the Baroque period, when palace façades were embellished with struggling giants and atlantes, bridges such as Prague's remarkable Charles Bridge lined with gesticulating saints, and almost every town square in the country adorned with tapering piles of statuary that offered thanksgiving to the Virgin for protection during a plague. The earliest of the great Baroque sculptors working in Bohemia was **Johan Georg Bendl** (c 1620–80), who is sometimes thought of as the sculptural equivalent of Škréta, combining as he does Baroque drama with powerful realism; though intimate with the sculpture of the Roman Baroque, he seems to have been trained in his native South Germany, which perhaps explains his particular genius for lime-wood carving. All the other main sculptors of the Bohemian Baroque took part in the decoration of the Charles Bridge, including Jan Brokoff (1652–1718) and Matěj Václav Jäckel (1655–1738), both of whom were influenced by Bernini. Brokoff's son, **Ferdinand Maximilian Brokoff** (1688–1731), began his career collaborating with his father on the Charles Bridge, but soon surpassed him both in technique and imagination, evolving a heavy monumental style enlivened with vivid touches of realism.

Brokoff would have been without equal in Bohemia if his career had not coincided with that of **Matthias Bernard Braun** (1684–1738), one of the most brilliant sculptors of the European Baroque. Born in the Oetz Valley in North Tirol and trained probably in Italy, Braun came to Prague in about 1710. The *Vision of St Luitgard*, which he executed that year for the Charles Bridge, is a dynamic sculptural group of astonishing technical virtuosity, and so painterly in its approach to stone that you can well believe the tradition which ascribes its design to the painter Petr Bendl. In later years the agitated, almost hysterical energy of his art was to make the work of Bernini seem quite restrained in comparison.

Braun had a large workshop, but his influence on the Bohemian sculptors of the late 18C was slight. The leading sculptor of this later generation was Ignác František Platzer (1717–87), whose art owes less to Braun than to the more Classical style of Austria's foremost 18C sculptor, Georg Raphael Donner.

The late 18C brought with it major changes in the structure of **patronage** in Bohemia. The expulsion by Maria Theresa of the Jesuits in 1775 and Joseph II's dissolution of most of the country's monasteries in the course of the 1780s greatly diminished the political and economic power of the Church. The country's artists and architects could thus no longer depend on what had once been their most stable source of income, and were forced to rely more on the nobility, who came to be based for much of the year in Vienna and would come to Bohemia principally for summer stays on their country estates.

From neo-Classicism to Art Nouveau

An elegant neo-Classicism of French derivation became the dominant architectural style in Bohemia from the 1770s onwards, to be followed after about 1800 by an '**Empire style**' inspired not so much by France as its name would suggest but by Viennese architects such as Georg Fischer, who was himself responsible for the design of Prague's most striking Empire building, the austerely impressive customs house known as the U hybernů (1808–11).

Later in the 19C, when an at times fantastically over-blown eclecticism came to characterise the architecture of Central Europe, nationalist sentiments found a partial expression in the **neo-Gothic**, of which one of the principal Czech exponents was **Josef Mocker** (1835–1899), Bohemia's answer to Eugène Emmanuel Viollet-le-Duc, and a man known for his drastic restoration and rebuilding of many of this country's medieval monuments, including Karlštejn and Prague's Powder Gate. The major buildings of this period associated with the nationalist revival were in a **neo-Renaissance** style, which was initiated in Bohemia by **Josef Zítek** (1832–1909). Zítek was trained in Vienna under the architects of the Vienna Opera House, E. van der Nüll and A. von Sicardsburg, and devoted much of his life to the building of Prague's National Theatre (1867–81); his style was perpetuated by his one-time collaborator Josef Schulz (1840–1917), who was the author of this city's equally grandiose, if rather less eloquent, National Museum (1881–83). A variant of the style was the **neo-Czech Renaissance**, which, at the turn of the century, brought back a fashion for stepped gables and sgraffito decorations.

Though Bohemia cannot boast Art-Nouveau architects of the same calibre as Hungary's Ödön Lechner or Austria's Otto Wagner, there are numerous fanciful buildings in this style to be seen here, most notably Prague's newly (and disastrously) restored Municipal House, which was built between 1903 and 1911 by Antonín Balšánek, Osvald Polívka and Josef Chochol. The later development of **Art Nouveau**, when decorative exuberance gave way to more rationalist tendencies, is represented in Bohemia principally by Jan Kotěra (1871–1923), a pupil of Otto Wagner and the Viennese Secessionists, and whose works helped pave the way for the remarkable generation of pioneering architects active in Bohemia in the early 20C.

Nationalism and 19th-century Czech art

The **nationalist revival** of the 19C provided a great rallying point for painters and sculptors, and gave them necessary encouragement at a time when the conditions for producing art here were generally unfavourable. The situation for Bohemia's artists at the end of the 18C could in fact hardly have been worse, thanks to a combination of the Church's diminished role as a patron and Prague's decline into a provincial backwater. Concern with the provincial nature of Prague's cultural life led finally in 1796 to a group of Bohemian nobles and rich Prague citizens founding The Society of Patriotic Friends in Art. To help compensate for the loss to Vienna of Prague's imperial collections, this society began amassing a collection of paintings and sculptures which would later form the basis of the Czech National Gallery. Of more immediate consequence to the city's art life was the foundation by the society in 1796 of the **Prague Academy of Fine Arts**, an institution at which most of Bohemia's leading artists of the 19C were to receive their basic training.

The majority of Bohemia's painters in the early years of the 19C were highly conventional, including the academy's first director, Josef Bergler (1753–1829)—who painted stiff mythologies and Baroque-style portraits—and its first professor of landscape painting, Karel Postl (1769–1818), an artist in the Claude tradition. The portraitist Antonín Machek (1775–1844) delicately portrayed the leading figures associated with the nationalist revival, while the landscapist Antonín Mánes (1784–1843)—the father of a great dynasty of painters—is notable principally for his romantic landscapes of sites associated with Bohemia's past. A more remarkable painter than either of these was **Josef Navrátil** (1798–1865), who painted still-lifes of extraordinary freshness and realism that only came to light long after his death. But by far the most important painter of the first half of the century was Mánes's son, **Josef Mánes** (1820–71), an artist of great versatility, equally adept at portaiture, landscape painting, nudes, Romantic historical works, and Classical allegories. His central position in Czech art is also due to his fascination with Slavic country-folk and close involvement with the nationalist revival. A tour around Silesia in 1846 first aroused his interest in traditional rural life, and this interest was further stimulated in the course of numerous stays after 1849 with the Silva Tarouca family in their estate in the Haná region, a part of Moravia known for its strong folk culture; in 1854 he undertook a long journey through Moravia, Slovakia and Silesia with the specific aim of recording folk costumes and traditions. He designed banners for patriotic organisations and, in the last years of his life, ensured his lasting popularity in Bohemia through his delightful scenes of the Czech and Slovak countryside for the astronomical clock on Prague's Old Town Hall.

Vienna and Munich were the principal art centres to which Bohemian artists were attracted in the first half of the 19C. By the middle of the century, however, Paris had superseded these places in popularity, and a number of the leading artists of this generation spent a long period of their lives there, including the Courbet-inspired portraitist and still-life painter Karel Purkyně (1834–68), the landscapist and genre painter Soběslav Pinkas (1827–1901) and Viktor Barvitius (1834–1902), who abandoned an early career as a history painter to devote himself to the portrayal of urban life. The only painter of this period to gain an international reputation was **Jaroslav Čermák** (1830–78), who painted scenes from Czech history in a style indebted to French artists such as Eugène Delacroix and Eugène Fromentin; as well as spending many years in France, he travelled extensively around Dalmatia, and produced a large body of work documenting the struggle of the Montenegran people against Turkish domination.

From the 1870s onwards, the situation for artists wishing to work in Bohemia itself was greatly improved and, following a pattern widespread throughout Europe, many of the artists who had lived for a long time in France began returning to their home country. The ambitious buildings that were erected in Prague in the last years of the century, such as the National Theatre, involved the collaboration of virtually all the country's important artists, and indeed this whole generation is referred to today as the **National Theatre Generation**. Two of these painters, František Ženíšek (1849–1916) and Vojtěch Hynais (1854–1925) produced spirited interpretations of often ridiculous Classical subject-matter, involving numerous female nudes; another, Václav Brožík (1851–1901), after specialising in quiet landscape studies in France, made a name for himself in Bohemia with two large canvases representing *Master Jan Hus before the Council of Constance* and *The Election of George of Poděbrady as King of Bohemia* (1898). The major landscapists to have worked in the National Theatre were Julius Mařák (1832–1899), famous for his romantic woodland scenes, and Antonín Chitussi (1847–91), who spent much of his early life working in and around the Fontainebleau forest near Paris, and later applied a Barbizon School manner to the depiction of his native Czech-Moravian Highlands. The central figure of this generation was **Mikoláš Aleš** (1852–1913), whose works can be paralleled with the historical novels of his contemporary Alois Jirásek. He endlessly depicted scenes from Bohemian history and folk-tales, and at the National Theatre collaborated with Ženíšek on a great patriotic cycle entitled *My Country* (now in Moravský Krumlov). Lively and very decorative, his style was ideally suited to book illustration and after 1882 he virtually abandoned oil painting to devote himself to graphic work, a move which may also have been connected with his constant financial difficulties.

Aleš today is little known outside the Czech Republic, in contrast to his contemporary **Alfons Mucha** (1860–1939), most of whose life was spent in Paris, where he gained enormous fame for his luxuriously flowing Art Nouveau posters, in particular a series of the 1890s featuring the actress Sarah Bernhardt. Though an essentially decorative artist he worked in fact in many different fields, and was sponsored by a Chicago industrialist and Slavophile, Charles Richard Crane, to paint a series of 20 enormous canvases entitled *Slav Epic* (also now in Moravský Krumlov). An immensely wealthy and celebrated artist, he settled permanently in Czechoslovakia in 1922, taking up residence in a Renaissance palace in Prague's Little Quarter and continuing his varied career through such activities as designing stamps and banknotes. Mucha's fame in his home country has recently been further perpetuated by the newly opened museum to him right in the heart of Prague's New Town.

To the end Mucha's art remained deeply rooted in the world of the turn of the century, as did that of the later artist **Max Švabinský** (1873–1962), another highly successful figure working in many fields, from oil painting to the design of stained-glass windows and mosaics. The strong Symbolist elements in Švabinský's paintings are also evident in those of J. Preisler (1872–1918), who executed decorative works reminiscent of those of Pierre Puvis de Chavannes and designed mosaics for a number of Art Nouveau buildings in Prague. The principal exponent in Bohemia of an Impressionist style of landscape painting was Antonín Slavíček (1870–1910), while Post-Impressionist tendencies can be seen in the work of **Jakub Schikaneder** (1855–1924), whose highly subtle paintings mark the transition between Czech art of the 19C and the experimental generation of the early years of the 20C. Schikaneder began his career painting peasant genre scenes in the tradition of the French painter Jules Bastien-Lepage, but ended it with haunting and almost abstract evocations of dusk scenes in Prague.

Bohemian sculpture, after a period of decline in the late 18C, was to enjoy during the following century a gradual renewal in vitality which was to lead eventually to one of the livelier periods in its history. The Prague Academy of Fine Arts was not to have its own sculpture school until 1896, but a number of aspiring sculptors went there to study drawing from the Antique, including Václav Prachner (1784–1832), who evolved a robust Classicism. Romantic historical subjects were the speciality of the brothers Josef Max (1804–55) and Emanuel Max (1810–1901), artists of German origin who, while often portraying scenes from Czech history, did so in a stiff and linear manner which owes more to German rather than Czech sculptural traditions. Very sensual modelling, which was to be one of the main characteristics of later Czech sculpture, was shown instead in the early works of Václav Levý, whose bronze of the legendary Czech bard Lumír (1848) in the Klatovy Museum is sometimes regarded as one of the first eloquent manifestations in sculpture of Czech national consciousness. However, Levý was unable to compete successfully with the Max brothers in Prague and in 1854 settled in Rome, where he fell under the cold and sterile influence of the religious art of the Nazarenes.

The second half of the century was dominated by **Josef Václav Myslbek** (1848–1922), a sculptor whose richly worked bronzes were to be admired by Auguste Rodin. In Myslbek's work a romantic Slavonic fervour vied with a strong neo-Renaissance element, and in the course of the slow evolution of his Wenceslas Monument in Prague (1888–1923) a wild and romantic portrayal of the saint gave way to a statelier and more sober one. One of the greatest of Myslbek's pupils was **Stanislav Sucharda** (1866–1916), who displayed particular brilliance as a sculptor of Symbolist metal reliefs, and was also responsible for one of the most exciting of Prague's monuments, the Palacký Monument (1898–1912), a work with a pictorial verve worthy of Matthias Braun. The other outstanding monument from turn-of-the-century Prague was the Hus Monument (1900–15) by **Ladislav Jan Šaloun** (1880–1946), one of the few sculptors of this period to have developed independent of Myslbek. This much-neglected and misunderstood work revealed a painterly approach to bronze which was anathema to Myslbek, who had instilled in his pupils a rigorous tectonic approach to sculpture and had encouraged them to avoid the more extreme forms of Art Nouveau. A comparably isolated artist who had rejected both Myslbek's training and principles was František Bílek (1872–1941), the author of elongated Art Nouveau works of great expressive power. The more mainstream Czech sculptors at the turn of the century were heavily influenced by Rodin, including two of Myslbek's more important later pupils, Josef Mařatka (1874–1937) and Bohumil Kafka (1878–1942). The former organised a major exhibition of Rodin's work in Prague in 1902, while the latter entered Rodin's studio in Paris in 1904; in later years Kafka was to devote himself to Romantic historical works, culminating in his statue of Jan Žižka on Prague's Žižkov Hill, which is claimed to be the largest statue in the world. Another of Myslbek's pupils was Jan.Štursa (1880–1925), who achieved particular notoriety for his exceptionally sensual female nudes, executed in a great range of styles, from the Classical to the highly realistic.

The 20th century

The vital role which Czech and Slovak artists played in the art and architecture of the 20C has come to be recognised only recently, and is likely to become ever more widely appreciated thanks to Prague's magnificent new Museum of Modern Art housed in the former Trade Fair Palace. The towering genius of the early years of the century was **František Kupka** (1871–1957), one of the pioneers of abstract painting in Europe, but someone whose work was greatly neglected in Czechoslovakia after the Second World War. After studying at the Prague Academy of Fine Arts, and later in Vienna, Kupka settled in Paris in 1895 and was thereafter to live mainly in France. In his early years he painted a number of vividly coloured Symbolist canvases, but worked principally as a satirical artist and book illustrator. From the start he had been fascinated by spiritualism and the occult, and from this had grown an interest in the spiritual symbolism of colour. Soon he began experimenting with linear rhythms and colour schemes that attempted to approximate to the effects of music, and even started to call himself a 'colour symphonist'. Inspired by high-speed photography after 1909, he went on to portray effects of movement, and this was to lead in 1912 to the pure abstraction of *Amorpha: Fugue in Two Colours* (now in the Museum of Modern Art), which created a sensation at the Salon d'Automne of that year. The lyrical abstraction of these years, which can closely be related to the work of Robert Delaunay and the Orphists, gave way in the 1920s to a more geometric abstract style. In 1923 he published in Prague an influential theoretical work entitled *Creation in Plastic Art* (*Tvoření v Umění v ´ytvarném*), and in 1931 was one of the founder members of the French-based Abstraction-Création Group.

In the years immediately before the First World War, when Kupka had been engaged in his experiments in Paris, Prague had emerged as one of the main centres of the European avant-garde. The more modern tendencies in Czech art had been represented for many years by the **Mánes Association of Artists**, which had been founded in 1887 in opposition to the Prague Academy of Arts, and had organised several highly influential exhibitions in the early years of the century. One of these was an exhibition in 1905 of the Norwegian artist Edvard Munch, which had been derided by both the public and critics alike and yet had been a decisive influence on the formation in 1907 of Bohemia's first avant-garde group of artists, **The Eight** (Osma). Four years later members of the short-lived Eight group were to found the Association of Plastic Arts, the membership of which included all the painters, sculptors and architects who were to be associated with **Czech Cubism**. A knowledge of French Cubism among Czech artists was at first derived largely from visits to Paris, but an important part in its dissemination here was also played by the art historian and future director of the National Gallery, Vincenc Kramář, an avid collector of the works of Picasso and Braque. The main Cubist painters in Czechoslovakia were Vincenc Beneš (1893–1979), Josef Čapek (1887–1945), Emil Filla (1882–1963), Antonín Procházka (1882–1945), Václav Špála (1885–1946) and the aptly named Bohumil Kubišta (1884–1918); most of these artists were to remain faithful to the principles of Cubism for the rest of their lives. Filla, the principal spokesman of this group, made two attempts at Cubist sculpture, but the leading artist in this style was **Otto Gutfreund** (1889–1927), perhaps the most outstanding Czech sculptor of the century. After evolving an idiosyncratic

'Analytical Cubist' manner by 1911, later in the decade Gutfreund moved closer to 'Synthetic Cubism' before abandoning Cubism altogether after 1920 and producing works in a style which came to be known as 'Objective Realism'. In these last years Gutfreund devoted himself to the realistic but dignified portrayal of the everyday world, which he represented with simple, stately forms, often making use of colour and terracotta; these works were to have an enormous influence on Czech sculptors of the 1920s, including Karel Dvořák (1893–1950), Jan Lauda (1898–1959), Karel Pokorný (1891–1962) and Bedřich Stefan (1892–1982).

A phenomenon unique to Bohemia and Moravia was the impact of Cubism on architecture. Believing that the ever more severe brick and concrete structures of the Secessionist architect Jan Kotěra had become far too rationalist, a group of architect members of the Association of Plastic Arts attempted to create a more self-consciously artistic architecture, using a simplified ornamental vocabulary comparable to the forms employed by Cubist painters such as Braque and Picasso. Pavel Janák (1882–1956) was the leader of this group, but some of the finest buildings in the style were those created between 1911–14 by **Josef Chochol** (1880–1956) at the foot of Prague's Vyšehrad: the façades of these structures were covered in faceted diamond-shaped forms that owe a debt not only to Cubism but also to the diamond or 'cellular' vaulting of the Bohemian architects of the late Gothic period. Another of the Cubist architects was **Josef Gočár** (1880–1945), who was inspired instead by the ordering of Bohemian façades of the Empire period, and came to evolve in the 1920s an academic Cubist style made up of cylindrical forms, most notably in the former Legio Bank in Prague.

The optimism and excitement that followed the creation of the Republic of Czechoslovakia in 1918 led to a period of quite exceptional cultural vitality and experimentation. Thanks to its situation at the heart of Europe, Czechoslovakia became a meeting-point for all the conflicting cultural fashions of the time, and appropriated and transformed such influences as Constructivism and Productivism from Russia, Dadaism from Zürich and Berlin, Futurism from Italy, the Bauhaus from Weimar and Dessau, and Purism and Surrealism from Paris. The great focal point of the Czech avant-garde of this period was a left-wing group which was formed in Prague's Union Café in 1920, and given the mysterious name of **Devětsil**, which is both the name of an obscure flower and a composite of two words meaning 'nine' and 'forces', the forces in question being probably the nine Muses of Parnassus. It was a group which experimented with most of the 'isms' of the 1920s, and included progressive figures active in all cultural fields, from architecture and the fine arts to design, poetry, music, drama, and film; honorary memberships were even given to Charlie Chaplin and Douglas Fairbanks, though it is unlikely that these two figures would have been aware of this honour. Its leader was the witty and charismatic Karel Teige, an experimental poet and collage artist who believed in the integration of all the arts, and whose theoretical writings included an article on the work of art in the age of mechanical reproduction which anticipated by some ten years Walter Benjamin's famous essay on this subject. Teige's aesthetic was based essentially on the reconciliation of the opposing extremes of utilitarianism and lyrical subjectivity, a dichotomy which he described in terms of '**Constructivism and Poetism**': 'Constructivism', he wrote, 'is a method with rigorous rules, it is the art of usefulness. Poetism, its living accessory, is the atmosphere of life ... the art of pleasure.' The Marxist utopianism of Devětsil was not to survive the growing totalitarianism of the 1930s, but when the group finally folded, in 1931, it had managed to maintain its delicate unity longer than all the other European avant-gardes of the 1920s.

One of the principal ideals behind Czech avant-garde architecture of the inter-war years was a belief in the beauty of the industrial age, and it is significant that several of the Devětsil architects, such as Jaromír Krejcar (1895–1949), were inspired by transatlantic steamers and other modern forms of transport, incorporating into their buildings such elements as portholes, the rounded windows of express trains, and terraces balustraded with railings as on a ship's deck: such conceits were typical of Devětsil, the geometry of the architecture being invested with a strong element of poetry, in this case derived from the glamorous associations of long-distance travel. However, with the rapid growth of Devětsil's architectural membership, the poetry of the buildings was made increasingly subservient to their utilitarian and purely abstract elements, Constructivism becoming replaced by an international **Functionalism** of a type promoted by Le Corbusier, Gropius and Mies van der Rohe. An intermediary building was the wonderful structure now housing Prague's Museum of Modern Art—the Trade Fair Palace: built beween 1924 and 1928 by Josef Fuchs and Oldřich Tyl (1884–1939), this incorporates a strong element of poetry (evident above all in the balustraded Great Hall) into a monument that was claimed by Le Corbusier to have shown him how Functionalism could be applied on a pioneeringly large scale. A more brutally Functionalist building of similarly vast proportions was Prague's Social Insurance Building of 1929–34, a gaunt concrete structure by Josef Havíček (1899–1961) and Karel Honzík (1900–60).

An architect of these years whose work ran contrary to all the prevailing Modernist trends was **Josip Plečník** (1872–1957), a Slovenian architect who had been invited to Prague by Jan Kotěra in 1911 to teach at the School of Decorative Arts. Later Plečník formed a close friendship with the President Tomáš Masaryk, who commissioned from him in the 1920s the restoration of Prague Castle. His interest in the architecture of the past, as well as in traditional craftsmanship and materials, has led him to be hailed in recent years as a precursor of Post-Modernism, though in reality his work was so idiosyncratic as to defy rigid categorisation. His Prague Church of the Sacred Heart is certainly one of the more bizarre masterpieces of Czech architecture between the wars, taking elements from such diverse sources as an Early Christian basilica and an Egyptian temple, and treating them with a boldness which is thoroughly modern.

The artists of Devětsil, in common with the Dadaists, rejected the notion of high art, though in their case they at first expressed this disdain through taking an interest in popular culture, devoting themselves at the beginning of the 1920s to what they termed '**Poetic Naivism**'. Inspired by ex-votos and anony-mous shop signs, but also by Henri Rousseau, the Czech Cubists, and the child-like figures in the paintings of the Czech artist Jan Zrzavý (1890–1977), several of the Devětsil members, such as the painter and art historian Adolf Hoffmeister (1902–73), created self-consciously naïf works. Soviet-style Constructivism had little impact on the painters of this generation, though it did influence one of the most original of the Devětsil sculptors, **Zdeněk Pešánek** (1896–1965), who experimented with kinetic art and also made a number of works involving electric light. Constructivism was also an important force behind the works of the pioneering **photographers**, Jaroslav Rössler (1902–90) and Jaromír Funke (1896–1945), both of whom were technically adventurous and flirted with pure abstraction. Two other outstanding photographers of these years were František Drtikol (1883–1961) and the one-armed Josef Sudek (1896–1976), the former specialising in female nudes in disturbing, geometrical settings, the latter concentrating on the abstract qualities of everyday scenes and objects, and also creating some of the most evocative images ever produced of Prague. The Devětsil leader Karel Teige employed photographs in his spirited and mysterious collages, which he described as 'Pictorial Poems'.

The free rein given to the poetic impulse and to the subconscious in the work of Teige and other Devětsil members created effects of pure Surrealism, which was perhaps the lasting legacy of the Devětsil artists. Not surprisingly, when Devětsil eventually closed, many of its members went on to found the **Czech Group of Surrealists**. The French Surrealist, André Breton, described Prague as 'the magic metropolis of old Europe', and it was only fitting that this city should have become between the wars one of the main European centres of Surrealism. The Czech Surrealists included the sculptor Ladislav Zívr (1909–80), who devised a number of strange assemblages, and Zdeněk Rykr (1900–40), an artist remarkable above all for his delicate collages made out of thread, tissues and other ephemeral materials. Among the other Surrealists were the versatile Jindřich Štyrský (1899–1942) and the morphological painters Josef Šíma (1881–1971) and Toyen (1902–1980). Another of the painters was Kamil Lhoták (1912–), who was to be one of the most interesting Czech artists active in the 1940s and 1950s, executing strange and sinister landscapes that beautifully evoked the uncertainty of the war years and their aftermath.

As a whole the art and architecture of Communist Czechoslovakia was unmemorable, and certainly cannot be compared in quality to the literature, theatre and cinema of those years. The revolutionary Functionalism of the 1920s and 1930s led under Socialism to the drabbest of housing schemes and civic buildings, while the visual arts of this period suffered from a lack both of imaginative patronage and of a true spirit of communal endeavour. Inevitably, the most interesting artists were the dissident figures who used a subversive and characteristically Czech sense of humour to mock at officialdom: one such person was **Jiří Kolář**, who began as a banned poet in the 1950s before going on in the early '60s to produce witty Teige-inspired collages involving words, images and political comment. With the thaw leading up to the Prague Spring of 1968 the Czech avant-garde was able once more to reassert itself, with artists such as Milan Knižak introducing Prague to the 'happening' by slaughtering chickens to the sounds of loud rock music.

In the post-Communist world of today many of the dissidents of old have become part of the new establishment, with even someone such as Knižak becoming appointed to the directorship of the Prague Academy of Art. Fortunately, even in this new era of near unrestricted freedom there still remains a place for wittily subversive figures such as the 'Situationist' artist **David Černý**, who achieved considerable notoriety in 1991 by painting the Soviet memorial tank in the Prague district of Smíchov a bright pink (which was, as he explained to journalists, the colour of an infant babe in arms, a symbol of inno-cence). More recently, Černý has placed a giant immobile metronome on top of the granite plinth in Prague that once supported a massive statue of Stalin. The novelist Bohumil Hrabal only regretted that the statue itself had not been around for Černý to have applied his pink paint to that as well: 'Can you imagine', he wrote, 'what a wondrous sight that would've been ...? In one fell swoop this would've made Prague the world centre for pop art; a happening like this here in Prague would've set the crown on that American school initiated all those years ago by Allan Kaprow, Claes Oldenburg and the rest ...'

Music

'The music claimed me there a long time', wrote the American traveller Bayard Taylor on a visit in 1846 to the exuberant Baroque church of St Nicholas in the Little Quarter of Prague. Most visitors to Prague today are likely to have a similar experience, and to find themselves transfixed by the sounds of classical music that seem to emanate from so many of this city's churches and palaces. For this is a part of Europe that has not only given birth to an exceptional number of composers, but which has also enjoyed a reputation for its vibrant musical life since at least the late 18C, when the English musical historian Dr Burney came here and opined that 'Bohemia is the conservatory of Europe.'

Early Czech music and the Church
The early history of Czech music is centred around St Vitus's Cathedral in Prague, which is documented as acquiring a new organ as early as 1245, and as already extending its choral resources by 1250. With the flowering of the arts initiated by Charles IV in the following century, the cathedral choir came to possess up to 100 singers, and a richly varied tradition of liturgical music began gradually to develop. The course of Czech music would soon, however, be altered radically by the rise of the Hussite movement.

With their opposition to anything in religion that might detract from the primitive simplicity of early Christianity, the Hussites disapproved both of the 'decadent' art of polyphony and of the use in churches of organs and other instruments; they encouraged instead **congregational music** and the aban-donment of Latin songs in favour of ones in Czech, a language previously forbidden in church music. In 1561, when the fashion for choral music was at its height, as many as 750 new Czech hymns were brought together in the *Samostatný Hymnal* by the future Bishop of the Hussite Church, Jan Blahoslav (d. 1561), who, three years earlier, had published the pioneering *Musica*, which was not only the first musical text-book in Czech, but also the first theoretical treatise of any description in this language. The powerful and often folk-influenced melodies of these songs—later a rich source of material for the 19C national school—would be perpetuated over the centuries by Bohemia's numerous **singing societies**, of which over 100 were still in existence near the end of the 18C, despite the ban after 1620 on all but Catholic ones. In few other countries were social singing societies to proliferate so early or to exist so long.

But the Hussite abolition of the Latin liturgy, and the partial and temporary ban on instrumental church music, had the additional effect in the early 16C of cutting off Bohemia from the innovatory developments of the Flemish school, whose impact was so enormous on the music of the European Renaissance. Bohemia had little contact with these developments until the reign of Rudolph II, who turned his court into a truly cosmopolitan centre by inviting to Prague such musical celebrities as the German Hans Leo Hassler (1564–1612), the Italian Filippo di Monte (1521–1603) and the Slovenian-born Jacob Handl (1550–1591), who, despite his place of birth, is sometimes regarded as Bohemia's first polyphonic composer of European standing. Though Rudolph's court orchestra (which numbered about 60 musicians) had little direct influence on Czech music generally, it seems to have served as a prototype for the many **domestic bands** that were established in the 17C and 18C in the châteaux and town-houses of the Czech nobility.

Czech music in the 18th century

The musicians employed by these aristocrats were usually liveried servants whose duties extended beyond music to humdrum domestic activities, as was the case with František Václav Miča (1694–1744), who, while employed by Count Johann Adam Questenberg as valet at Jaroměřice, organised the other servants into an orchestra and composed in 1730 the first Czech opera—*The Origin of Jaroměřice*. The most famous employee of this kind was the Bohemian-born violinist and composer **Heinrich Biber** (1644–1704), who worked as a teenager in the orchestras founded by Prince-Bishop Karl von Liechtenstein-Castelcorno at Kroměříž and Olomouc. Biber was an extraordinarily original composer who retuned stringed instruments to produce unusual notes (an effect known as *scordatura*), and used these to great naturalistic effect in the evocation of battle scenes, or even—on one occasion—a gall-bladder operation.

In 1670 Biber left Olomouc on a mission to collect violins from the Austrian town of Absam, and never returned to Bohemia. Most other, but by no means all, Czech composers of the 17C and 18C followed Biber's example and spent the greater part of their careers working in German lands. Of those who stayed behind several made fascinating use of local folk motifs, notably the Czech composer **Jan Jakub Ryba** (1765–1815), whose delightful and unconventional *Christmas Mass* of 1796 is still regularly performed every Christmas Eve in the Prague Church of St James. This work, with its rich folk influences, is sometimes said to have paved the way for 19C nationalist composers such as Smetana.

In the meantime Czech composers were making a considerable name for themselves throughout Europe. **Jan Dismas Zelenka** (1679–1745)—one of several distinguished composers to have studied at Prague's Clementinum (another was Christoph Gluck)—was employed for the last 35 years of his life as a musician at the Court of Dresden: the author of stunnningly inventive works that made considerable demands on instrumentalists (especially the wind-players), he acquired such a reputation at Dresden that he was invited in 1723 to compose music for the coronation in Prague of the Habsburg emperor Charles VI.

Two of the best known operatic composers largely active abroad were **Jiří Benda** (1722–1795) and **Josef Mysliveček** (1737–81): the former—one of a large family of Bohemian musicians—worked in Berlin for 28 years as a Kappelmeister to the Duke of Gotha, pioneering during this period the dramatic use of the spoken word against a musical background (that is, 'melodrama', in the original meaning of this term); Mysliveček, meanwhile, settled in Italy aged 26 and wrote operas there that earned him the title of *Il divino Boemo*, or 'The divine Bohemian'.

Mozart in Prague

A large number of Czech composers were inevitably drawn to Vienna, including the prolific Křititel Vaňhal (1739–1813)—the author of more than 100 symphonies and 90 masses—and Leopold Koželuh (1747–1818), who succeeded Mozart as chamber composer to the Viennese court. Mozart himself was particularly influenced by the family of Mannheim-based Bohemian musicians led by **Johann Stamitz** (1717–1757), who was born as Jan Václav Stamic in the Czech town of Hávlíčkuv Brod. The symphonic compositions of Stamic and the 'Mannheim School', with their change in emphasis away from strictly observed counterpoint towards harmonic contrasting of attractive melodies, were fundamental to Mozart's musical development.

Mozart's debt to Bohemian music would be amply repaid, for it was perhaps thanks above all to Mozart that the Czechs today are so famed internationally as a music-loving nation. Though Mozart went as a child to Bratislava, Olomouc and Brno, he did not have any real contact with Bohemia until as late as January 1787, when he came to Prague with his wife Costanza to attend the production of his **Marriage of Figaro**, a work that had been improperly understood in Vienna. His English biographer Edward Holmes, writing in 1845, said of this production that 'the success of Le Nozze di Figaro, so unsatisfactory at Vienna, was unexampled at Prague, where it amounted to absolute intoxication and frenzy.' All this proved understandably exhilarating to Mozart, whose rapturous response to the city and its people was evident in a letter he wrote describing to his Viennese friend Baron Gottfried von Jacquis his attendance at a ball where 'the cream of the beauties of Prague is wont to gather':

'*You* ought to have been there my friend! I fancy I see you running, or rather, limping, after all those pretty girls and women! I neither danced nor flirted with any of them, the former because I'm too tired, and the latter arising from my natural bashfulness. I looked on, however, with the greatest pleasure while all these people flew about *in sheer delight* to the music of my 'Figaro' arranged for contredanses and German dances. For here they talk nothing but 'Figaro'. Nothing is played, sung or whistled but 'Figaro'. No opera is drawing like 'Figaro'. Nothing, nothing but 'Figaro'. Certainly a great honour for me!'

Shortly afterwards he composed, while still in the city, his '**Prague Symphony**'; and he returned here with Costanza later in the year to perform and to compose his opera **Don Giovanni**, which he dedicated to the 'good people of Prague', who, it would seem, were equally taken by him ('The people of Prague', wrote his contemporary biographer Niemetschek, 'were charmed by his affability of manner and unassuming behaviour'). On this second visit, in the autumn, he stayed at first at an inn called *The Three Lions* before moving on to the house of the Czech composer František Xaver Dušek and his wife Josepha (1753–1824), an accomplished singer. This house on the outskirts of Prague (it survives today as the Mozart Museum) proved almost an over-congenial setting for the composer, who found himself constantly distracted from his work by all the laughter, conversation and playing of bowls that took place in this most unusually warm of autumns. Finally, in the course of an animated party given here at the end of October, one of the guests is said to have reminded Mozart that the première of *Don Giovanni* was scheduled for the following night, and that the overture for this had still not been written. The story then goes that Mozart duly retired to his room at about midnight, ordered some punch and asked Costanza to try and keep him awake by talking. Though the overture was ready by the time the copyists came to collect it at seven in the morning, the copyists were not as quick as the composer had been, and the audience had to wait 45 minutes for the performance to start, at seven forty-five that evening. Whether this story is true or not, **Don Giovanni** was certainly composed at remarkable speed, and its overture must have been performed sight unseen.

'My opera Don Giovanni', recorded Mozart, 'was received with the greatest applause.' Some time later, Josef Haydn, replying to a letter sent to him by the director of the opera house, wrote that 'Prague ought to retain him, and reward him well too; else the history of great genius is melancholy, and offers posterity but slight encouragement to exertion ... I feel indignant that this *unique* Mozart is not yet engaged at some royal or imperial court.'

Mozart came back to Prague in August 1791, alone and in such poor health that he was observed continually taking medecine. Commissioned to compose an opera to accompany the coronation in this city of the Emperor Leopold, he begun this work—**La Clemenza di Tito**—in the carriage in which he had travelled, and completed it in Prague 18 days later. He stayed again with the Dušeks, where he was side-tracked this time not so much by any activity organised by his hosts but by the billiards in a neighbouring coffee-house. Yet even when playing billiards, Mozart's creative mind was busily at work, and he kept on interrupting the game to take out a pocket book and scribble down notes while humming away: he later astonished everyone at the Dušek household by performing here soon afterwards the quintet from the first act of what would be his last work, *The Magic Flute*.

The Prague public, worn out by all the revelry that the emperor's coronation had entailed, did not respond to *La Clemenza di Tito* with the same enthusiasm that had been hoped for by the composer, who died in Vienna later in the year. An enormous affection for Mozart has none the less been maintained in Prague over the centuries, and he has now come to be treated here not only as an honorary Czech, but also as a person integral to the stereotypical image of the city—a status enormously enhanced by the filming here in 1984 of Miloš Forman's film, *Amadeus*.

Mozart's visits to Bohemia have been given so much emphasis that it is easy to forget the important stays here made by other leading European composers from the late 18C onwards. The spa towns of Teplice, Marianské Lázné and Karlovy Vary were especially lively musical centres, and attracted such figures as Ludwig van Beethoven, Frédéric Chopin, Johannes Brahms and Richard Wagner (who began conceiving *Tannhäuser* while staying at Teplice in 1843). Prague too had a great appeal to composers of the Romantic generation, beginning with Beethoven, who paid at least four visits to the city between 1796 and 1812. From 1813 to 1816 the German composer Carl Maria von Weber was musical director of the German Opera House that was founded here in 1807; and from

1840 onwards Franz Liszt became a regular visitor to the city, meeting up here
with, among others, Hector Berlioz, Robert Schumann and a Czech composer
who drew heavily on Liszt's work and that of Wagner to formulate a truly
national Czech style—Bedřic Smetana (1824–84).

Smetana and Czech nationalism

The eldest son of a successful brewer from Litomyšl, Smetana grew up a
German-speaker, and was never fully to master the Czech language despite a life-
long dedication to the Czech nationalist cause. Whereas Liszt and Chopin were
only able to flourish in Western Europe, Smetana found in his homeland a
perfect environment for the nurturing of his talents: here he could follow closely
the great revival of interest in Czech culture and history while being exposed to
the latest developments in European music. After attending schools in Jindřichův
Hradec, Jihlava, Prague and Plzeň, he settled in Prague, where he immediately
revealed his political sympathies by composing in 1848 a work entitled *The
March of the Prague Students' Legion*. In that same year he composed his piano
work *Six Characteristic Pieces*, which he dedicated to Liszt, who became a friend
and mentor, and indeed advised him in 1856 to move to Sweden, where many
other Czechs had taken taken refuge in the wake of 1848.

It was after his return to a more liberal Bohemia in 1861 that Smetana
composed the works that would soon turn him into a national figurehead. The
country's new mood of optimism was epitomised by the inauguration in 1862
of a provisional Czech National Theatre for the performance of opera, ballet and
plays. Encouraged by this, and swearing allegiance to the school of Wagner,
Smetana set himself the task of creating a repertory of **Czech operas**, starting
off with *The Brandenburgers in Bohemia*, which, though composed in 1863, was
not performed until 1866, when he was appointed director of the National
Theatre. Later in that same eventful year he produced here the even more
successful **The Bartered Bride**, which remains to this day the most popular of
Czech operas.

Smetana's national consciousness was expressed not only in his subject-
matter but in his lofty and monumental compositions, which attempted to
merge the achievements of European pioneers such as Wagner, Liszt and
Schumann with a highly personal language derived from Czech folk music: in
contrast to other 19C Romantics, he never quoted nor imitated folk melodies but
tried to capture instead their essential spirit. A stirringly patriotic climax to his
work was reached with his cycle of six 'symphonic poems' collectively known as
My Country ('Má Vlast', 1874–79). *Vltava* and *The Fields and Forests of Bohemia*
celebrated the beauties of the Bohemian landscape, while *Tábor* and *Blanik*
evoked two of the greatest periods in Bohemian history. The two remaining
works of the cycle, *Vyšehrad* and *Šárka*, turned to the same legendary past that
inspired his opera *Libuše*, the première of which in 1883 was chosen to open the
magnificent neo-Renaissance structure constituting the new National Theatre.
Remarkably this last decade of critical triumph for Smetana was marked by
rapid physical and mental deterioration: made suddenly deaf as early as 1874,
he died insane ten years later.

Antonín Dvořak

After Smetana's death, the role of inspirational figure to the new generation of Czech musicians was inherited by a composer 17 years his junior, and with a notably different background and character—Antonín Dvořák (1841–1904). Born in the village of Nelahozeves, just to the north of Prague, he was the son of the village butcher and publican, and began his career as a butcher boy. Lacking the education and resources of the young Smetana, he gained his interest in music entirely through his zither-playing father, who conducted the village band. After becoming a violin-player in this band from the age of nine, Dvořák went to Prague when he was 16, and became a pupil of the organ school attached to the Bohemian Church Music Society. So poor that he had to keep himself by playing the viola in cafés and the organ in a mental home, he was even unable to afford to go to concerts ('As for Mozart and Beethoven', he later reminisced, 'I only just knew that they existed.'). In 1862, when he was 21, he was accepted as viola player in the provisonal National Theatre orchestra conducted by Smetana, and in 1875 he was awarded a grant for impecunious musicians by an Austrian government commmittee that included Brahms, who became therafter a keen promoter of his music.

Dvořák's roots in Czech peasant culture, and his lack of early exposure to classical music, gave him far greater credentials than Smetana as a musician closely wedded to the Czech soil. And yet, ironically, his aims as a composer were more overtly international than those of Smetana, and the folkloric elements of his music more integrated still into compositions betraying strong influences from Beethoven, Schumann, Brahms and, above all, Wagner. International success came with the publication in 1878 of his *Moravian Duets* and *Slavonic Dances*, the latter drawing on folk-dances from all the Slav countries but without ever borrowing existing tunes. Invited thereafter to England and the United States (where he held the post of artistic director of the New York Conservatory between 1892 and 1895) he became known especially for his symphonic works. Though he even referred to his famous symphony in E minor, subtitled *From the New World*, as 'genuine Bohemian music', his symphonies at their best transcend personal and national sentiments to achieve a truly universal significance.

Working under the shadow of both Smetana and Dvořák, but likewise considered as one of the founders of Czech national music, was **Zdeněk Fibich** (1850–1900), who wrote Wagner-inspired operas and concert melodramas. Unlike his more famous Czech contemporaries, he took almost no interest in folk music, and has since become virtually unknown outside the Czech Republic, where his works are still regularly performed.

Janáček's new musical language

Though barely four years younger than Fibich, the composer Leoš Janáček (1854–1928) was a late developer whose music belongs essentially to the 20C. Born in the North Moravian town of Hukvaldy, he became at the age of ten a choir-boy at the Augustinian Monastery at Brno, where he was greatly influenced by the monk Pavel Křížkovský (1820–1885), a Moravian composer of strongly nationalistic tendencies who was an ardent transciber of folk-songs. Janáček went on to pursue his studies in Prague and Leipzig, but remained so attached to his native Moravia that he returned afterwards to Brno, where he stayed for the rest of his life.

Isolating himself in this way from Prague led to his being treated at first as a composer of essentially provincial importance; but it was also the avant-garde nature of his work that hindered its early appreciation. In addition to collecting and notating the folk-songs of Bohemia, Slovakia and Moravia, he embarked in the early 1890s on the far more unusual task of recording on paper the melodic and rhythmic characteristics not only of the spoken word but also the sounds made by animals and inanimate objects. Calling these musical descriptions of real sounds **'Speech Melodies'** or 'Melodic Curves', he later boldly announced that 'no-one can become an opera composer who has not studied living speech'. 'Speech Melodies' encouraged him to abandon verse for prose in his own operas, the most famous of which was written in 1903, just after the death of his daughter Olga, whose dying rattle he had naturally recorded. Known originally as 'Her Step-Daughter' (*Její pastorkyňa*), this was first performed in 1904 in Brno, where it was a complete failure. Not until 1916, when it was premièred in Prague under the catchier title of **Jenůfa**, was its greatness finally recognised and Janáček acknowledged as an avant-garde composer of the stature and originality of Claude Debussy, whose new musical language had much in common with his own independently created one.

Stimulated by this late success, the elderly Janáček went on to produce most of the other works for which he is best remembered today, including the operas *The Makropolous Affair* (1926), *The Cunning Little Vixen* (1923), and *The Journeys of Mister Brouček on the Moon in the 15th Century*, a proto-Surrealistic piece based on the tales of the 19C author Svatopluk Čech. Just one year before he died he wrote his most important choral work, the *Glagolithic Mass*, an exultant work of almost barbarous joy in which 'Melodic Curves' are combined with the old Slavonic rite.

Whereas Janáček managed eventually to achieve a reputation as both an avant-garde and a popular composer, the same was not true of the far more prolific **Bohuslav Martinů** (1890–1959), who, despite being the only other 20C Czech composer of major international status, was heavily neglected during the Communist era, and is only now beginning to feature more regularly in the Czech classical repertory. The son of a Moravian bell-ringer, and indeed brought up in the village bell-tower of Polička, he was a largely self-taught composer much drawn in his mature music to the works of Debussy, Igor Stravinsky and Albert Roussel. Moving to France in 1923, where he came to be regarded as a leading light of the School of Paris, he was to spend almost all his remaining life away from Czechoslovakia while continuing to write music that expressed both his yearnings for his homeland (most poignantly in his *Fifth Symphony* of 1946) and his deep attachment to its musical traditions (for instance, in his 1937 choral work *Kytice*, which has a text drawn from collections of Czech and Slovak folk songs).

The persistent influence of folk music on Czech classical composers in the 20C is also illustrated in the work of Martinů's contemporary Alois Hába (1893–1973), who was a professor of composition at the Prague Conservatory from 1923 to 1953 and, like almost all the important Czechoslovakia-based musicians of the inter-war years, a member of the Přítomnost Society for Contemporary Music. Haba's main claim to fame is as one of the 20C most convinced exponents of composing in semi-tones, quarter tones and sixth tones (**microtone music**). Interestingly, he was originally prompted to embark on his life-long study of 'micro-intervals' largely as a result of his encounter with the modified scales used by Czech and Slovak folk singers.

Jazz and dissent

A major new influence on Czech music from the 1920s onwards was jazz, which soon developed into a national mania. One of the classical composers effected was **Erwín Schulhoff** (1894–1942), who, in addition to the challenge of composing an oratorio on the subject of *The Communist Manifesto* (1932), wrote a *Jazz Oratorio* and other jazz-related works. He was also a member of the Jazz Orchestra founded in 1936 at the celebrated avant-garde venue known as The Liberated Theatre (Osvobozené Divadlo), which was associated with the Devětsil actor-playwrights Jiří Voskovec and Jan Werich. The orchestra director was Jaroslav Ježek (1906–42), who wrote jazz music to accompany Voskovec's and Werich's absurdly satirical pieces.

The jazz-obsessed novelist Josef Škvorecký, in his books *The Bass Saxophone* (1980), *Talking Moscow Blues* (1989) and *Heading for the Blues* (1998), has beautifully recorded how jazz in Czechoslovakia was transformed from the Second World War onwards from a music of pure entertainment into a **music of protest**—'a sharp thorn in the sides of the power-hungry men, from Hitler to Brezhnev'. The Nazis, for reasons largely of misleading propaganda, allowed former Jewish members of the Jazz-Quintet Weiss to regroup at Terezín as 'The Ghetto-Swingers'. However, they generally considered jazz, with its African rhythms, as decadent music, as did their Communist successors, under whom musical life in Czechoslovakia reached its lowest point.

During the Stalinist era Czech composers were not allowed to stray far from an officially sanctioned Romantic style often incorporating folk music: the orthodox *Wallachian Symphony* (1952) by the previously experimental Hába is a typical example of this. A more liberal attitude to musical expression set in during the early '60s, and a number of interesting classical composers emerged during the last three decades of Communist power, including the electronic specialist Mikoslav Kabeláč (b. 1908), and the jazz-inspired Alexej Fried (b. 1922).

But the role of music as a symbol of personal freedom was assumed principally by **popular music**, which acquired in the 1960s and '80s some of the same emotive, epoch-making qualities that had characterised the works of Smetana and other nationalist composers of the 19C. The spirit of the Prague Spring of 1968 was epitomised in the mini-skirted figure of the singer Marta Kubišova, whose impromptu planting of a kiss on Dubček's lips was one of the key images of her generation. And it was, strangely enough, the censoring of a punk group unpromisingly named 'The Plastic People of the Universe' that led to the creation of Charter 77, the most sustained charter of human liberties in the history of Communist Europe.

Visions of Prague
The city through the eyes of travellers and writers

Tho' the latitude's rather uncertain
And the longitude too is vague
The persons I pity, who know not the city,
The beautiful city of Prague.
                    William Prowse, *The Beautiful City of Prague*

Prague, a city so frequently described as 'the golden' or 'the beautiful' or even 'the most beautiful city in the world', is a place that inevitably raises enormous expectations in the first-time visitor. But when I first came here, shortly after the fateful summer of 1968, my bright fairy-tale imaginings had to contend with what seemed to me a Kafkaesque reality: the beauty was undeniable, but so too was a sense of gloom and oppressiveness that filled me with mounting panic as I wandered through empty nocturnal streets, escaping occasionally from the constant drizzle into the smoky blur of beer cellars pierced by grotesque cackles and hostile drunken glances.

Travel literature is littered with hasty appraisals such as these; but, in the case of Prague, native writers, no less than over-impressionable foreigners, have generally agreed that this is a city where beauty, melancholy and anguish have tended to exist in almost equal measures. 'There are evenings', wrote the Prague writer Miloš Jiránek in 1908, 'when Prague, our filthy, gloomy, tragic Prague, is transformed by the golden light of sunset into a blonde fairy-like beauty, a miracle of light and brilliance.' André Gide referred to Prague as 'a glorious, suffering and tragic city', while the level-headed historian Peter Demetz prefaced his recent book on the city with the words 'I love and hate my hometown.'

The leading Prague novelist of today, Ivan Klíma, searching to define the 'spirit of Prague', concluded that this is a 'city of paradoxes'. One need only reflect on the extent to which the rapturous epithet of 'city of the hundred spires' is due to the four centuries of building work undertaken by the country's Catholic oppressors. But one should also consider the contrast between the city famously characterised by the French Surrealist André Breton as the 'magic capital of old Europe', and the pragmatic, down-to-earth, beer-drinking city that Kafka and other intellectuals found irritatingly small and cramped.

Perhaps no other city but Prague could have nurtured such opposing literary contemporaries as the ascetic, teetotal vegetarian Franz Kafka (the ultimate representative of the city's German-Jewish intellectual community) and the fat, drunken philistine Jaroslav Hašek (the creator of the quintessentially Czech anti-hero, Schwejk). Revealingly, even two of the greatest books ever written about Prague are works that take a diametrically opposed approach to the city. One is Angelo Maria Ripellino's *Magic Prague* (1973), a brilliant, difficult and densely argued book that takes off occasionally into flights of fictional fantasy; the other is Peter Demetz's recent *Prague in Black and Gold* (1997), a solid work of revisionist history that avoids imaginative simplifications and gives greater emphasis to Rabbi Löw's pedagogical reforms than to his golem, to the sober philosophy of T.G. Masaryck than to the *fin-de-siècle* fantasists and mystics beloved by Ripellino.

'I catch myself wondering whether Prague really exists or whether she is not an imaginary land like the Poland of King Ubu,' confesses Ripellino, who is severely criticised by Demetz for having promoted the fanciful, distorted vision of Prague that had been created by foreigners, developed by turn-of-the-century Czech and German Decadents, and then taken up again in the 1960s by the dissident left in reaction against the drab uniformity of Socialist Realism. But, as the Canadian translator Paul Wilson pointed out in his excellent *Prague: A Traveler's Literary Companion* (1995), 'Prague is far more than the sum of its physical parts or its history. It is a city of the mind and the imagination, a city that exists as vividly in poetry and painting and music and legend as it does in brick and stone.'

In the eyes of foreigners this rich imaginary city does not begin properly to take shape until well into the 19C. Up till then foreign conceptions of Prague had to rely largely on sober descriptions that did not bear out any exotic notions that might have been formed on the basis of the city's remoteness and important history. **Hester Lynch Piozzi**, an adventurous member of Dr Johnson's circle, recalled how her mentor had lost his temper once at a man 'for not being better company' despite his having 'travelled into Bohemia and seen Prague': '"Surely", added Dr. Johnson, "the man who has seen Prague might tell us something strange, and not sit silent for want of matter to put his lips in motion."' But when Piozzi herself finally visited Prague in the 1780s, she had to confess to 'have brought away nothing very interesting I fear; unless that the floor of the opera-stage there is inlaid.' Among her only other observations was that the food here was 'incomparable' (see p 23) and that 'here everything seems at least five centuries behind-hand.'

During the Romantic era, too, with its taste for the medieval and the bizarre, foreign accounts of Prague remained at first remarkably low-key, even when written by the future gushing author of *Tales of the Alhambra*, **Washington Irving**. Irving came here in November 1822, at a time when many of the palaces of the Little Quarter had fallen into ruins after their owners had departed for Vienna. In his diary notes he commented on the 'curious' architecture of many of the houses, and on how he found the people 'better looking than any we had seen yet in Moravia'; and he revealed a typically Romantic fascination with decayed splendour in his evocation of the collapsing, geese-ridden Čzernín Palace. But otherwise all he could say about Prague was that it had 'a fine, old continental look'.

Much more eloquent and forthcoming was Irving's contemporary and fellow Hispanophile the **Vicomte de François-René Chateaubriand**, who arrived on a May evening in 1833, and embarked on a walk up to the Hradčany: 'I climbed up silent, gloomy streets, without street-lamps, to the foot of the tall hill which is crowned by the immense castle of the Kings of Bohemia. The building outlined its black mass against the sky; no light issued from its windows: there was there something akin to the solitude, the site and the grandeur of the Vatican, or of the Temple of Jerusalem, seen from the Valley of Johoshaphant ... As I climbed I discovered the town below me. The links of history, the fate of men, the destruction of empires, the designs of Providence presented themselves to my recollection, identified themselves with the memory of my own destiny ...'

By the following decade, when the city was visited by **J. Bayard Taylor**, the author of *Views A-Foot. Or Europe Seen with Knapsack and Staff* (1846), Prague had already come to be perceived in a largely fantastical light. Under the blue haze that was present when Bayard Taylor made his own ascent up to the Hradčany, Prague looked 'like a city seen in a dream'. After eccentrically describing Prague as a 'half-barbaric, half-Asiatic city', he went on to write that the 'fantastic Byzantine architecture of many of the churches and towers, gives the city a peculiar oriental appearance; it seems to have been transported from the hills of Syria. Its streets are full of palaces, fallen and dwelt in now by the poorer classes. In a word, it is, like Venice, a fallen city.' As with so many later 19C travellers he acquired a certain morbid fascination with the then horribly decrepit Jewish Quarter, which he stumbled on by chance, and left hurriedly, pursued by beggars and other more sinister types.

The nightmarish quality of Prague hinted at by Bayard Taylor was exploited by **George Eliot**, whose visit to the city in 1858 led the following year to the writing of her short novel about the supernatural, *The Lifted Veil*, a novel so strange that no one would publish it until nearly 20 years later. This work begins with the narrator relating a disturbing vision he has had of Prague's Charles Bridge under a harsh sunlight: 'The city looked so thirsty that the broad river seemed to me a sheet of metal; and the blackened statues, as I passed under their blank gaze, along the unending bridge, with their ancient garments and their saintly crowns, seemed to me the real inhabitants and owners of this place ...' What is particularly unsettling is that he had yet to go to Prague, and—presumably like most Victorians—had only the haziest idea of what it must be like: 'I had seen no picture of Prague: it hung in my mind as a mere name, with vaguely-remembered historical associations—ill-defined memories of imperial grandeur and religious wars.' Eventually, when he finally comes to the city and escapes from his party to rush off and see for himself the Charles Bridge, he finds his vision to be borne out entirely by the reality. It is indicative perhaps of the tourist priorities of the time that the people he is with should want to start their tour of the city not with its famous bridge nor even with the Hradčany but with the Jewish Quarter—a part of the city that now comes to be central to the nascent image of Prague as a centre of magic, mystery and evil.

The ever more feverish interest taken by foreigners in Prague from the mid-19C (culminating in Marion Crawford's best-selling novel of 1882, *The Witch of Prague*) coincided with the emergence of a native literary tradition inspired by this city. The Prague-born **Jan Neruda**, in his *Tales of the Lesser Quarter* (1878) celebrated with ironic concision and humour the often eccentric everyday lives of those living in his own picturesque home district below the castle; the satirist Svatopluk Čech, meanwhile, used the setting of a well-known beer cellar in the castle precinct as the drunken starting-point for the fantastical exploits of one Matě Brouček, who travelled even to the moon and back to the 15C.

The gentle wit and whimsy of Czech authors such as these were in contrast to many of the writings of Prague's Germans and Jews, who captured in their works the dark, sinister and claustrophobic city that the Prague-born poet Rainer Maria Rilke found unbearable in its 'heaviness' and in its 'incomprehensible and confusing' presence. Egon Erwin Kisch dedicated himself to the city's underworld, night life and labyrinth of covered passages, while Gustav Meyrink, in his enormously successful novel *The Golem* (1915), took over from Marion Crawford in popularising the city's many alchemists and practitioners of the occult.

But the writer whose works did most to establish the image of a nightmarish Prague was of course **Franz Kafka**, who, as an agnostic in a German-speaking Jewish community that faced prejudices from both Czechs and Germans alike, was ideally placed to explore alienation and paranoia. The centre of his world was the Old Town Square and its surroundings, where he spent most of his childhood and youth, witnessing during these years the destruction of the decayed ramshackle Jewish Quarter where he was born. 'The unhealthy old Jewish town within us', he once commented, 'is far more real than the hygienic town around us.' This phrase is indicative not only of his morbid obsessiveness but also of his transformation of the city's topography into a geography of the heart and the mind.

The only one of Kafka's fictional works specifically to mention places in Prague was his novella *Description of a Struggle* (1904–05), which deals with two strangers leaving a party and walking by moonlight across the Charles Bridge and up on to the Petřín Hill: more concerned with mood than with plot, this is a hallucinatory account of a journey through a deserted nocturnal Prague that has rarely been so brilliantly evoked as a city of the dead. In all his other works, notably the posthumously published novels *The Trial* (1925) and *The Castle* (1926), the setting, though unspecified, can easily be imagined as Prague, with the cathedral referred to in the first of these novels being taken as St Vitus's and the eponymous castle as the Hradčany—an association that would acquire an added resonance during the Communist era, when the place was the focal point of a corrupt power and a monstrous bureaucracy.

Whereas the humdrum reality of modern Prague was glossed over in Kafka's expressionistic vision of the city, it frequently impinged on the fantasies of the growing number of foreign travellers now coming to Prague. One of the more critical of these was the poet and essayist Arthur Symons, who, while finding little to admire in the city's 'over-emphatic, unaesthetic ... bastard kind of architecture' ('Renaissance crossed with Slavonic'), was able to let his imagination loose in the Jewish Quarter, especially in the cemetery, where 'it seemed to me as if one were seeing all the graves of all the people who had ever died.' For him the Jewish Quarter was the one corner of Prague which had 'kept more than any other its medieval aspect'; however, by the time his essay on the city eventually appeared (in 1903), this district had already been pulled down, making more noticeable still the modern Prague which had been 'growing up in the image of Vienna, with tall characterless buildings, and modish shops'.

The clash between the real and the imagined Prague, the old and the new city, was highlighted by the popular novelist Vernon Lee, who confessed in her book *The Sentimental Traveller* (1921) that ever since childhood the 'mere name of Prague had awakened emotions of mystery and wonder.' Inevitably she had to pay for such 'imaginary raptures' in the course of 'three dreary, chilly autumn days in the Prague which exists outside the fancy ...' However, there were moments of escape from this Prague of 'electric trams' and 'intolerably gloomy' weather: walking at dusk into the 'silent emptiness' of the Hradčany she was able to relive her childhood imaginings through an encounter there with a strange and fascinating woman whom she romantically perceived as a princess.

Extremes of elation and depression were reached in the respective responses towards Prague of the writers Patrick Leigh Fermor and Albert Camus, both of whom were here in the mid-1930s. Leigh Fermor, looking back on his visit over 40 years later, remembered how the city had seemed to him 'not only one of the most beautiful places in the world, but one of the strangest'. Camus instead perceived a Prague of unrelieved grimness: lonely, frightened and constantly sickened by the 'cummin-flavoured food' (see p 23), he would later retain of the city little more than the 'smell of cucumbers soaked in vinegar, which was sold at every street corner to eat between your fingers, and whose bitter piquant flavour would awaken and feed my anguish as soon as I had crossed the threshold of my hotel.'

The one foreign writer of the early years of the 20C who managed successfully to bring together the conflicting moods of Prague was the French poet **Guillaume Apollinaire**, who, though paying only a brief visit to the city in 1902, profoundly influenced the Prague avant-garde of the 1920s and '30s, and made such an impact here that he is commemorated today by a street named after him. Apollinaire's experiences in Prague—the subject of his prose story *Prague Flâneur*—were distilled to their essence in the poem *Zone*, which appeared in 1918 in a Czech translation by Karel Čapek, with illustrations by the latter's brother Josef. The short section of this long and innovative poem that deals with Prague opens with the poet sitting happily in a suburban garden, where he is distracted from his writing of *Prague Flâneur* by the sight of a beetle asleep inside a rose. The next lines recall a panic attack the poet had while visiting the Wenceslas Chapel in St Vitus's Cathedral: looking here for the precious stone that is said to bear the features of Napoleon, Apollinaire discovered instead his own sad face. The image of the famous backward-moving clock in the Jewish Town Hall then sets him on a journey into his own past, which continues as he climbs up to the Hradčany and listens in the evening to 'Czech songs being sung in the taverns'.

Apollinaire's technique of compiling apparently disconnected images was emulated by the writers associated with Poetism, a major Czech movement of the inter-war years that—under the influence of French Surrealism—advocated free association and the impulse of the subconcious. The leading writer associated with the movement was **Vitězslav Nezval** (1900–58), who, after beginning his career as a 'proletarian' poet, reacted against doctrinaire rhetoric in favour of a style that was better able to express what was contradictory and paradoxical in experience. Prague, the ultimate symbol of this contradictoriness, provided him with one of his major themes, and inspired perhaps his finest collection, *Prague with Fingers of Rain* (1936). His love for Prague was by no means immediate, as is indicated in his poem *Walker in Prague*, which evokes the Camus-like state of solitude and depression in which his days were spent here after first arriving in the city in April 1920:

Like a practical joke the Castle suddenly stands before me
I shut my eyes it was a mirage
A fragment of memory the tears are welling we are in Prague
I try in vain to sleep in the room where a man once shot himself
Thus I walked for days and nights on end
Unspeakably dejected
Everything was strange I did not dare to remember
Until one day
I met a memory
It was a friend
He took me along under his umbrella
We sat in a room the piano was playing at last I shall be able to
    love you Prague

The theme of falling in love with Prague was taken up again in the title poem of *Prague with Fingers of Rain*, which, after an incantatory repetition of the line 'That I learned to love her in a way no one loved her before', ends with the words:

For time flies and there's so much left I want to say about you
Time flies and I have still not said enough about you
Time flies like a swallow lighting up the old stars over Prague

Another poet whose early development was comparable to that of Nezval was **Jaroslav Seifert**, who also moved from Proletarianism to Poetism, and was similarly influenced by Apollinaire, to the extent even of fantasising about sitting next to the French poet in Prague's *Café Slavia* (see p 169). He too was an obsessive lover of Prague, which, at dusk, seemed to him 'more beautiful than Rome'. In later years, when he went on to confirm his unofficial status as Czech national poet after becoming the first Czech recipient of the Nobel Prize for Literature, he came to view Prague through an increasingly romantic haze, as is illustrated in his poem *View from Charles Bridge*:

Day after day I gaze in gratitude
on the Castle of Prague
and on its Cathedral:
I cannot tear my eyes away
from that picture.
It is mine
and I also believe it is miraculous.

The complex spirit of Prague is one that in recent years has been evoked more vividly in fiction than in poetry, including works by such disparate foreign authors as Philip Roth and Bruce Chatwin. The former's *The Prague Orgy* (1985) is an absurdly funny yet deeply serious portrayal of the city's dissident scene in the 1970s, while the latter's *Utz* (1989) is a sparsely told tale set near the Jewish Cemetery and commenting obliquely on the golem story. Prague has also been a powerful presence in the works of the many Czech authors who, since the 1960s, have made their nation's literature one of the most translated into English. Though the city has been evoked only partially by both Milan Kundera (who is far more concerned with ideas than with specific places) and Josef Škvorecký (whose novels are set mainly in rural eastern Bohemia, with the major exception of his marvellous *Miss Silver's Past*, 1969), the place is of paramount importance to those other two leading Czech writers of modern times, **Ivan Klíma** and **Bohumil Hrabal**.

In his stimulating essay *The Spirit of Prague* (1994), Klíma gave particular emphasis to this city's intensely human aspects—the absence in its centre of any tall building or triumphal arch, the local dislike of ostentatiousness, the paucity of public monuments and memorials. This is exactly the modest Prague that serves as the backgound to his largely autobiographical works, such as *My Golden Trades* (1992), which describes with quiet humour and delicious irony the ridiculous variety of jobs he was forced to undertake during the Communist period. Communism, as Klíma himself has acknowledged, at least enabled Czech writers to have a far greater insight than they might otherwise have had into the everyday lives of the city's inhabitants. This was certainly true of Hrabal, whose experiences while working compacting wastepaper and books were put to brilliant allegorical and humorous use in his short work, *Too Loud a Solitude* (1976). Indeed Hrabal regarded himself less as a writer than as a teller of stories related to him either at work, or, more usually, in the numerous Prague bars that he used to frequent. Yet, in contrast to Klíma's delicate and understated approach to the city, Hrabal's vision of Prague was one in which a Hašek-like earthiness merged at times into the zany and the fantastical, as in his profoundly entertaining *I Served the King of England* (1989), which is an account of Bohemia's 20C history as seen from the grotesquely distorted viewpoint of a diminutive waiter with a preternatural gift for survival and the giving of sexual pleasure.

Younger Czech writers, whose works are only now beginning to be known outside the Czech Republic, have continued to perpetuate a vision of Prague based on such polarities as the magical and the coarse, the disturbing and the ludicrous, the intimate and the broadly expressionist. One of the more imaginative of these new talents is Michal Ajvaz, whose Kafkaesque novel *The Other City* (1993) includes a particularly powerful nocturnal scene set high up in the tower of the Little Quarter Church of St Nicholas. Here, as he observes the deserted moonlit cityscape around him, the narrator meets a mysterious beautiful young woman, on kissing whom he is suddenly attacked by a shark: 'I remained alone with the shark on the gallery of the tower above the sleeping city.'

In the post-Communist Prague of today, in a city that is daily becoming more crowded, more garish, more Americanised, and more like any other European capital, one might have expected writers to have observed the place in a more normal light. And yet the very speed with which all these changes have come about has appeared to many to contain its own element of magic and the unreal, so much so that the authoress Daniela Hodrová, in her essay *I See a Great City* ..., asked herself whether 'this had all been just a dream—the kind in which the prisoner dreams that he has become king?' The bizarreness and surreal absurdities of the city's sudden recent transformation have been sharply chronicled by one of the hippest of Prague's current writers, **Jáchym Topol**, a former singer and songwriter and co-founder of what is now known as *Revolver Review* in deference to the strangely persistent local cult of John Lennon:

'The city was changing', runs the refrain of Topol's short story *A Visit to the Train Station* (1993). 'Iron grills and shutters pulled down for years and gone to rust were given fresh coats of paint and often a sign with somebody's name on it. Dusty cellars and dirty beer joints in what used to be the Jewish Quarter were cleverly converted into luxury stores. You could find steamer trunks from the last century, a book dictated by Madonna herself with a piece of her chain included, pineapples and fine tobacco, diaries of dead actresses and trendy wheels from farmers' waggons, whips and dolls and travel grails with adventurer's blood in them, coins and likenesses of Kafka, shooting galleries with all the proletarian presidents as targets, rags and bones and skins, anything you could think of.'

Appropriately, the narrator observes this changing Prague in the state that epitomizes the city's maelstrom of conflicting emotions in which painful reality comes fast on the heels of hearty indulgence, good humour and magical intoxication—a violent hangover.

Further reading

General, travel literature, fiction and poetry

No other European city apart from Barcelona has been the recent subject of so
many **general books** as Prague. The two that stand out head and shoulders
above the rest are Angelo Maria Ripellino's *Magic Prague* (first English paperback
edition 1995) and Peter Demetz's *Prague in Black and Gold* (1997). The former,
though a difficult read and almost oppressively erudite, is filled with exciting,
fanciful ideas and wonderful esoteric information; the latter, in contrast, is a
clear, sturdy and eminently readable work of scholarship that does its best to
deprive the city of its 'magical' reputation. Those in search of a lightweight,
romantic and old-fashioned account might be better off with Count Francis
Lützow's *The Story of Prague* (London, 1902). The most famous photographic
introduction to the city is Josef Sudek's stunning *Praha* (Prague, 1948).

Among **early travellers'** impressions of the city are those contained in
Hester Lynch Piozzi's *Observations and Reflections. Made in the course of a journey
through France, Italy and Germany* (1789; edited by Herbert Barrows, Ann Arbor,
Michigan, 1967); Volume 5 of the *Memoirs of Chateaubriand* (1833; translated
by Alexander Feixara de Mattos, 6 volumes, London, 1902); *The Journals of
Washington Irving* (1822; edited by William P. Trent and George S. Hellman,
Boston, 1919); and J. Bayard Taylor's *Views A-Foot. Or Europe Seen with Knapsack
and Staff* (1846). Mozart's stay in the city is documented in *The Letters of Mozart
and his Family* (edited and translated by Emily Anderson, Basingstoke, 1985), as
well as in such early accounts as Edward Holmes' *The Life of Mozart* (1845;
reprinted with introduction and additional notes by Christopher Hogwood,
London, 1991) and Edward Moricke's *Mozart's Journey to Prague* (1850–51;
translated by Leopold von Loewenstein-Wertheim, London, 1957).

Of the travellers' accounts that proliferated from the late 19C onwards, one of the
most interesting if also misguided ('the Bohemians have produced nothing beautiful in any of the plastic arts' runs a typical sentence) is Arthur W. Symons's
eloquent essay on Prague in his book *Cities* (London, 1903); a wholly uncritical
approach towards the city is taken instead in B. Granville Baker's *From a Terrace
in Prague* (London, 1923), which is almost contemporary with Vernon Lee's similarly romantic *The Sentimental Traveller. Notes on Places* (Leipzig, 1921). Albert
Camus' bitter tale of his experiences in the city, included in his *Selected Essays and
Notebooks* (Harmondsworth, 1984), is a good antidote to the ecstatic reminis-
cences featured in Patrick Leigh Fermor's *A Time of Gifts* (London, 1979), which
is written in the author's characteristically indigestible flowery style. Accounts of
a more recent Prague include those that appear in V.S. Pritchett's *Foreign Faces*
(London, 1964), Stephen Brook's *The Double Eagle: Vienna, Budapest and Prague*
(London, 1988), Rory Maclean's semi-fictional *Stalin's Nose: Across the Face of
Europe* (London, 1992) and Geoffrey Hodgson's readable if pedestrian *A New
Grand Tour. How Europe's Great Cities Made our World* (London, 1995).

Undoubtedly the most enjoyable preparation you can make before visiting Prague
is to immerse yourself in the wealth of novels and poems written about the city. F.
Marion Crawford's occult classic *The Witch of Prague* (London, 1976), Philip Roth's
amusing *The Prague Orgy* (Harmondsworth, 1985) and Bruce Chatwin's beautifully
enigmatic *Utz* (London, 1989) are perhaps the three best-known **foreign works**

of fiction set in Prague; also worth reading is Martha Gellhorn's autobiographical novel *A Stricken Field* (London, 1986), which deals with the experiences of an American journalist working in Prague after the Munich pact of 1938.

Apollinaire's influential poem *Zone*, with its famous section on Prague, is featured in Oliver Bernard's *Apollinaire: Selected Poems* in the Penguin Modern European Poets series (Harmondsworth, 1965). For English translations of **Czech poetry** inspired by Prague see *Three Czech Poets: Vitězslav Nezval, Antonín Bartušek, Josef Hanzlík* (translated by Ewald Osers and George Theiner, Penguin Modern Poets, Harmondsworth, 1971) and *The Selected Poetry of Jaroslav Seifert* (translated by Ewald Osers, London, 1986).

Two classics of **Czech fiction** are Jan Neruda's *Prague Tales* (1878; translated by Michael Henry Heim, with an introduction by Ivan Klíma, London, 1993) and Alois Jirásek's *Old Czech Legends* (1890s; translated by Marie K. Holeček, London, 1992). The best known works of historical fiction by Prague-born authors are Gustav Meyrink's *The Golem* (1913–14; translated by M. Pemberton, London, 1985) and Leo Perutz's *By Night Under the Stone Bridge* (1953; translated by Eric Mosbacher, London, 1991), both of which are set in Rudolphine Prague. Franz Kafka's *The Complete Novels* (London, 1992) and *The Complete Short Stories* (London, 1994) are available as Minerva paperbacks.

One of the most outstanding Czech writers active at the beginning of the Communist period was Jiří Weil, whose *Life with a Star* (1947; first published in English in 1988) and *Mendelssohn is on the Roof* (posthumously published in 1960, and translated into English by Marie Winn in 1988) are unforgettable evocations of Jewish experience in Prague during the Second World War: moving and bleak at times, they are also savagely ironic and blackly humorous. Among the more recent Czech novels, short stories and essays that have particular relevance to Prague, some of the most entertaining are Bohumil Hrabal's *The Death of Mr Baltisberger* (1990), *I Served the King of England* (London, 1989) and *Total Fears* (Prague, 1998); Ivan Klíma's *My Merry Mornings: Stories from Prague* (London, 1993), *My Golden Trades* (London, 1992) and *The Spirit of Prague* (London, 1994); and Ludvík Vaculík's *A Cup of Coffee with my Interrogator: the Prague Chronicles of Ludvík Vaculík* (London, 1987). Elena Lappin's excellent anthology *Daylight in Nightclub Inferno: Czech Fiction from the Post-Kundera Generation* (North Haven, Connecticut, 1997) includes a lengthy extract from the *The Other City* (1993), a haunting novel by Michal Ajvaz, who is also featured in Paul Wilson's admirable *Prague: A Traveler's Literary Companion* (San Francisco, 1995), a collection of Czech writings about the city.

Details of other literary works describing Prague are given in James Naughton's useful *Traveller's Literary Companion to Eastern and Central Europe* (Brighton, 1995), as well as in Susie Lunt's *Prague* (World Bibliographical Series, Volume 195, Oxford, 1997), which is the most important bibliography of the city as yet available in English.

History

One of the best general introductions to Czech history remains Robert Seton-Watson's *A History of Czechs and Slovaks* (second edition, Hamden, Connecticut, 1965). Bede Jarrett's *The Emperor Charles IV* (London, 1935) serves as a readable introduction to the greatest of Prague's medieval rulers, while Howard Kaminsky clarifies many of the complexities of the Hussite period in *A History of the Hussite Revolution* (Berkeley and Los Angeles, 1967). **Rudolphine Prague** is especially well chronicled in English, notably by R.J.W. Evans in his celebrated *Rudolf II and his World: A Study in Intellectual History, 1572–1612* (Oxford, 1984), and by the many authors of the massive exhibition catalogue *Rudolph II and Prague* (edited by Eliška Fučíkova, London, 1997). Other studies relating to this latter period include Frederick Thieberger's *The Great Rabbi Loew of Prague* (London, 1955); *The Prague Ghetto in the Renaissance Period* (edited by Otto Muneles, Prague, 1965); Max Caspar's *Kepler* (London, 1959); and John Alleyn Gade's *The Life and Times of Tycho Brahe* (Princeton, 1947).

Useful background material for the **later history of Hapsburg rule** in Prague is provided by C. Veronica Wedgwood's fascinating and scholarly *The Thirty Years War* (London, 1992), Michal Sroněk and Jaroslava Hausenblasova's *Gloria & Miseria 1614–1648: Prague During the Thirty Years War* (Prague, 1998) Lawrence D. Orton's *The Prague Slav Congress of 1848* (Boulder, Colorado, 1978), G.B. Cohen's *The Politics of Ethnic Survival: Germans in Prague 1861–1914* (Princeton, 1981), and Zdeněk Zeman's *The Break-up of the Habsburg Empire* (Oxford, 1963). Zeman was also the author of *The Masaryks: The Making of Czechoslovakia* (London, 1976), which, together with Karl Čapek's *Masaryck Tells his Story* (London, 1951) and Paul Selver's *Masaryck: A Biography* (London, 1949), helps chart some of the most exhilarating years in Prague's 20C history. Further details of the historical and cultural backround are given in such splendid literary biographies as Ernst Pawel's *Franz Kafka: The Nightmare of Reason* (London, 1984), Lionel B. Steinman's *Franz Werfel: The Faith of an Exile* (Waterloo, Ontario, 1985) and Sir Cecil Parrot's *The Bad Bohemian: The Extraordinary Life of Jaroslav Hašek* (Loondon, 1978), which is almost as entertaining as anything that Hašek himself wrote. A useful survey of Prague cultural life from the 1880s right up to the 1960s is Peter Hrubý's *Daydreams and Nightmares* (New York, 1990).

Among the numerous works in English documenting aspects of Prague's history from the **Second World War** right up to the **Soviet invasion** of 1968 are Callum MacDonald's *Prague in the Shadow of the Swastika: A History of the German Occupation, 1939–1945* (Prague, 1995), Meir Cotic's *The Prague Trial. The First Anti-Zionist Show Trial in the Communist Bloc* (London, 1987), *Stalinism in Prague: The Loebl Story* (New York, 1969) and Harry Schwartz's *Prague's 200 Days: the Struggle for Democracy in Czechoslovakia* (London, 1969). These works can be supplemented by a wide range of engrossing personal memoirs, above all Heda Margolius Kovaly's *Prague Farewell* (London, 1988), Rosemary Kavan's *Love and Freedom: My Unexpected Life in Prague* (London and New York, 1988), Sir Cecil Parrot's *The Serpent and the Nightingale* (London, 1977), Edwin Muir's *An Autobiography* (London, 1980), Alexander Dubček's *Hope Dies Last: The Autobiography of Alexander Dubček* (London, 1993) and Alan Levy's engrossing accounts of his harrowing involvement in 1968 and its aftermath, *Good Men Still Live (I am the Other Karel Čapek)* (Chicago, 1974) and *So Many Heroes* (Sagaponach, New York, 1980).

For an excellent analysis and eyewitness description of the **Velvet Revolution** of 1989 see Timothy Garton Ash's *We the People: The Revolution of 89 Witnessed in Warsaw, Budapest, Berlin and Prague* ... (Cambridge, 1990) and *The Uses of Adversity. Essays on the Fate of Central Europe* (Cambridge, 1989).

Art and architecture

Remarkably, there is still no good general history of Czech art and architecture written in English. However, those interested specifically in architecture can turn to Brian Knox's *The Architecture of Prague and Bohemia* (London, 1962), which remains an invaluable introduction to the subject. There are also a number of detailed **architectural guides** to Prague, notably the densely and tediously written *Prague: Eleven Centuries of Architecture* (various authors, Prague, 1992), which nevertheless provides most of the necessary facts, as well as a wealth of useful plans, elevations and line drawings. A more accessible architectural work is Léon and Xavier de Koster's *14 Promenades dans Prague*, which is useful even to those who do not understand French, thanks to the exceptional clarity of its layout and admirably concise information.

The **medieval period** is covered by a number of poorly translated and barely readable books such as V. Denkstein's and A. Matouš's *Gothic Art of South Bohemia* (Prague, 1955), Eric Bachmann's *Gothic Art in Bohemia: Architecture, Sculpture and Painting* (Oxford, 1977) and Václav Mencl's *Czech Architecture of the Luxemburg Period* (Prague, 1955). Far better, but in French, is Karel Stejskal's *L'Empéreur Charles IV: L'Art en Europe au XIVe siecle* (Paris, 1980). But the definitive work for some time to come on 14C Czech art is likely to be the enormous exhibition catalogue *Magister Theodorious, Court Painter of Emperor Cahrles V* (ed. Jiří Fajt, Prague 1998).

Thomas da Costa Kauffmann has written a difficult but stimulating account of the Czech **Renaissance and Baroque periods** in *Court, Cloister and City: The Art and Culture of Central Europe 1450–1800* (London, 1995); he is also the author of *The School of Prague: Painting at the Court of Rudolph II* (Chicago, 1988). Jiřina Hořejší's *Renaissance Art in Bohemia* (London, 1979) and Oldřich Blažícek's *Baroque Art in Bohemia* (London, 1968) are to be enjoyed largely for their illustrations, as is also the case with Milan Pavlík's and Vladimír Uher's superlatively produced *Prague Baroque Architecture* (Amsterdam, 1998).

The city's **Art Nouveau** monuments are beautifully photographed in Petr Wittlich's *Prague—Fin de Siècle* (London, 1992), while the exhibition catalogue *Czech Modernism, 1900–1945* (Phoenix, Arizona, 1989) provides the best overview of early 20C Czech art and architecture. The most detailed architectural survey of Prague during this period is Rostislav Šacha's *The Architecture of New Prague, 1895–1945* (Boston, 1997), which, though difficult to read as a continuous text, serves as an especially useful guide to the city's modern buildings. A portable alternative to this massive tome is Ivan Margolius's literally pocket-sized *Prague: A Guide to Twentieth-Century Architecture* (London, 1994). More specialist works for the enthusiast of the modern city are Karel Teige's *Modern Czechoslovak Architecture* (London, 1947), the exhibition catalogue *Czech Cubism: Architecture, Furniture and Decorative Arts, 1910–1925* (edited by Alexander von Vegesack, Montreal, 1992), the guidebook *Cubist Prague 1905–25* (various authors, Prague, 1995), and Damjan Prevlovšek's *Jože Plečnik, 1872–1957 – Architectura perennis* (Yale University Press, 1998).

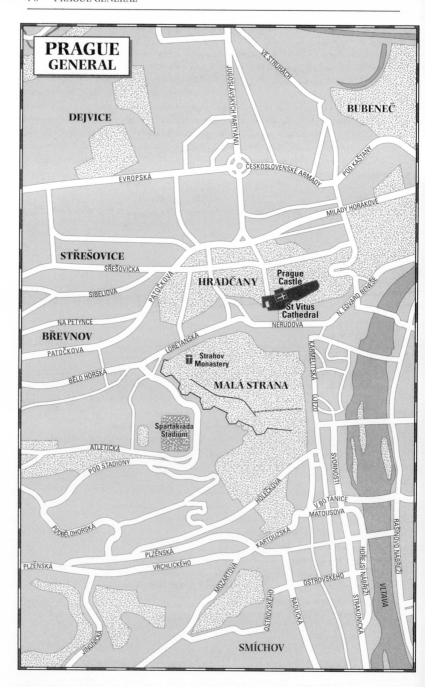

PRAGUE
GENERAL

DEJVICE

BUBENEČ

VE STRUHÁCH

JUGOSLÁVSKÝCH PARTYÁNU

ČESKOSLOVENSKÉ ARMÁDY

EVROPSKÁ

POD KAŠTANY

MILADY HORÁKOVÉ

STŘEŠOVICE

SŘEŠOVIČKA

PATOČKOVA

HRADČANY

Prague
Castle

St Vitus
Cathedral

N. EDVARD BENEŠE

SIBELIOVA

NA PETYNCE

NERUDOVA

BŘEVNOV

PATOČKOVA

LORETÁNSKÁ

KARMELITSKÁ

ÚJEZD

Strahov
Monastery

BĚLO HORSKÁ

MALÁ STRANA

Spartakiada
Stadium

ATLETICKÁ

SVORNOSTI

POD STADIONY

HOLEČKOVA

V BOTANICE

MATOUSOVA

RAŠÍNOVO NÁBŘEŽÍ

PODBĚLOHORSKÁ

KARTOUZSKÁ

HOŘEJŠÍ NÁBŘEŽÍ

PLZEŇSKÁ

VRCHLICKÉHO

MOZARTOVA

OSTROVSKÉHO

STRAKONICKÁ

VLTAVA

PLZEŇSKÁ

OSTROVSKÉHO

RADLICKÁ

JINONICKÁ

SMÍCHOV

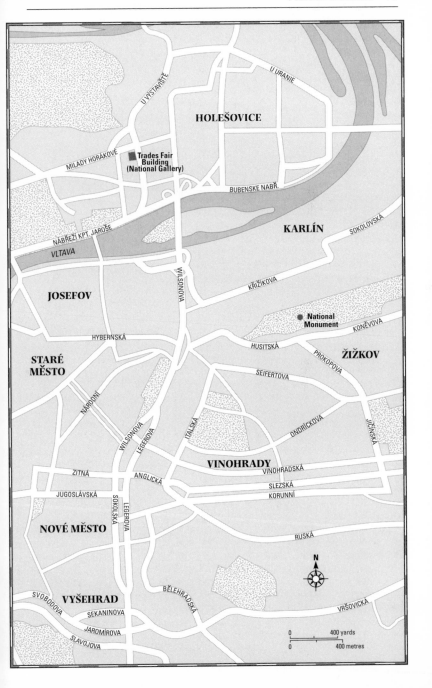

HOLEŠOVICE

U VYSTAVIŠTĚ

U URANIE

MILADY HORÁKOVÉ

Trades Fair
Building
(National Gallery)

BUBENSKE NABŘ.

NÁBŘEŽÍ KPT. JAROŠE

KARLÍN

SOKOLOVSKÁ

VLTAVA

JOSEFOV

WILSONOVA

KŘIŽIKOVA

National
Monument

KONĚVOVA

HYBERNSKÁ

HUSITSKÁ

ŽIŽKOV

STARÉ
MĚSTO

PROKOPOVA

SEIFERTOVA

NÁRODNÍ

WILSONOVA

LEGEROVA

ITALSKÁ

ONDŘÍČKOVA

JIČÍNSKÁ

ZITNÁ

ANGLICKÁ

VINOHRADY

VINOHRADSKÁ

JUGOSLÁVSKÁ

SOKOLSKÁ

LEGEROVA

SLEZSKÁ

KORUNNÍ

NOVÉ MĚSTO

RUSKÁ

N

SVOBODOVA

VYŠEHRAD

BĚLEHRADSKÁ

VRŠOVICKÁ

SEKANINOVA

JAROMÍROVA

SLAVOJOVA

0   400 yards
0   400 metres

The Guide

Planning your walks

Prague is divided into ten postal districts, the sights of tourist interest being mainly to be found in Praha I, which extends on either side of the Vltava river, and comprises the five historical townships of the Staré Město (Old Town), Malá Strana (Little Quarter), Hradčany (Castle District), Nové Město (New Town) and the former Jewish enclave within the Staré Město known as the Josefov. Although this forms a relatively small area that is easily manageable on foot, the wealth of monuments to be seen within is such that at least one week is needed to begin to do justice. Those with only two or three days to spare should devote their attention largely to the streets and monuments along the so-called Royal Road, notably the Powder Gate, Celetná Street, Old Town Square, Karlova Street, Charles Bridge, St Nicholas in the Little Quarter, Nerudova Street and Prague Castle; additional nearby sights that should certainly not be missed are the Jewish Museum in the Josefov, the Týn Church, the Municipal House, the National Theatre, the Loreta, the library of the Strahov Monastery, the gardens of the Wallenstein Palace, the National Gallery in the Sternberg Palace and Frank Gehry's 'Fred and Ginger' building. Even with little time at your disposal you should also make every effort to see the Prague that lies beyond the increasingly commercialised and over-prettified centre. Among the major outlying attractions are the citadel of Vyšehrad (and the 'Cubist' buildings at its foot), Jože Plečník's Church of the Sacred Heart, and the National Gallery's recently opened Collection of Modern Art at the Trade Fair Palace, which is in many ways the city's most outstanding art gallery.

Walking is by far the best way to get to know the city centre, using perhaps as your starting-points the metro stations of Staroměstká, Musek, Náměsti Republicky and Malostranská. If travelling beyond Praha I, you would be well advised to purchase one of the maps or atlases published by the Prague firm Kartografie, which outline the routes followed by the city's efficient network of trams and buses. One confusing anomaly of the Czech Republic is the dual numbering of all the buildings: the numbers that you should look out for are those in blue and white, which have odd numbers on one side of the street and even on the other.

1 · The Old Town (Staré Město) and the Jewish Quarter (Josefov)

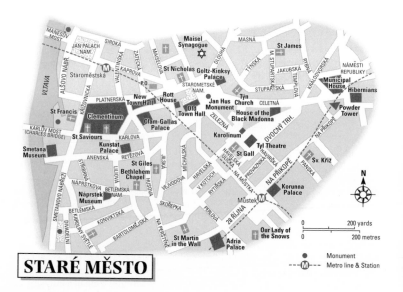

STARÉ MĚSTO

● Monument
---Ⓜ--- Metro line & Station

Along the Royal Route

The **Staré Město**, or Old Town, is bordered to the north and west by the river Vltava, and to the south and east by a long thoroughfare (comprising Národní třída, Na příkopě and Revoluční) marking the line of the medieval fortifications.

The Powder Gate

The Powder Gate (Prašná brána) stands on the **Náměstí Republicky**, which divides the pedestrian Na příkopě from its northern continuation, Revoluční. **Open** daily 10.00–18.00.

History of the Powder Gate

Originally known as the New Tower, the dark and sinister Powder Gate, 65m tall, was commissioned in 1475 by Vladislav Jagiello on the site of one of the 13 gates forming part of the Old Town's defensive system, a system which had been made redundant following the founding of the New Town in 1348. The Gate, adjoining at one time the building which served from 1383 to 1484 as the seat of the Royal Court of Bohemia, was intended purely as a monumental entrance to the Old Town, and marked the beginning of the Royal Route used by the Czech kings on their way to be crowned in St Vitus's Cathedral. When in 1484 Vladislav Jagiello moved the Royal

Court back to Prague Castle, work on the gate was abandoned, and the incomplete structure was given a temporary roof and put to use—until the end of the 17C—as a storehouse for gunpowder. Heavily damaged during the Prussian siege of Prague in 1737, it was left in a ruined state until the late 19C. Its present appearance is due largely to reconstruction work carried out between 1875 and 1886 by Josef Mocker, who provided the structure with its turreted upper gallery, steeply pitched roof and flamboyant Gothic decoration. The writer Max Brod recalled how every afternoon at 2 o'clock he would wait at the foot of the newly restored tower for his friend Franz Kafka, who invariably would arrive late: 'My anger', wrote Brod, 'at his lateness would rapidly dissolve as soon as the tall, thin figure appeared, who, more often than not, would be wearing an embarrassed smile.'

The profuse neo-Gothic ornament which covers the Powder Gate contains, alongside late 19C statues of Czech kings and other pseudo-medieval figures, fragments of the original sculptural decoration carried out by Matěj Rejsek of Prostějov after 1478; during the summer months you can climb up to the tower's upper gallery, the best point from which to study the layout of Prague's Old Town.

Before entering the Old Town, you should take a look at two of the other monuments on the náměstí Republiky. Facing the gate, at the eastern end of the square (No. 3), is the house called **The Hibernians** (U Hybernů), which occupies the site of a former church and monastery belonging to the Hibernian Order (Franciscans of Irish origin). The monastery building, erected in 1637–52, is a simple structure now used for offices; far more impressive is the adjoining former church, which was transformed by Georg Fischer in 1810 into a grandiose Customs House, inspired in its design by the former Mint in Berlin, and constituting one of the finest examples in Prague of the Empire style (the building now serves as a space for ambitious art exhibitions).

Municipal House

Meanwhile, flanking the northern side of the Powder Gate, and indeed dominating the whole square, is the Municipal House (Obecní dům), still the most remarkable Art Nouveau building in the Czech Republic, despite recent restoration that has made its beauty seem somewhat tawdry. **Open** Mon–Sat 10.00–18.00.

History of the Municipal House

The Municipal House stands on the site originally occupied by the Royal Court of Bohemia, a building dating back to the late 14C and later converted first into a seminary, then into a barracks, and finally into a cadets' school, which was pulled down in 1902–03. The idea of erecting the Municipal House was that of the Czech Patriotic Society, which envisaged a building which would serve as a social and cultural centre for the Czech community in Prague, complete with café, restaurant, concert hall, and rooms for civic functions and assemblies. The architects chosen for the task, after a public competition which closed in 1905, were Antonín Balšánek and Osvald Polívka. Work on the building was undertaken between 1906 and 1912, and involved the collaboration of many of the leading Czech painters and sculptors of the turn of the century, including Ladislav Šaloun (the sculptor of the Hus Monument in the Old Town Square; see below), Max Švabinský (who created the stained-glass windows in St Vitus's Cathedral) and Alfons Mucha, who had accepted the commission in the mistaken belief that he had been asked to carry out all the decoration (a protracted and heated correspondence in the press concluded that it would not be fitting for a single artist to assume responsibility for the whole work). The most important meetings to have taken place in the building were held at the end of the First World War, concluding with the proclamation here, on 28 October 1918, of the independence of Czechoslovakia and the issuing of the new republic's Constitution. As for the concert hall, this continues to be one of Prague's most important cultural venues, hosting each year the inaugural concert of the Prague Spring Musical Festival; among the famous musicians to have performed in the hall are Sviatoslav Richter, David Oistrakh, Yehudi Menuhin, Mstislav Rostropovitch and Pablo Casals.

This large, irregularly-shaped building, once so wonderfully evocative of the city's turn-of-the-century splendour, now has the garish, artificial look of some modern pastiche. The restoration that was completed in 1997 has been rightly described by Daniel Špička, director of the Prague Centre for the Preservation of Architecture, as a textbook case of how not to renovate the city's buildings. Fortunately no amount of crude restoration can entirely diminish the genuine decorative brilliance of the structure, the exterior of which is impressive above all for its central **ironwork canopy**, which is coloured with stained glass and topped by bronze figures of lamp-bearers executed by K. Novák. Above the canopy is a large lunette decorated by Karel Špillar with a mosaic, *Homage to Prague*; crowning this is a cupola, while on either side are sculptural groups by Ladislav Šaloun representing respectively the *Humiliation and Rebirth of the Czech Nation*. Numerous other sculptures adorn the exterior, including a statue by Čeněk Vosmík of the main architect of the adjoining Powder Gate, Matěj Rejsek, and a relief by Šaloun commemorating the first assembly in 1918 of the National Committee of the Czechoslovak Republic.

Inside the building you find yourself in a vestibule adorned with bronze statues of *Flora* and *Fauna* by Bohumil Kafka. To the right a door leads into a **restaurant**, with large views of Prague by Josef Tomec and Antonín Záhel, and paintings by Josef Wenig representing *Hop-Growing*, *Viticulture*, and *Prague welcoming its Visitors*; to the left of the vestibule is the similarly elegant **café**, featuring at one end a niche containing a statue

Detail of the Municipal House

of a nymph made of white Carrara marble by Josef Pekárek. A further restaurant and a late-night bar are situated in the basement, where you will find coloured drawings by Mikoláš Aleš and a folkloric fantasy by Jakub Obrovský entitled *Harvest Time*.

The Concert Hall and Civic Rooms are to be found on the first floor, and can be visited during the day by guided tour (temporary exhibitions are also held in some of the newly renovated rooms). The large, ochre-coloured **Concert Hall**, named after the composer Smetana, has a central section domed in stained glass, and two wide balconies flanked by large murals by Karel Špillar representing Music, Dance, Poetry and Drama. In between the stage and two prominent boxes at the front of the hall (the box on the left is that used by President Havel), are two dynamic stucco groups by Ladislav Šaloun portraying scenes from Dvořák's *Slavonic Dances* and Smetana's opera *Vyšehrad*. Among the other first-floor rooms are the small and exquisitely tasteful neo-Classical pastiche called the **Sweetshop**, the rather brasher **Oriental Room**, and the **Němcová Salon**, decorated all over with stuccowork inspired by folkloric themes. Other rooms on this floor have ambitious large-scale paintings, for instance the **Rieger Hall**, which has two long painted panels by Max Švabinský (*Czech Spring*) containing portraits of leading Czech writers, artists and musicians such as Jan Neruda, Božena Němcová, Josef Mylsbek, Josef Mánes, Mikoláš Aleš, Bedřich Smetana and Antonín Dvořák. Pride of place among the Civic Rooms must go to the **Hall of the Lord Mayor**, the windows of which occupy the central position on the building's façade. All the furniture and furnishings, and every detail of the decoration of this circular room are by Alfons Mucha, including allegorical murals on the walls and shallow ceiling, the pale blue stained-glass windows, the Lord Mayor's chair, and the elaborately embroidered curtains.

After leaving the Municipal House, turn left and then left again into the narrow side-street U Obecního domu, which flanks the northern side of the building. On the right-hand side of this street is another fine building of the turn of the century, the newly and brashly revamped **Hotel Paříž**, which was built in 1907 by Jan Vejrych and regarded in its time as a model example of the Art Nouveau style. There are colourful figurative decorations on the corner façade of its gabled, Gothic-inspired exterior, while inside are an attractively panelled café and a mirrored restaurant with blue mosaics. A fantastical description of this hotel appears in Bohumil Hrabal's novel, *I Served the King of England*: 'The Hotel Paříž was so beautiful it almost knocked me over. So many mirrors and brass balustrades and brass door handles and brass candelabras, all polished till the place shone like a palace of gold.' It is here that the picaresque narrator of the novel meets the head waiter who 'served the King of England', and where he himself makes his reputation by serving Haile Salasse at a Gargantuan banquet centred around a stuffed and roasted camel.

At the end of U Obecního domu turn left into the short U Prašné brány, where you will pass at No. 1 an Art Nouveau apartment block built by Bedřich Bendelmayer in 1903–04, and featuring inside an elegant semi-circular staircase. The street brings you back to the Powder Gate and to the eastern end of Celetná.

Celetná, the pedestrian street at the start of the Royal Route, is one of the showpiece streets of the Old Town, and is lined principally with recently restored houses of medieval origin that were given pastel-coloured façades during the

House of the Black Virgin

Baroque period. At No. 31, on the right-hand side of the street, is a palace built in 1750 by K.I. Dientzenhofer for the Master Minter Josef Pachta of Rájov; until 1784 the Mint itself was situated in the palace at No. 36 on the opposite side of the street, a building which Pachta erected in 1759 on the site of the medieval Mint, and featuring atlante figures of miners by the Baroque sculptor I.F. Platzer.

At No. 34 Celetná is one of the more interesting modern buildings in the Old Town, the building known as the **House of the Black Virgin** (Dům U černé Matky Boží). Built as a department store in 1911–12 by Josef Gočár, this corner house is one of the masterpieces of Czech Cubism, and has two prominent cornices as well as heavy prism-shaped forms painted a dark maroon; its name is derived from a curious survival of the Baroque building it replaced—a 17C statue of the Virgin that in 1921 inspired Jaroslav Seifert's poem *Prayer on the Pavement* ('I raised my eyes towards the Black Virgin / Standing there / and keeping her protecting hand over my head / and I prayed...'). Major restoration carried out in 1993–94 attempted to bring back as much as possible the look of the original interior: partition walls and ceilings were demolished, revealing reinforced concrete beams reminiscent of Gothic vaulting. Although plans to recreate the original first-floor café have been abandoned, the building now houses part of the **Czech Museum of Fine Arts** (České muzeum výtvarných umění), which displays on the top two floors a small but choice collection of Czech Cubist paintings, sculptures and works of applied art culled both from its own holdings and those of the Museum of Decorative Art, the National Technical Museum, and various regional museums; among the works are paintings by Filla, Čapek and Špala, a mirror by Pavel Jának, and a sofa, sideboard and other furniture by Gočár. Curiously the beautiful roof-top views from the building become progressively more Cubist the higher you climb. **Open Tues–Sun 10.00–18.00.**

Opposite the building, at No. 23 Celetná, is to be found another statue of the Virgin, this one by a pupil of Matthias Braun and attached to the undulating Baroque façade of the palace built for the Schönpflok family. Continuing to walk on the right-hand side of Celetná, turn right just after No. 17 and walk through the covered passage leading towards the Malá Štupartská, on which stands the former **Monastery church of St James** (sv. Jakub), which was founded by Minorites in 1232 and completely remodelled by Jan Šimon Pánek between 1689 and 1702. The tall twin-towered west façade has rich stuccowork by

O. Mosto, executed in 1695 and featuring representations of SS James, Francis and Anthony of Padua.

The enormously long and imposing interior, which has retained the medieval three-aisled plan and tall, Gothic proportions, is profusely white-washed and gilded, and contains ceiling frescoes of the *Life of the Virgin* by F. Voget (1736), and 22 altars. The main altarpiece, supported by an exuberant gilded framework of angels high above the chancel, is a painting by V.V. Reiner of the *Martyrdom of St James*. Three of the altars on the right-hand side of the nave are by Peter Brandl, and were executed around 1710; another work by Brandl (the St Joseph Altar of 1708) is on the left-hand side of the nave, where an altar by J.K. Liška representing *St Valburg* can also be found. This side of the nave also boasts one of Prague's grandest funerary monuments, the *Monument to Jan Vratislav of Mitrovice*, designed by J.B. Fischer von Erlach in 1721 and containing sculpted figures by F.M. Brokoff.

The church is famous for its acoustics and the sung High Mass on Sundays is well worth attending, as is the annual Christmas Day service featuring the Christmas Mass by the Czech composer Ryba. Pleasing music might well be necessary to make you forget the building's most gruesome feature—a 400-year-old decomposed human forearm which hangs on the right-hand side of the west wall. This was put there both as a warning and as a record of a miracle involving the Virgin's tight-fisted response to a man who had attempted to steal her jewels from the high altar: the thief's arm, unable to free itself from the Virgin's grip, had eventually to be cut off by a local butcher.

Turning right on leaving the church and taking the first turning to the left, Tynská, you will reach (at No.6) the medieval **House of the Golden Ring** (dum U zlatého prstenu), which has now been taken over by the collection of 20C Czech art belonging to the Prague City Gallery. The long and rambling building, with its whitewashed vaulted rooms and views of the Týn Church, provides a characterful setting for a comparatively small selection of mainly early 20C Czech works, including Max Svabinsky's powerful *Destitute Land* (1900), sculptures by Bílek, boldly handled landscapes by Antonín Slavícek (among which is an unfinished view of Prague Cathedral of 1912), Indian-inspired paintings by Otakar Nejedly (who spent several years in Southern India and Ceylon at the beginning of the century), delicate fantasies by Zrzy, Sima, and Toyen, Cubist and other works by Filla, and Surrealistic photo montages by Jirí Kolar. The labelling and information panels are in Czech and English, and, as with the Museum of Modern Art in the Trade Fair Palace, the collection is arranged under such enigmatic and generally unhelpful headings as 'Rigid Unrestful'. **Open** Tues–Sun, 10.00–18.00

Instead of visiting just now the Týn Church (the apse of which directly faces the museum's entrance), turn left down Stupartská to return to the covered passage leading to Celetná, where you will emerge directly in front of the spacious beer cellar at No. 22 known as **At the Vulture** (U Supa), which is housed on the ground floor of a pale green, late 18C building with a German inscription dating back to the days when the royal jeweller Gindle had his shop here.

Continuing west on the left-hand side of Celetná, you will come, at No. 12, to the elegant **Hrzán Palace**, a building of Romanesque origin remodelled to a design by G.B. Alliprandi in 1702, and with sculptural decorations on the façade by pupils of F.M. Brokoff; the father of Franz Kafka, Hermann, had a haberdashery shop on the premises after 1882. Further down the street, at No. 2, is the house where the Kafka family lived in 1888–89, and where Albert Einstein is said to have first explained his Theory of Relativity. Between 1896 and 1901 the Kafka family lived on the opposite side of the street, at No. 3, where the writer's street-facing bedroom inspired one of his earliest stories, *The Window onto the Street*. At the adjoining No. 5 is the 17C **Týn Presbytery**, occupying the site of a 12C hospice for foreign merchants; a short and narrow alley between the two houses leads to the south portal of the Church of Our Lady before Týn (see below).

Old Town Square

Celetná comes to an end at the spacious Old Town Square (Staroměstské Náměstí), one of Europe's most beautiful squares.

History of the Square

Situated at what was formerly the junction of several trade routes, the Old Town Square served as the market-place of the Old Town in the 11C and 12C centuries. An important point on the traditional processional route of the Bohemian kings, and overlooked by the former Hussite Church of Our Lady before Týn, the square was later to witness some of the most significant—and tragic—events in the history of Prague, and came almost to symbolise the struggles and aspirations of the Czech people. Jan Želivský— the Hussite leader whose storming of the New Town Hall in 1419 had sparked off the Hussite Wars—was executed here in 1422; 56 other Hussites, including the officer Jan Roháč of Dubé, were executed on the square 15 years later. At the Old Town Hall, George of Poděbrady was elected King of Bohemia in 1458, and in 1621, 27 of the Protestant leaders who had taken part in the Battle of the White Mountain were beheaded outside the building. One of these was the pioneering surgeon Jan Jessenius, an ancestor of Kafka's great love, Milena Jesenská. Before his tongue had been taken out prior to the execution he had said, 'You are treating us shamefully, but I want you to know that others will come who will bury with honour our heads, which you have desecrated and put on show.' In 1945 large crowds welcomed the arrival here of Soviet troops, and three years later Klement Gottwald proclaimed from the balcony of the Kinský Palace the accession of the Communists to power. A rather different response to the Soviet army was shown in 1968, when, at the end of the 'Prague Spring', Soviet tanks advanced on the square, their arrival being greeted not by applause but by Molotov cocktails.

The square is surrounded by a picturesque jumble of medieval to Baroque buildings, to which recent restoration has given a toy-like cleanliness and cheerful range of light and vivid colours. Though most of the square is now traffic-free, it is the tourist heart of Prague, and you would be best advised to come here early in the day to appreciate the place before it fills up with a vast and noisy crowd in which buskers, street vendors and money-changers now jostle with the foreigners. Rising on steps near its centre and dominating the whole space is the extraordinary bronze **Monument to Jan Hus**, a disgracefully undervalued work of the early years of the century, considered by some to be completely out of place in the square, but which is surely one of the most powerful public monuments in any European city, and one which brilliantly complements its surroundings.

History of the Monument

The Monument to Jan Hus was the masterpiece of the idiosyncratic sculptor Ladislav Šaloun, who began planning the work as early as 1898, and struggled with it for the next 17 years, making constant changes throughout this period of gestation. The monument was intended to be unveiled in 1915, on the occasion of the 500th anniversary of the burning of Jan Hus for heresy. The unveiling went ahead as planned, but few worse moments could have been chosen for the com-pletion of a highly emotive monument symbolising the Czech national consciousness and the fight for Czech independence. The Austrian authorities did not permit any speech or unveiling ceremony of any kind to take place, but within a few days the work was completely covered with flowers, and all that showed of it was a solitary finger pointing menacingly to the sky. At this time there still stood next to the monument a Marian column erected in 1650 to commemorate the Peace of Westphalia—the treaty which brought the Thirty Years War to an end. In 1918, only five days after the decla-ration of independent Czechoslovakia, this symbol of Catholic and Habsburg domi-nance, with its sculpted angels tram-pling over devils, was

The Jan Hun Monument by Ladislav Šaloun

pulled down, leaving only Jan Hus to preside over the square. The continuing power of the latter monument was attested in the wake of the Soviet invasion of August 1968, when it was shrouded in black drapes.

Šaloun's monument to Hus, which bears at its base the preacher's words 'The truth will prevail', features the figure of Hus rising above a struggling sea of gesticulating people, in a defiant posture reminiscent of one of Rodin's *Burghers of Calais*; the power of this detailed yet unified composition lies to a large extent in the way in which—even on the brightest of days—it forms against the light and cheerful background of the square a dark and menacing profile, vividly reminding the spectator of the bleaker moments in Czech history.

Church of Our Lady Before Týn

The eastern end of the square is overshadowed by the most prominent building in the Old Town, and one of those most closely associated with the Hussite cause, the Church of Our Lady Before Týn. As with most medieval churches in Bohemia it does not rise directly above the square, but is set back behind a row of arcaded houses, comprising in this case a house of Romanesque origin with a tall late 18C façade (No. 15, at the south-eastern end of the square), and the attractive **Týn School** (No. 14), which has a late 14C ground floor and a pair of stepped 16C gables recalling those of the Scuola Grande di San Marco in Venice; the architect Matěj Rejsek of Prostějov was a teacher at the school in the late 15C. Walking through the second of the school's four arches will take you to the west portal of the church (alternatively you could enter the church through its south portal by following the alley alongside the Týn Presbytery at No. 5 Celetná; see above). For many years much of the exterior of the Týn has been encased by scaffolding, and access to its very restricted site has been extremely limited; entry to the building can only be guaranteed at times of services, and this situation is likely to persist for several more years.

History of Týn Church

The origins of the Týn church are in a Romanesque building first mentioned in 1135 as the property of the foreign merchants' hospice in Celetná. Work on the present structure was begun in 1365, and by the 1380s the north portal, the side aisles, the walls of the nave and much of the east end had been completed. The reformist preachers K. Waldhauser and Milíč of Kroměříž were already preaching in the building by the end of

View of Týn Church

the 14C, and early in the following century the place was to become the main church of the Hussites in Prague; it was to remain associated with the followers of Jan Hus until 1621. The nave was vaulted by 1457, a year before the accession to the throne of the Utraquist monarch George of Poděbrady, who was to be one of the church's greatest benefactors. Under George the northern of the west façade's twin towers was erected (the southern one dates from the early 16C), as was this façade's tall gable. The gable was adorned with a statue of George and a gold chalice symbolising the Utraquist cause, but these were removed after the Battle of the White Mountain in 1620, and replaced with an image of the Virgin whose halo was made from the gold of the chalice. A severe fire in 1679 led to the rebuilding of the nave vault and extensive remodelling of the interior.

The twin-towered exterior of the church is a gloomy pile of exposed masonry, the principal decoration being concentrated on the north portal, where there is a late 14C tympanum of the Crucifixion from the workshop of Peter Parlér (the original is now in the National Gallery in Prague Castle). The north portal can be reached along the narrow Týnská, which runs along the northern side of the Týn School, and off which there is a gateway (just to the east of the church) leading into the merchants' courtyard which gave this area its name (*týn* means 'enclosure'); the courtyard, used from the 11C to 18C for the stocking and selling of goods, and as a customs house, retains only the ground-plan of the medieval structure, the oldest surviving part being the mid-16C loggia of the Granovský House.

The interior of the Týn church, in need of restoration, is a dark three-aisled hall space with crumbling, unadorned plaster from the Baroque period. At the western end of the north aisle is a Gothic baldachin by Matěj Rejsek (1493) which was originally situated above the tomb of the Hussite bishop A.L. Mirandola. The outstanding work of art in the building is the intricately carved *Baptism of Christ* by the Monogramist I.P. (c 1526), on the pier immediately to the right of the south portal. Attached to the south aisle pier directly in front of the main apse is the red marble tombstone of the Danish astronomer Tycho Brahe, who died in 1601 as a result of trying to hold back his urine while in the presence of the Emperor Rudolph ('I don't want to die like Tycho Brahe' is the Czech expression for 'I'm desperate for a pee'). The high altar of the Ascension (1649) is by Karel Škréta.

Returning to the Old Town Square and continuing to walk north along its eastern side, you will come next to the **House at the Stone Bell** (Dům U kamenného zvonu) at No. 13, a narrow-fronted structure, the Baroque cladding of which was recently removed to reveal its original late 14C stonework; the interior, now used for concerts and small exhibitions, features a small chapel with fragments of 14C murals. Adjoining it, at No. 12, is one of the most elegant of the city's 18C palaces, the **Goltz-Kinský Palace** (1755–65), which was built by Anselmo Lurago to a design supplied by K.I. Dientzenhofer, and richly stuccoed by C.G. Bossi. The twin pediments of the façade are a clever solution to the building's position at the corner of the square, and show how the architects were anxious not to destroy the unity of the multi-gabled square by providing a single enormous pediment. **Open** Tues–Sun 10.00–18.00.

Goltz-Kinský Palace

One of the many distinguished visitors to have stayed in the palace was the Swedish dynamite magnate Alfred Nobel, who fell in love here with the future Bertha von Suttner (née Kinský), whose early years were spent in the building: Bertha, who became famous as a pacifist and the author of *Down with the Weapons*, was said to have been very influential in determining Nobel's decision in later life to found the Nobel Peace Prize, of which she herself was one of the first recipients. In the late 19C part of the palace was turned into a state-run German-language secondary school, one of whose pupils was Franz Kafka, who came here in September 1891 and—despite irrational fears of failing his final exams—graduated from the institution ten years later; between 1912 and 1918 a ground-floor room on the southern side of the palace served as the new premises of his father's ever more successful haberdashery business. But the palace's eminence in modern Czech history was not finally sealed until 21 February 1948, when, from one of its main balconies, Klement Gottwald proclaimed to an assembled crowd of thousands the coming to power of the Communist regime. At his side was a man called Clementis who was executed four years later for high treason, and later airbrushed from all the many photographs of the scene; this incident is recalled in the opening passages of Milan Kundera's novel *The Book of Laughter and Forgetting* (first published in English in 1980). The building has now been taken over by the Kafka Foundation, which has converted the family's former premises here into an excellent bookshop and plans to open above this a large museum and library devoted to the writer. For the time being the Prague National Gallery continues to hold exhibitions of prints and drawings in an upstairs room.

The northern side of the square was radically altered at the end of the 19C, at around the same time that the pompous Pařížská třída was built. At the north-eastern corner of the square, adjacent to the Goltz-Kinský Palace, is the late 17C former Pauline Monastery (Klášter paulánů), but the space between here and Pařížská is now taken up by the enormous, neo-Baroque building housing the Ministry of Domestic Trading. The **Church of St Nicholas** (sv. Mikuláš) was once tucked away at the very corner of the square, at the junction of Pařížská and U radnice, but, since the destruction in the Second World War of the northern wing of the Town Hall, has now a prominent, exposed position, and indeed is one of the square's great glories. **Open** Tues–Fri 10.00–12.00, also Wed 14.00–16.00.

History of the Church of St Nicholas

The original Church of St Nicholas was founded by merchants in the late 13C, and served until the building of the Týn church as the parish church of the Old Town. The reformist preacher Jan Milíč gave sermons here in the 1360s, and in the following century the building was taken over by the Utraquists, who were to keep it for over two centuries. In 1635 the church was presented to the Benedictines, who had it rebuilt between 1650 and 1660. During the rule of Abbot Anselmo Vlach it was demolished and replaced by the present structure, which was built in 1732–35 by K.I. Dientzenhofer. The monastery was abolished in 1787, and for a while the church was used as a concert hall before being handed over to the Russian Orthodox Church in 1871. Since 1920 it has been the property of the Czechoslovak Hussite Church, which was founded in that same year. A thorough restoration of the building was completed in 1990.

The church, which has recently been given a dazzling coat of white paint, is a centrally planned structure with an unusual design which was determined to a large extent by the once cramped nature of the site. Dientzenhofer, wishing to create a structure which would powerfully reaffirm the Catholic faith in the wake of the building's Utraquist past, was forced by the restricted site to put the emphasis on verticality. The twin-towered southern façade of the church, adorned with sculptures from the school of Braun, has an arrangement recalling that of Borromini's Sant' Agnese in Rome, but the architectural elements have been elongated in the creation of soaring proportions.

The spectacular interior, now also a brilliant white, is dominated by the enormously tall central dome, and gives one the impression of being inside a wedding cake. There are ceiling frescoes by the Bavarian artist P. Assam of scenes from the Old Testament and the lives of SS Nicholas and Benedict but—unusually for Dientzenhofer—the painted decorations are subservient to the exceptionally rich stucco framework by Bernard Spinetti.

Adjacent to the west façade of St Nicholas, on Maislova, is the site of the house where Franz Kafka was born on 3 July 1883; not until 1965, when the Communist regime finally accepted Kafka as a 'revolutionary critic of capitalist alienation', was the present bronze commemorative bust by Karel Hladík attached to it. The house, known as **At the Tower** (U Věže), originally belonged to the Benedictines, but by Kafka's day had been turned into a warren of small apartments at the southernmost end of the Jewish ghetto; largely destroyed by fire in 1887, but replaced in 1902 with a new structure that retained the original Baroque portal, the building now features a small **Kafka museum**. Open Tues–Fri 10.00–18.00, Sat 10.00–17.00.

Old Town Hall

Immediately to the south of St Nicholas is a small garden laid out on the site of the demolished northern wing of the Old Town Hall. The heavily restored Old Town Hall (Staroměstská radnice), which projects into the southwestern corner of the Old Town Square, is the square's principal tourist attraction. Its history is a complex one, the place being an assemblage of several buildings, the earliest of which dates back to the beginning of the 14C. **Open** Mon 11.00–17.00, Tues–Sun 09.00–17.00.

To understand the Town Hall's genesis you should walk slowly around the exterior, beginning with the eastern end, which incorporates part of the ground floor of the original building—a private house which the civic authorities purchased from one Wolflin of Kámen in 1338. A tower was added to this in 1364, and a chapel—with an oriel window projecting east—built on its first floor by 1381; on the wall underneath the oriel is a plaque bearing the names of the 27 Protestants executed on the square in 1621, the exact place of the execution being marked on some nearby paving stones. The block which was attached to the northern end of Wolflin's house was a late 15C addition, rebuilt in the late 18C, and again in the early 20C; it was burnt down by the Nazis on the penultimate day of the Second World War, and plans to put up a modern extension on its site seem to have been abandoned. Walking the length of the southern side of the Town Hall, from east to west, you will come immediately to the famous **Astronomical Clock**, which was added to the south façade of Wolflin's house in 1410.

History of the Old Town Hall

Installed originally by the master clocksmith Mikoláš of Kadaň in 1410, the clock was rebuilt in 1490 by a teacher at the Charles University, Master Hanuš of Růže According to legend Hanuš was blinded to prevent him from creating another such marvel in Prague, but the blind man then climbed up the tower and stopped the clock. The true story is that the clock's mechanism was not to be perfected until Jan Táborský repaired it between 1552 and 1560, after which it required no further alterations. Only its decorations have been changed, the painted calendar on the lower level being executed by J. Mánes in 1865 (the original is in the National Gallery at St Agnes Convent), and the coloured figurines on all three of its levels being carved by V. Sucharda in 1948. The middle level comprises the clock proper, which both tells the time and gives the position of the sun and moon. Just before the striking of each hour a large crowd gathers in front of the clock to watch an impressive spectacle which begins with a skeleton (on the upper right corner of the clock) raising an hour glass and pulling a funerary bell; windows subsequently open on the upper level, and a macabre procession of Apostles and allegorical figures (such as a miser gloating over a sack of gold) files past.

West of the clock is a portal of 1470–80, attributed to Master Rejsek, and constituting the main entrance to the building. Further west is the former **Kříž House**, purchased by the civic authorities in 1360 and featuring a fine Renaissance window of 1520 bearing the Latin inscription *Praga caput regni* ('Prague, capital of the kingdom'). In 1458 the Town Hall was extended by the purchase of the house now attached to the west, a property belonging previously to Mikeš the Furrier and which was to be remodelled in a neo-Renaissance style in 1878 by the architect A. Baum. The complex was enlarged yet further in 1835 with the purchase of the adjoining house called **At the Cock**, an originally Romanesque structure given an Empire façade in 1830. Finally, in 1896, the Town Hall bought the splendid property adjacent to the western end of At the Cock, **At the Minute** (Dům U minuty), a house where the Kafka family had lived from 1889 right up to the time of its purchase. The exterior of the house is covered with sgraffito decorations that are among the finest in Prague; these monochrome works, representing Classical and biblical scenes and allegorical figures of the Virtues, were executed around 1611 and restored in 1919 by J. Čapek, the brother of the writer Karel (they were to be restored again after the 1945 fire).

The interior of the Town Hall can only be visited with a guided tour, and these take place at irregular intervals throughout the day, and attract great crowds of tourists. Though it has been much altered over the centuries and was badly gutted in 1945, it retains on the second floor the late Gothic **Council Chamber** of 1470. The late 19C **Assembly Room** on the same floor was dominated until recently by two large canvases by V. Brožík, *Master Jan Hus at the Council of Constance* and *The Election of George of Poděbrady as King of Bohemia* (these are now in the Troja Château; see p 203); the Gothic vaulting in the vestibule of the building has a mosaic decoration of 1937, executed after designs by M. Aleš, and representing the story of the mythical Countess Libuše. A visit to the Town Hall is complemented by a climb up its 70m-high **tower**, from where an excellent view can be had.

Before leaving the Old Town Square, you should walk along the southern side of the square, which is lined with an especially attractive row of arcaded houses. The neo-Gothic one at No. 16 (at the entrance to Celetná) has sgrafitted decorations by M. Aleš, most notably a representation of St Wenceslas on horseback. Further west, at No. 20, is the **House at the Golden Unicorn** (Dům U zlatého jednorožce), which has an 18C façade with a Gothic portal; the cellar is a Romanesque structure of the 13C, while the late-Gothic vaulting in the vestibule was designed by Matěj Rejsek in 1496. A plaque on the outside of the building records that in 1848 the composer Bedřich Smetana established here his first music school.

Along Karlova

The Old Town Square leads at its narrow southwestern corner into the quieter and triangular-shaped **Small Square** (Malé Náměstí), which is centred around a small **fountain** surrounded by a Renaissance ironwork grille of 1560. One of the oldest spaces in the Old Town, this was inhabited in the 12C by French merchants; fruit markets were held here during the Middle Ages. Though a number of the houses have Romanesque cellars, the present appearance of the square is due mainly to 18C and 19C remodelling. One of the most prominent of the buildings is the one at No. 3, which was rebuilt in a neo-Renaissance style in 1890 for the ironmongery firm of V.J. Rott; the name of Rott appears on the recently repainted façade, which is covered all over with figurative and ornamental motifs based on designs supplied by M. Aleš. An excellently preserved neo-Baroque pharmacy of the last century is incorporated into the late 18C house at No.

No 3 Malé Náměstí, with ornamental designs by M. Aleš

13, adjoining which, at the southwestern corner of the square, is the site of the former American Reception Centre—a landmark in the history of Prague's post-1989 transformation, and a place where you could buy T-shirts inscribed with the words, 'Prague. Czech it out'.

Although this reception centre has now gone, Americanisation of the worst kind has done much to destroy the character of the neighbouring **Karlova**, along which you can continue heading west along the processional route of the Bohemian kings. As much of a showpiece as Celetná, but narrower and more winding, and with houses that are picturesquely askew, this street has sadly lost much of its former fairy-tale charm through its recent encrustation of competing neon signs, brash eateries and other tourist establishments.

At the junction of Karlova and **Husova**, the first street that you cross, are three interconnected buildings forming another branch of the **Czech Museum of Fine Arts** (České muzeum výtvarných umění), this one devoted entirely to temporary art exhibitions are put on. The part of the gallery on Karlova is an elegant 18C structure, but the building where the gallery's main entrance is situated, at No. 21 Husova, is a Renaissance house crowned by an attractive pair of stepped gables; the interior of the gallery, featuring a Romanesque cellar, successfully incorporates the surviving medieval elements into a bright modern setting. Just to the south of the entrance, at No. 19 Husova, is the beer cellar called **At the Golden Tiger** (U zlatého tygra), a popular former haunt of the writer Bohumil Hrabal, and mentioned in several of his writings, for instance in a short piece entitled *The Magic Flute* (1989): 'And I was at the Golden Tiger, deep in thought, saying to myself, as I always do, that if the Gods loved me I would expire in front of a glass of beer ...' A phantasmagorical oil painting of Hrabal has now been hung on one of the walls, and there is also a colour photograph of him having a beer in the bar with President Clinton in 1994.

One of Prague's raunchiest Bohemian meeting-places of the early 20C, the **Cabaret Montmartre**, was situated around the corner from here, at No. 7 Řetězová (the first turning to your right as you continue south down Husova).

Returning to Karlova along Husova, and deviating this time to the north, you will pass almost immediately the most celebrated of Prague's Baroque palaces, the **Clam-Gallas Palace**. Built between 1713–19 for Count J.W. Gallas, it was the work of the great Viennese architect Johann Bernard Fischer von Erlach, aided by two of the leading artists of his day, the sculptor Matthias Braun and the Italian painter Carlo Carlone. The main façade, hemmed in on the narrow Husova, is in many ways remarkably Classical, with its large central pediment, simple fenestration, and largely undecorated walls. At the same time, however, it is given a dynamic Baroque quality by Braun's sculptural additions—the row of figures (replaced mainly by copies) along the attic and, above all, the powerful, struggling atlantes who support the two portals, which are unusually situated at the sides of the façade. The dramatic elements of the exterior are continued inside in the exciting Grand Staircase, where there are further works by Braun in addition to sumptuous stuccowork by Santino Bussi and an exhilarating ceiling painting by Carlone representing *The Triumph of Apollo*. The whole building, boasting a number of other ceilings by Carlone, and beautifully restored in the 1980s, now houses the city archives, and is officially closed to visitors.

The northern side of the palace abuts into the Náměstí Primátora Dr. Vacka, where you will find, immediately on turning right into the square, a **fountain** attached to the palace's garden wall. Within its niche is a copy of a famous sculpture executed in 1812 by the Romantic artist Václav Prachner (the original has now been taken to the National Gallery at Zbraslav): entitled *Vltava* but popularly called Terezka, it is a vigorous portrayal of a female nude, and tradi-

Cabaret Montmartre

It was founded in 1911 in a seedy beer-cellar forming part of a then run-down building appropriately known as the The Three Wild Men on account of a popular local legend claiming that a strange trio of cannibals lived here in the late 17C (hence the mural on the building's exterior of what looks like a group of Hell's Angels). The interior consisted originally of two large rooms with a dance-floor, grotesque Cubist parodies by V.H. Brunner, and—according to one of its *habitués*, Egon Erwin Kisch—'mysterious cubist and futurist images' left by some of the clients in lieu of paying their bills; the place was rebuilt after 1918 to Cubist–Futurist designs by Jiří Kroha, who created rooms nicknamed 'Heaven', 'Hell' and 'Paradise'. The clientele comprised a wide variety of the city's literary and artistic coteries, including the German-Jewish writers in the circle of Kafka and Brod, gypsy painters and actors from the Lucerna Cabaret, and Czech anarchist poets; inevitably, another of the regulars was the ubiquitous Hašek, who generally turned up late and drunk, splattering beer over a wide radius, and often creating such a stir that he had to be thrown out. Soloists from the National Theatre sang here during their off-hours, while Kisch made a name from himself inventing dances such as the 'Ape Man' and the 'Paralytic's Dance' (also known as the 'Holešovice Apachee'). Accompanying these on the piano was a local celebrity with the wonderful name of Emča Revoluce (Emma Revolution), who also danced the tango with the famous head-waiter known as Hamlet, an ex-actor with a mass of curly hair. Presiding over all this was the cabaret's owner and founder Josef Waltner, an actor and variety singer who, attired in the long robe of a 'high priest' and flanked by two female 'acolytes', would read out from a book that brought together local anecdotes, quips and repartee. There is talk today of turning the whole place into a Museum of Prague Bohemianism.

tion has it that an old man living in the neighbourhood fell in love with this image and left all his money for her in his will.

The rest of the square is taken up by the northeastern corner of the vast Clementinum (see below), the grim Municipal Public Library (1924–28) and, on the eastern side of the square, the **New Town Hall**. The latter, built in 1908–11 by O. Polívka, is a grey and heavy Art Nouveau structure enlivened by some fine and prominent statuary: the allegorical figures and reliefs around the main portal are by S. Sucharda and J. Mařatka, while the niche figures at the two corners of the façade are by L. Šaloun, and include a wonderful sandstone representation of Rabbi Löw (1910).

The short Seminářská, at the southwestern corner of the square, will take you back to Karlova, passing at the junction of the two streets, at No. 3 Karlova, the toy-like corner house known as **At the Golden Well** (Dům U zlaté studně), a Renaissance structure later adorned with stucco figures of saints by Ulrich Mayer; the latter were added in 1701, shortly after an outbreak of plague, and include two saints normally invoked at times of plague, SS Anthony and Roch.

Continue walking west along Karlova and you will find at No. 18, at the junction with the next street, Liliová, a pink Renaissance house named **At the**

Golden Serpent (U zlatého hada), with a 19C plaque of a snake on the outside. In the early 18C the house was occupied by the Armenian coffee-merchant Deodatus Damajan, who sold coffee in the streets of Prague before opening here the first coffee-shop in Prague (later he opened another shop at the Three Ostriches—U tří pštrosů—on the other side of the river); the place today is an unappealingly decorated restaurant. Further west along the southern side of Karlova, at No. 4, is a plaque marking the house where the German astronomer J. Kepler lived between 1607 and 1612, formulating during this period his first two laws concerning the movement of the Earth around the Sun; the tower within the courtyard of the house is said to have been used by Kepler as an observatory.

At the Golden Serpent

The Clementinum and its churches

The whole northern side of the Karlova, from Seminářská right up to the end of the street, is lined by the former Jesuit College of the Clementium, the largest complex of buildings in Prague after the Castle, and covering an area of two hectares.

As part of his campaign to strengthen the Catholic faith in Bohemia, the Habsburg Emperor Ferdinand I summoned the Jesuits in 1556 to Prague where they took over the former Dominican church and monastery of St Clement. At the western end of Karlova, overlooking Knights of the Cross Square, the Jesuits began building in 1593 the Church of the Holy Saviour, the construction of which was later to involve two of the leading architects of the early Baroque in Bohemia, Anselmo Lurago and Francesco Caratti. By the middle of the 17C the teaching establishment which the Jesuits had founded alongside the church had been turned into a university college, endowed with an important library. From 1653 onwards Caratti began work on the university buildings, a task which was to entail the pulling down of much of the Old Town and was not to be completed until 1748, under the direction of F.M. Kaňka. With the expulsion of the Jesuit order in 1773, the Clementinum was given over to the Charles University, which shortly afterwards transferred here its own library.

This library has now been amalgamated into the Czech National Library, which takes up most of the complex and boasts such precious works as the Vyšehrad Codex of 1085. **Open** Mon–Fri 08.00–22.00, Sat 08.00–19.00.

Walking down Karlova from Seminářská you skirt the southern side of the former Dominican **Church of St Clement**, which is incorporated into the southern walls of the Clementinum. The church was rebuilt in 1711–15 by F.M. Kaňka, and is now used by the Greek Catholic Church. The recently restored interior, which is rarely open, is covered with ceiling paintings of the life of St Clement by J. Hiebel, who was also responsible for the illusionistic framework in the chancel, a work clearly inspired by the Italian quadratura specialist Padre Pozzo. More remarkable are the outstanding and emotionally charged series of statues of the *Evangelists and Fathers of the Church* by Matthias Braun and his workshop, decorating the niches of the piers.

Adjacent to the western end of St Clement, and attached to the apse of the Holy Saviour, is the **Italian Chapel**, the rounded exterior of which affects the course of Karlova, and gives drama to the street; built around 1590 (but with an interior redecorated in the 18C), it is the earliest example in central Europe of an elliptically planned structure. The grandest of the churches associated with the Clementinum is that of the **St Salvator**, which was begun in 1593 and not completed until 1714. The Italianate west façade, facing Knights of the Cross Square, is inspired by that of the Jesuit's mother church in Rome, but has a three-arched portico which was added by Francesco Caratti in 1653–59; the sculptures on the portico's balustrade, as well as those on the pediment above, were executed by Jan Bendl in 1659. The interior, with alterations by both C. Lurago and F.M. Kaňka, has rich stucco decorations by Bendl, and also a ceiling painting of the *Four Continents* by K. Kovář (1748); among the furnishings is a confessional (1675) which Bendl decorated with sculptures of the Apostles.

Running north of the church of St Salvator along Křižovnická is the earliest and most grandiose of the Clementinum's façades, begun by F. Caratti in 1653 and featuring stucco medallions of Roman emperors by Antonio Cometa. An arch by the side of the church will lead you inside the complex, where you will find four large and greying courtyards, one of which has a statue by Emmanuel Max of a *Prague Student* (1847), a work commemorating the role played by students in defending the Charles Bridge during the Sack of Prague by the Swedes in 1648; in another of the courtyards is an 18C **observatory tower** crowned by a bronze of *Atlas* (1722). The interiors of the Clementinum, which can only be visited with special permission, are remarkable for their Rococo rooms by F.M. Kaňka, most notably the **University Library** of 1727, a sumptuous gilded space with a ceiling painting by J. Hiebl of *The Temple of Wisdom*, and walls enlivened by salomonic columns.

The small and busy **Knights of the Cross Square** (Křižovnické Náměstí) derives its name from the hospice brotherhood to which the protection of the Judith's Bridge, the predecessor of the Charles Bridge, was entrusted in the 13C. The former **Monastery and church of St Francis**, which once belonged to

this order, stand adjacent to the church of the St Salvator, and were rebuilt in the late 17C. Designed by Jean-Baptiste Mathey, and carried out by Carlo Lurago, the centrally-planned church has a dome based closely on that of St Peter's in Rome. The interior is ringed with dark Slivenec marble altars, and adorned with a ceiling painting of the *Last Judgement* by V.V. Reiner (1722–23); in the crypt are the foundations of the original three-aisled structure of the 13C. Just outside the church is a cast-iron **Memorial to Charles IV**, designed by A. Hähnel in 1848 to commemorate the fifth centenary of the foundation of the Charles University. The western end of the square is marked by the **Tower of the Old Town Bridge**, a late 14C structure which served as a model for the Powder Gate and has rich sculptural decorations from the workshop of Peter Parléř, including, above the gate, representations of St Vitus (the bridge's patron saint) flanked by St Wenceslas and Charles IV; the structure was heavily restored and considerably embellished by Josef Mocker in the 1870s. The view from the top is in many ways the finest in all Prague, embracing the Old Town, the Little Quarter and a grand sweep of the Vltava. Viewing gallery **open** daily June–Sept 10.00–18.00, Oct–May 10.00–17.00.

Tower of the Old Town Bridge

The southern Old Town

The arch of the tower leads on to the Charles Bridge, along which the coronation processions would pass on their way to St Vitus's Cathedral. Leave the Royal Route and head south from the square along the **Smetena Embankment** (Smetanovo Nábřeží) to visit the southern half of the Old Town. The first turning to the right is the short Novotného Lávka, which takes you on to a tiny spit of land jutting out into the Vltava and dominated by the former **municipal water tower** (a structure of 1489 reconstructed at the end of the 19C). The furthermost building, originally a part of the municipal waterworks, was built in 1885 in a Czech Renaissance style, and is covered with sgraffito decorations representing the *Siege of the Old Town by the Swedes*, and executed after designs by M. Aleš, F. Ženíšek and J. Koula. Inside is the crammed café/bar/theatre/ nightclub called **Lávka**, which is perhaps best appreciated during the summer months while sitting at its shaded riverside terrace. Upstairs (**open** daily, except Tues 10.00–17.00) is a drably modern display of exhibits relating to the life and work of the composer **Bedřich Smetana**, who is also commemorated outside by a statue by J. Malejovský

(1984), which bizarrely shows him with his back turned to one of his principle sources of inspiration, the Vltava.

Across the Smetana Embankment from Novotného lávka is Anenská, which leads after a few metres into the intimate Anenské Náměstí. Immediately to your right on entering the square (at No. 4) is a Rococo palace built c 1765 by Jan Josef Wirch for Count Hubert Karel Pachta of Rájov. The Pachtas were great patrons of music, and Mozart, his wife Costanza, and Beethoven were among those who have stayed here. Attached to this palace, at No. 5, is an early 19C building which was transformed in the late 1950s into one of Prague's most influential small theatres, the **Theatre on the Balustrade** (Divadlo Na zábradlí).

History of the Theatre

The Theatre on the Balustrade rose to prominence in around 1960 under the directorship of the visionary, dictatorial and totally impractical director Ivan Vyskočil, whom Václav Havel recalls in his book *Disturbing the Peace* (1990): 'Sometimes his behaviour was outrageous: for example, he'd say, "Tomorrow we're going to try out whatever comes into our minds", but then he wouldn't come to the rehearsal, although he was the only person in the troupe capable of that kind of creativity.' Leon Grossman took over the directorship of the theatre shortly afterwards, and it was under him that it experienced its greatest years, putting on acclaimed productions of Jarry's *Ubu Roi*, Beckett's *Waiting for Godot*, and a dramatisation of Kafka's *The Trial*. The theatre is perhaps best remembered today for its associations with Václav Havel, who worked here between 1960 and 1968, establishing himself as a playwright through such works as *The Garden Party*, *The Memorandum* and *The Increased Difficulty of Concentration*. Since the events of November 1989, Havel's plays and those of his banned contemporaries have returned to the repertory here, and alternated for a while with the mime productions of Fialka and his troupe. Fialka's internationally renowned Pantomime, which acquired in later years the status of a tourist attraction, was housed in this theatre from the time the place was founded up to Fialka's death in the spring of 1991.

On the opposite side of the square to the theatre is the former **Convent of St Anne** (Klášter sv. Anny), which was founded by Dominican nuns in 1313 inside a monastery which had belonged up to then to the Order of the Knights Templar. After 1330 the nuns built a Gothic church on the site of the Templars' Romanesque rotunda, the foundations of which were excavated in 1954–57; the convent itself was rebuilt in the late 17C, and has an imposing main façade of 1676. The church—where Christoph Willibald Gluck used to play the organ in the early 18C—survives to this day, though has been put to other uses since the abolition of the convent in 1782; the whole complex, for many years the centre of the printing works of Schönfeld, is used today partly as lithographic studios, and partly as rehearsal rooms for the National Theatre.

The former convent extends east of the square all the way to the continuation of Anenská, Řetězová, on which stands, at No. 3, the **House at the Stork's** (Dům U Čápa), one of the more remarkable survivals in Prague of Romanesque domestic architecture, containing as it does a ground floor which has remained little changed since around 1200; the building, which can be visited, belonged in the 15C to George of Poděbrady.

Return along Anenská to the Smetana Embankment, and walk south by the side of the Vltava. Shortly you will come to a small garden containing Prague's answer to London's Albert Memorial—a neo-Gothic **Monument to the Emperor Franz I**, who died in 1846. Erected in 1844–46 by J.O. Kranner, it features at its base a series of allegorical figures by Josef Max, executed in a style which owes nothing to Czech art but much to German sculpture and engravings of the late 15C and early 16C; the equestrian statue of Franz I which once crowned the monument was taken down in 1918, and now languishes in that sculptural mortuary comprising the Lapidarium of the National Museum.

Due east of the garden, along Konviktská, is the tiny **Rotunda of the Holy Rood** (Rotunda sv. Kříže), one of Prague's oldest buildings. Dating back to the early 12C, it was well restored by Vojtěch Ullmann in 1862–65, and ringed by an attractive iron-work grille designed by Josef Mánes; the interior, restored again in the late 1970s, contains fragments of 14C wall-paintings, including a scene of the *Coronation of the Virgin*.

Head south from the Rotunda down Karolíny Světlé and turn left along Krocínova into Bartolomějská. Towards the end of the latter street, you will pass on your left the former Jesuit church of **St Bartholomew** (sv. Bartoloměje), which was built by K.I. Dientzenhofer in 1726–31, and has a richly decorated west façade and ceiling paintings by V.V. Reiner; next to it is a former Jesuit College intended for young noblewomen, and built in 1660 on the site of a centre for reformed prostitutes. Turn left at the end of the street into Průchodní, which leads into **Bethlehem Square** (Betlémské Náměstí). On the western side of the square, at No. 1, is the **House at the Hálaneks**, which was formed of three 15C houses that were remodelled at the end of the 16C. **Open** Tues–Sun 09.00–12.00, 13.00–17.30.

History of the House at the Hálaneks

In the middle of the 19C the House at the Hálaneks came into the hands of Vojta Náprstek (1826–94), a manufacturer and academic who was responsible, among other things, for introducing to Prague such modern appliances as the refrigerator, the washing machine and the sewing machine. An enthusiast of anthropology, he arranged lectures on the subject in his house, and opened here first a library and then a museum of anthropology. Thanks to numerous bequests from Czech travellers, Náprstek was soon able to build at the back of his house a large modern extension to this museum, designed in 1886 by A. Baum and B. Münzberger.

Náprstek's institution, subsequently administered by the National Museum, is known today as the **Náprstek Museum of Asian, African and American Cultures**, and is housed in its entirety in the extension of 1886. This grand red-brick block forms a complete contrast to the intimate arcaded courtyard which precedes it. The collections are clearly displayed and, in the case of those on the top floor dedicated to Australasia, with considerable imagination. **Open** Tues–Sun 09.00–12.00; 12.45–17.30.

Bethlehem Chapel

The north side of the Betlémské náměstí is dominated by the austere twin-gabled chapel, the Bethlehem Chapel, which gives the square its name. **Open** Apr–Oct daily 09.00–18.00; Nov–March 09.00–17.00.

History of the Bethlehem Chapel

In 1391 followers of the reformist preacher Milíč of Kroměříž decided to build a church where the Mass would be said in Czech. The Catholic authorities agreed only to the construction of a chapel, but when it was completed in 1394 the building turned out to be large enough to contain a congregation of 3000. The fame of the place was secured in the following decade when it became associated with the extraordinary rise of Jan Hus, leader of the Hussite movement.

The Bethlehem Chapel was to remain the spiritual centre of Hus's followers long after their master's death. His friend, Master Jakoubek of Stříbro, succeeded him as preacher here from 1414 to 1429, and in 1521 the German peasant leader Thomas Münzer proclaimed from the chapel's pulpit his Utopian social views; from 1609 up to the Battle of the White Mountain in 1620, the chapel belonged to the Union of Czech Brethren, one of whose preachers was the future father-in-law of the educational reformer Comenius, J.A. Komenský. Taken over subsequently by the Jesuits, the building was destroyed three years after the expulsion of the Jesuit Order in 1773, and a private dwelling put up in its place. In 1919 part of the chapel was unearthed under the house, and further archaeological excavations in 1949 revealed that all except the southern wall of the chapel had been used in the construction of the later building. The decision was then taken to reconstruct the Bethlehem Chapel in its original state, the idea being to create a memorial to the Hussites who, according to remarks made at this time by Klement Gottwald, were already 'fighting for Communism' 500 years ago. A rather cynical view of the place during the Communist period was expressed by one of the characters in Josef Škvorecký's novel *The Miracle Game*: 'Petrofim couldn't even work up any plausible enthusiasm for the Bethlehem Chapel, reconstructed—mainly to attract tourists—on a spot where it was thought the great Jan Hus might once have preached.'

The box-like interior of the chapel, which was reconstructed in 1950–52 by Jaroslav Fragner, has pseudo-medieval wall-paintings and wooden furnishings, and is focused on the pulpit rather than the altar. A door on the eastern side leads into the house where Jan Hus and other preachers lived: inside you will find a partial recreation of a domestic interior of the early 15C, and displays relating to the Hussite movement.

After leaving the building turn left and then left again into Husova, on which stands—a short way to the north on the right-hand side—the **Church of St Giles** (sv. Jiljí). Founded in the 13C and rebuilt between 1310 and 1371, this church has a sturdy, twin-towered west façade which has been little altered since the 14C, when the building was the principal base of the reform preacher Milíč of Kroměříž; the tall interior, however, was remodelled by F. Špaček after 1733

Jan Hus

Born in 1373 of peasant parents in the south Bohemian village of Husinec, Hus studied at Prague University before entering the Church, where he soon made such a name for himself that he became confessor to King Wenceslas IV's wife, Queen Sophie. He was at first unwavering in his devotion to the Church of Rome, but the papacy's corruption at the time of the Schism—as exemplified in its selling of indulgences in the streets of Prague—was to turn Hus into one of its most violent opponents. In 1402 he began denouncing the morals of the clergy from Prague's Bethlehem Chapel, finding international support for his views two years later following the arrival in Prague from England of two disciples of the English reformer John Wycliffe, James and Conrad of Canterbury. He would continue preaching from the chapel up to 1413.

The preachings of Hus won him an enormous following among the Czech people and at Prague University led to the development of a great rift between the Czechs and the Germans, the latter all taking the side of the Church of Rome. In 1409 Hus scored a major victory when he managed to persuade Wenceslas IV to impose the Decree of Kutná Hora, whereby the voting system in the university was changed greatly in favour of the Czechs, a decision which led to an exodus from Prague of 2000 German students and many professors, who went on subsequently to found the University of Leipzig in Saxony. The success of the Czech reform movement incited the new pope at Rome, Alexander V, to authorise the archbishop of Prague to destroy all the writings of Wycliffe and to punish those who read and preached his doctrines. When Hus persisted in his preachings, he was excommunicated, and all those who supported him were threatened with the same fate, even if they only offered him food and drink; it was further stipulated that all religious services were to be suspended in every town which he entered. Wenceslas IV persuaded Hus to leave Prague for a while, in the hope that his absence from the city would help to calm the situation. In his 20 months of voluntary exile Hus produced most of his finest writings, but also continued to preach, finding his congregations in the villages and farms around his native Husinec. In the meantime Wenceslas's brother Sigismund induced the church authorities to call a Council at Constance to settle the dispute between the rival pontiffs. Sigismund also suggested that Hus should attend this council to refute the charges of heresy, promising him a safe-conduct and a free return to Bohemia whatever the outcome. Hus was burnt at the stake at Constance on 6 July 1415.

and has been cloaked with massive gilded capitals, rich stucco decoration by B. Spinetti and ceiling frescoes by V.V. Reiner comprising a central panel of the *Celebration of the Dominican Order*, and two flanking ones representing the *Legends of St Giles and St Thomas Aquinas*.

Head east of the church along the tiny Zlatá, turn right into Jilská, and then immediately left into Vejvodova; this will take you into Michalská, where you turn right again, and then first left into **Havelská**. At its northeastern end Havelská widens into a narrow square, enlivened today by Prague's last surviving open-air market, and dominated by the **Church of St Gall** (sv. Havla). The latter, a 13C foundation, was remodelled around 1722 by Pavel Bayer and Jan Santini-Aichel, who gave the church its powerful, undulating façade. Between here and the former Fruit Market (Ovocný trh) to the northeast is the **Estate Theatre** (formerly the Tyl Theatre), an elegant neo-Classical building designed by Antonín Haffenecker in 1781.

History of the Theatre

The oldest theatre in Prague, the Tyl Theatre opened in 1783 with a performance of Lessing's play *Emilia Galotti*. Four years later the first ever performance of Mozart's opera *Don Giovanni* took place here, and early in the following century the place acquired further musical renown when the German composer K.M. Weber was director of its operatic ensemble. The property after 1799 of the Czech Estates, the theatre was known up to 1945 as the Estates Theatre, after which it was renamed in honour of the Czech dramatist J.K. Tyl (1808–56), whose comedy *Fidlovačka*—from which the song and future Czech national anthem, 'Where is my Home', is taken—had been premièred here in 1834.

Adjoining the theatre, at No. 9 Železná, is the **Carolinum**, the original building of the oldest university in central Europe. Founded by Charles IV in 1348, the university building is also claimed to be the oldest still in use in Europe, though in fact very little of the medieval structure remains, the principal survival being the charming oriel window on the southern side, facing the Fruit Market. The structure was extensively rebuilt by F.M. Kaňka after 1718, at the time when the university was in the hands of the Jesuits; further major reconstruction took place after the Second World War.

Continue north up Železná, and turn left into Kožná, where, at **No. 1**, is a house with a beautiful Renaissance portal featuring two bears. A plaque indicates that the house was the birthplace of the journalist Egon Erwin Kisch (1885–1948), who devoted much of his writing to accounts of his native Prague, including *Prague Adventures* and *Tales from Prague's Streets and Nights*. Another of his works was dedicated to the city's covered passages, and it is singularly appropriate that from No. 10 Kožná you can walk through such passages all the way back to Jilská. Kisch's birthplace stands at the corner of Melantrichova, where you turn right to rejoin the southern side of the Old Town Square.

The Jewish Town (Josefov)

Walk to the opposite side of the square and enter Pařížská, a good starting-point for a tour of the northern half of the Old Town. This long straight avenue, built at the end of the 19C, is lined with large, oppressively ornamented blocks, featuring fantastical corners composed of irregularly shaped balconies and openings piled up one on top of the other. Its creation constituted one of the few major plans of urban renewal within the Old Town of Prague, cutting as it did a great swathe through a slum area crammed with picturesque but decayed old houses inhabited largely by the city's Jewish population.

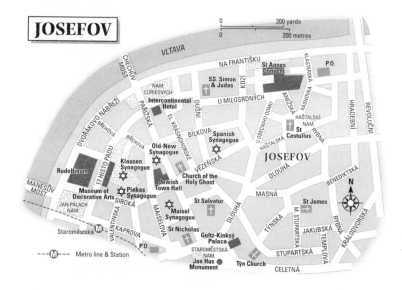

Before reaching the main monuments of Jewish Prague, take the first turning to the right, and then turn right again into Salvátorská, on which stands at No. 8 an innovative brick building constructed for the **Stenc Fine-Arts Publishing House** by Kotěra's student Otakar Novotný in 1908–11; exposed brickwork is uncommon in Bohemia, and reveals here Novotný's great interest in the works of Frank Lloyd Wright and the Dutch architect Hendrik Petrus Berlage.

Return to Pařížská and continue walking north, crossing at the end of the next block the large intersecting street of **Široká**. At No. 9 Široká, just to the west of its junction with Pařížská, is an Art Nouveau apartment block, built by Karel Mašek in 1908 and boasting a magnificent portal flanked by sculpted female allegorical figures; adjoining this, at No. 11, is a neo-Gothic apartment of 1906 by Matěj Blecha, with an oval Art Nouveau stairwell. Continuing north along Pařížská, you will find at the end of the next block to the left the *U Velké Synagogy*, a newly revamped restaurant which, in its former days as a modest beer-hall with a little-spoilt turn-of-the-century interior, was another of the haunts of the writer Bohumil Hrabal.

The monuments of Jewish Prague

Immediately beyond this establishment there is a sudden interruption in the line of Pařížská's turn-of-the-century blocks to reveal incongruously, just below the pavement level on the left-hand side, three of the main survivals of Jewish Prague—the Jewish Town Hall, and the Old-New and High Synagogues. The first two buildings, together with several other neighbouring monuments, form part of the **Jewish Museum**, which since 1994 has been administered by the city's Jewish community. The Jewish Museum is today one of the city's obligatory tourist sights, and the throngs of visitors who descend upon this restricted area lead to unpleasant congestion and long queues to enter some of the monuments. An extremely expensive (almost £9 or $14 at the time of writing) entrance ticket covering all the various parts of the museum can be purchased from any of the quarter's ticket offices (male visitors to both the Old-New Synagogue and the Jewish Cemetery are also provided with the small cap known as a yarmulka).

■ The sites in the Jewish Museum are open (with some variations) Apr–Oct Sun–Fri 09.30–18.00, Nov–Mar Sun–Fri 09.30–17.00.

Architecturally and historically the most important of the museum's sites is the **Old-New Synagogue** (Staronová synagoga), which is also Prague's most outstanding early medieval building. The oldest functioning synagogue in Europe, it dates back to the middle of the 13C, and owes its unusual name to the fact that it was originally called the 'New Synagogue' until another 'new' one was built in the vicinity. After noting on the exterior the unusually tall, stepped brick gables (a 15C addition), you enter a narrow, barrel-vaulted vestibule that was originally the main hall of the synagogue until the present one was added after c 1270 (it later became the women's gallery); in the 17C metal boxes were placed in this vestibule for the collection of Jewish taxes.

The actual main hall, one of the finest examples in Central Europe of the Cistercian Gothic style, is reached through a 13C portal with an exquisitely carved vine tree bearing 12 bunches of grapes that refer to the 12 tribes of Israel. There are numerous further references to the figure 12 both in the decoration and in the plan of the hall itself, a harmonious double-aisled vaulted hall-nave. Leaf ornament of the 13C decorates the tympanum of the shrine on the east wall containing the Torah (a parchment scroll of the five Books of Moses, or Pentateuch). In the middle of the hall stands a pulpit or almenar, surrounded by a beautiful Gothic grille of the late 15C; above this hangs a flag donated to Prague's Jews in 1648 by the Emperor Ferdinand, who wanted to thank them for helping him fight off the Protestant Swedes. The benches lining the walls are early 19C, while on the walls themselves are traces of medieval frescoes and inscriptions of 1618 recording certain sections of the Psalms.

Directly facing the south portal of the building is the entrance to the **High Synagogue**, which was built in 1568, extended at the end of the following century, and remodelled and given its present façade in the 19C; used until recently for the display of synagogical metalwork and textiles, it has now become once again a functioning synagogue, and is closed to the public.

Adjoining the synagogue, and until the 19C connected to it by a door, is the picturesque **Jewish Town Hall**, founded by Maisel in the late 16C, but completely rebuilt in 1763 when it was given its toy-like wooden turret, complete with a Hebraic clock which tells the time backwards ('The hand of the clock in the Jewish quarter is turning backwards /And you are passing slowly backward through the history of your life', wrote Apollinaire in his visionary poem *Zone*).

Walking south from here down Maislova, and crossing Široká, you will come at No. 10 to the **Maisel Synagogue**, which was commissioned and paid for by Mordechaj Maisel in 1590, later rebuilt in a Baroque style, and then given a wholly neo-Gothic appearance by A. Grotte between 1893 and 1905; at present the newly restored building contains an uninspiring display relating to the

The ghetto, the golem and the Nazi occupation

Jews began settling in Prague from at least the 10C onwards, though it was not apparently until the mid-13C that they began forming a ghetto in the district around the Old-New Synagogue; in accordance with the Third Lateran Council of 1179 this ghetto was separated from its Christian surroundings by a wall. Despite fires, pogroms and even a law of 1541 banishing Jews from the whole of Bohemia, the ghetto flourished, and by the 17C an estimated 7000 people were crowded into the area. Two of its most influential figures were active during the reign of Rudolph II, one being the Emperor's finance minister, Mordechaj Markus Maisel, who was responsible for the paving of the ghetto and the building of the Maisel Synagogue and the Jewish Town Hall. The other great Jewish figure of this period was the Rabbi Löw, a man much respected by Rudolph II and the leading aristocratic families of the time, and under whose influence the Jewish community in Prague enjoyed the most privileged period in their history. A prominent theologian, Löw was the author of many writings that became an inherent part of Hasidic teaching, such as his homily On the Hardening of Pharaoh's Heart. But Löw was to be remembered above all for his reputed supernatural powers, a reputation doubtless enhanced by his being a passionate devotee of the Cabbala, whereby he believed that the whole of human history, past, present and future, could be read in the Torah. Numerous fanciful tales are told of Löw, but none more famous than that of his creation—from the mud of the Vltava—of Yossel the Golem. Though sometimes portrayed as a guardian of the ghetto and even as a figure of fun, Yossel has usually been imagined as a figure like Frankenstein's monster, who ends up running amok (as in Gustav Meyrink's sinister novel The Golem of 1915 and in the German expressionist film of the same name by Paul Wegener).

The law requiring the Prague Jews to be contained in the ghetto was abolished in 1781 by Emperor Joseph II, whose ultimate intentions were to assimilate Jews fully into the rest of the population, destroying their language and culture by forbidding Hebrew and Yiddish for business transactions, and forcing the Jews to Germanise their names (it was not until 1867 that Jews were assured all civil rights equal to those guaranteed to Czechs and Germans). In 1850, when the ghetto had been almost entirely infiltrated by outsiders and only 10 per cent of the former Jewish population was left, this area of Prague was turned into a municipal district known as Josefov in honour of Joseph II. The emperor would not, perhaps, have entirely appreciated the honour, for this district was by now a festering slum, more over-populated than any other area in the city, without water-supply or drainage, and with a notorious reputation for low life: decrepit smoke-filled bars and brothels, marked by poles hung with red lanterns, stood provocatively alongside the houses of the remaining Orthodox Jews, whose sabbath chants would sometimes be interrupted by the shouts and songs of drunken revellers and prostitutes.

Despite the protests of poets, students, architects and others, this whole area was largely razed in 1895, leaving only the buildings of historical interest still standing (the 21,700 waggonloads of rubble were used as landfill to protect a district that was still constantly under the threat of floods). Later the Nazis, far from wishing to destroy these surviving monuments, planned to turn them into a 'Museum of Jewry', so as to record for posterity the culture of what they believed would soon be an extinct race. A museum of Jewish art had existed since the beginning of the century but, as a result of the Nazis' confiscation of Jewish property, its holdings were swelled to become the largest collection of synagogical art in the world. The museum's growth coincided with the dwindling of the Jewish population of Bohemia and Moravia to a tenth of its former size: a memorial in Prague's Pinkas Synagogue records the names of 77,297 Jews killed during the Nazi occupation of the country. Today only a small community of Orthodox Jews remains in the traditional Jewish quarter of Prague.

The former Jewish ghetto has always held a strong fascination for visitors to Prague, and a number of foreign writers have evoked the place in their works, for instance the popular 19C American novelist, Marion Crawford. In her novel, *The Witch of Prague* (1882), Crawford evokes the ghetto with an unsavoury mixture of romantic fascination and deep repellence: 'Throngs of gowned men, crooked, bearded, filthy, vulture-eyed, crowded upon each other in the narrow, public place ... a writhing mass of humanity, intoxicated by the smell of gold, mad for its possession, half hysteric with the fear of losing it, timid, yet dangerous, poisoned to the core by the sweet sting of money, terrible in intelligence, vile in heart, contemptible in body, irresistible in the unity of their greed—the Jews of Prague two hundred years ago.' More recently the former ghetto provided the main setting for the English novelist Bruce Chatwin's compelling novella, *Utz* (1988), which deals with a collector of Meissen porcelain figures living in the same district where the Rabbi Löw had fashioned his golem.

history of the Jews in Bohemia and Moravia from the 10C up to the period of their emancipation in the 18C. Heading instead north along Maislova from the Old-New Synagogue you will find at the end of the street (at No. 21) an elegant and beautifully decorated Art Nouveau apartment block, built by František Weyr and Richard Klenka in 1911; facing its northern side, at No. 2 Břehová, is another fine building of this period, designed by Bedřich Bendelmayer.

Returning to the Old-New Synagogue and heading due west along U Hřbitova you will shortly reach the **Klaus Synagogue**, which dates back to 1694 and has a stuccoed, barrel-vaulted interior containing today a large collection of Hebraic manuscripts and prints. Next to this is the entrance to the Old Jewish Cemetery, which is flanked on its western side by the former **Ceremonial Hall**, which was designed by F. Gerstl in 1906 for the Jewish Burial Society: taking the form of a tiny neo-Romanesque castle, it features a display of children's and other drawings depicting conditions at the Terezín ghetto and concentration camp.

Within the **Old Jewish Cemetery** (Starý židovský hřbitov)—the Jewish Museum's most popular attraction—are 20,000 tombstones jumbled together among trees in a manner which, until recently, echoed at times the visiting conditions (today's tourists are obliged to walk single-file along a designated

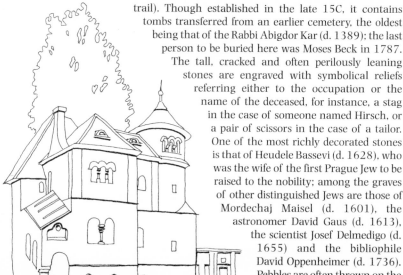

trail). Though established in the late 15C, it contains tombs transferred from an earlier cemetery, the oldest being that of the Rabbi Abigdor Kar (d. 1389); the last person to be buried here was Moses Beck in 1787. The tall, cracked and often perilously leaning stones are engraved with symbolical reliefs referring either to the occupation or the name of the deceased, for instance, a stag in the case of someone named Hirsch, or a pair of scissors in the case of a tailor. One of the most richly decorated stones is that of Heudele Bassevi (d. 1628), who was the wife of the first Prague Jew to be raised to the nobility; among the graves of other distinguished Jews are those of Mordechaj Maisel (d. 1601), the astronomer David Gaus (d. 1613), the scientist Josef Delmedigo (d. 1655) and the bibliophile David Oppenheimer (d. 1736). Pebbles are often thrown on the graves as a gesture of respect towards the dead. The grave with the greatest accumulation of these is that of the most famous person to be buried

Ceremonial Hall in the Old Jewish Cemetery

here, the Rabbi Löw, on top of whom visitors also throw bank notes in the hope that this man with supernatural powers will grant them their wishes. A beautiful description of the cemetery appears in Bruce Chatwin's novella, *Utz*: 'It was now early evening and we were sitting on a slatted seat in the Old Jewish Cemetery. Pigeons were burbling on the roof of the Klausen Synagogue. The sunbeams, falling through sycamores, lit up spirals of midges and landed on the mossy tombstones, which, heaped one upon the other, resembled seaweed-covered rocks at low tide.'

Today's designated trail through the cemetery will lead you to the **Pinkas Synagogue**, which is attached to the cemetery's southern wall. Founded by Rabbi Pinkas in 1479, this was rebuilt in 1535, and enlarged and remodelled by Juda Goldsmid de Herz in 1625. The hall, turned after the Second World War into a memorial to the Jewish victims of the Nazis, was closed in 1968 for restoration that was interminably and suspiciously protracted by the Communists. Only recently completed, the restored walls are once again entirely blanketed with the names, personal data, and home towns and villages of the 77,297 Jews killed by the Nazis in Bohemia and Moravia (of this number, 36,000 were from Prague).

Continuing east along Široká you will come, at the end of the cemetery wall, to the large riverside square which since 1989 has been named after the 1969 'martyr' Jan Palach, to whom there is a small memorial containing a bust made from a death mask. The four-span concrete bridge (the Mánesuv most) that leads from here to the Malá Strana dates back to 1911–14 and includes reliefs by such leading sculptors of the time as František Bílek and Jan Štursa. On the northern side of the square stands the imposing late 19C **Rudolfinum**, which, despite its conventional neo-Renaissance detailing, was greatly admired for the boldness of its layout by the Cubist architect Pavel Janák, who featured it in his book *Art Treasures of Bohemia* (1913): built between 1875 and 1884 by Josef Zítek and Josef Schulz, it functioned originally as an art gallery and concert hall before serving from 1918 to 1939 as the seat of the Czech parliament; after the war it was used again for cultural purposes and is now one of the main venues of the annual music festival known as the Prague Spring.

Turning right as soon as you enter the square from Široká, and walking north from it along 17. **Listopadu**, the next building you come to is the **Museum of Decorative Arts** (Umělecko-průmyslové muzeum), a French-style neo-Renaissance structure rising above the western side of the Old Jewish Cemetery. **Open** Tues–Sun 10.00–18.00.

The museum, founded in 1885 with a largely didactic purpose, was at first housed in the Rudolfinum while awaiting its eventual transference to the present building, which was completed by Josef Schulz in 1900; the façade is covered with reliefs by Bohuslav Schnirch and Antonín Popp representing the different branches of the decorative arts in Bohemia, and the coats of arms of the Bohemian towns most re-nowned for these arts.

The museum itself, frequently empty and looked after by a particularly charming group of elderly women, is one of the great little-known attractions of Prague. Its collections, ranging from the Middle Ages up to the present day and with the main emphasis on Bohemia and Moravia, include glass, ceramics, porcelain, woodwork, furniture, metalwork, clocks, textiles, costumes, prints, posters and photographs. Despite the great size of the building, only a small proportion of its objects is on display, and much of the space is often used for temporary loan exhibitions.

The rooms have ceilings attractively decorated with turn-of-the-century grotesque work, and the display is endearingly old-fashioned and crowded, the overall effect—enhanced by the occasional dramatic lighting—being that of great wealth and variety, as in a Netherlandish still-life painting. Among the finest of the objects permanently on show are the numerous pieces of Bohemian Baroque glass, and the superlative collection of Meissen porcelain figurines. A small selection from its unrivalled holdings of Czech Cubist works can currently be seen at the Czech Museum of Fine Arts on Celetná (see pp 84–85).

Continuing north along 17. listopadu will take you to the Náměstí Curieových, a riverside square standing at the northern end of Pařížská, and bordered to the south by the fussy modern block of the luxurious Hotel Intercontinental (1968–74), and to the west by the Law Faculty of Charles University, an Art Deco structure designed by J. Kotěra in 1919. Head south of the square along Pařížská and turn left beyond the Hotel Intercontinental to reach, on the eastern side of a small garden, the ulice Elišky Krásnohorské; here, at Nos 10–14, there is a remarkable 'Cubist' block built by Otakar Novotný in 1919–21 as the Prague Teacher's Co-operative.

Continuing south along this street, you will shortly rejoin Široká, passing on

Cubist building by Otakar Novotný, 1919–21

your left just before doing so the **Church of the Holy Ghost**, a single-aisled structure of 1346 remodelled after a fire in 1689; in front of the building stands a statue of St John of Nepomuk (1727) by F.M. Brokoff. Turn left along Široká, and then turn left into Dušní, where, directly facing the eastern end of the Church of the Holy Ghost, is the **Spanish Synagogue**, a neo-Moorish structure designed by J. Niklas in 1882 for the city's Sephardic Jews; the interior, with its elaborate stucco decorations inspired by those of the Alhambra in Granada, is due to reopen in late 1998 with a permanent exhibition documenting the history of Czech Jews from the late 18C up to 1945. Walk north along Dušní until you reach the 17C–18C **Church of SS Simon and Jude**, the choir of which has an organ on which both Mozart and Haydn played.

Convent of St Agnes

U milosrdných, which runs east of the church, will take you to the present entrance of the former Convent of St Agnes (Anežský klášter), a large and important medieval complex. The convent, which is sometimes known by the ridiculous name of the 'Bohemian Assisi', was founded for the Poor Clares by Wenceslas I in 1233, probably on the request of his sister, Agnes of Bohemia, who would become the first abbess, as well as the patron saint of Bohemia. **Open** Tues–Sun 10.00–18.00.

The museum installed in the convent is centred around a large cloister, which has largely retained its mid-13C appearance, apart from the upper level of the eastern side, which features a Renaissance arcade built by the Dominicans. At the cloister's southeast corner is a door leading into the convent's two adjoining churches: the earliest of the two was dedicated to St Francis and completed by the mid-13C; however only its presbytery has survived, and this is known today as the **Mánes Hall** and is used for concerts. Projecting east of this structure is the spacious and elegant **Church of St Saviour**, which dates from the 1280s, and is a fine example of French Gothic influence.

The convent now contains the 19C Czech paintings belonging to the National Gallery. Stairs off the east side of the cloister climb up to the collections on the first floor, which have been collectively dismissed as 'junk' by Sadakat Kadri, the lively and idiosyncratic author of the *Cadogan Guide to Prague*. Although

Saint Agnes

Born in 1211 as the third and youngest of King Přemysl Otakar I's daughters from his second marriage, Agnes spent most of her childhood being used as a pawn to try to secure useful political alliances. After being promised at the age of three to a Silesian prince who subsequently died, she was offered to the ten-year-old son of Emperor Frederick II, who was then taken away from her by the daughter of Duke Leopold VI of Vienna; marital negotiations were later entered into with Henry III of England, but after being protracted for several years, these were finally dropped, mostly on account of the dowry. When, finally, Frederick II himself tried on two occasions to marry her, she decided she had had enough of worldly suitors and made the sensible decision to betrothe herself instead to Christ. She was 23 at the time.

She entered the Prague convent of the Poor Clares in 1234, one year year after its foundation; after her hair had been shorn off and all her riches given away; she remained here until her death in 1292, by which time the present large complex was almost complete. Throughout her many years at the convent she remained fanatically devoted to her order's ideals of poverty, while accepting the concessions necessitated by their transference from Italy to the cold climate of Prague: papal permission was eventually given for fasting hours to be shortened and wool stockings and double or fur-lined tunics to be worn. The story of her legendary life, written 50 years after her death, praised the simplicity of her life-style, her humble devotion to her fellow nuns (whose clothes she washed and mended) and her frugal diet of raw onions and fruits.

Agnes's arguments against a Church too deeply involved in worldly power and magnificence did not prevent her convent from being taken over by the Hussites in 1420 for use as an arsenal. Occupied again after 1555 by the Dominicans, and then partially rebuilt in the wake of the Old Town fire of 1689, the convent was dissolved for good by Joseph II in 1782, after which the whole complex fell into decay and its buildings were usurped as craft workshops and poor people's homes. Extensive restoration work was begun in the 20C, and in the course of this the foundations of a neighbouring Minorite monastery of the early 13C were discovered. Agnes herself, beatified in 1874, was finally canonised on 12 November 1989, four days before the Velvet Revolution. Restoration of her convent is at last nearing completion.

mediocrity indeed predominates, numerous surprises are to be had, as well as much insight into the subject-matter that has always preoccupied Czech nationalists. The paintings displayed in the well-modernised upper rooms are arranged chronologically, beginning with Classical landscapes by Procházka and ending with the rural genre scenes and cityscapes of Jakub Schikaneder, with whose late works Czech art is brought into the 20C.

After leaving the Convent of St Agnes head south down the short Anežská (passing at No.2 the charming *U Červeného Kola* restaurant), at the end of which

19C Czech printing at the Convent of St Agnes

Among the more important Czech artists working in the early 19C were the painter of romantic Gothic interiors, Ludvík Kohl, the portraitist Antonín Machek, the mythological painter František Tkadlík, and the landscapists August Piepenhagen and Karel Postl, the latter being the first professor of landscape painting at the Prague Academy. Two other major names are Josef Navrátil—the author of a stunningly simple and realistic series of still-lifes—and Antonín Mánes, who is represented here by a number of romantic landscapes imbued with nationalist sentiment, most notably his view of the ruins of Kokořín Castle (1839). Two of Mánes's sons were painters, the most famous being the elder one, Josef, whose work dominates Czech 19C art. The paintings of his that are on show here reveal his extra-ordinary variety, and range from such academic canvases as *Petrarch and Laura* (1845–46) to a series of remarkably fresh landscapes painted in the 1850s and 1860s (for instance *Gmunden, and the Mountain Hut*); among his other works here are lively portraits of *Luisa Bělská* (1857) and *Anna Václavíková* (1862), detailed drawings of national folk costumes, a pair of mysteriously lit nudes (*Dawn* and *Evening*, 1857), and two large-scale oil studies for banners (one for the Říp Association at Roudnice, 1863–64, and the other for the Smíchov Luke's Choir, 1868).

Of Mánes's younger contemporaries, the only one to achieve an international reputation was Jaroslav Čermák, who specialised in ambitious scenes of Czech history, such as *The Hussites defending the Pass* (1857). Čermák, a Byronic figure with the painterly pretensions of a Delacroix, became an active witness to history by going off to record the war between Turkey and Montenegro, the subject of several scenes in the museum. Academic landscapists of this period include Bedřich Havránek, Alois Bubák, and Adolf Kosárek, while one of the finest of the genre painters was Soběslav Pinkas, who did numerous scenes of Prague life, such as *Children on Kampa Island* (1854).

From the 1850s onwards an increasing number of Czech artists spent long periods in France, including Pinkas himself, Viktor Barvitius, Karel Purkyně, and Antonín Chitussi. Barvitius was the author of the delightfully detailed and atmospherically lit genre scene, *Thursday in Stromovka Park* (1865); Purkyně meanwhile was an artist who fell strongly under the influence of Courbet, as can be seen in his powerful portrait of *Jech the Smith* (1860) and in the boldly painted still-lifes *The Snow Owl* (1862) and *Onions and Partridges* (1862). Chitussi painted many landscapes while staying in and around Paris, and on his return to Czechoslovakia did numerous Barbizon-inspired scenes in the region where he was born—the Czech Moravian Highlands.

Towards the end of the 19C many of the leading Czech artists were engaged in the decoration of the Prague National Theatre, including the landscapist Julius Mařák, and the specialists in allegorical and Classical scenes involving female nudes, Vojtech Hynais and František Ženíšek. The most important of the artists of the so-called National Theatre Generation was the prolific Mikoláš Aleš, among whose works in the museum is a series of cartoons for his series *Legend of My Country*, which he painted for the

National Theatre; many other of his drawings and decorative designs are to be seen here, as well as numerous historical canvases such as *The Meeting of George of Poděbrady with Matthias Corvinus* (1877), *Milica and the Yugoslavs* (1876), and *Hussite on the Baltic* (1877), a bleak snow-covered landscape featuring a lone rider on horseback in front of the tomb of one of his comrades.

The turn-of-the-century Czech artist best known outside the Czech Republic, Alfons Mucha, is represented here only by very slight works. In compensation there is a superb group of paintings by Jakub Schikaneder, ranging from the Bastien-Lepage-inspired *Autumn* (1884) to the large, suggestive and almost monochromatic city scenes of the first and second decades of the 20C, such as *Winter Evening in the Town* (1907–09) and *Embankment* (1916–18).

you will come to the **Church of St Castullus** (sv. Haštal), which dates back to the early 14C. Though the main nave and chancel were remodelled following the fire of 1689, the south aisle has been preserved in its medieval state, as has the remarkable twin-aisled extension which was added to the north side of the church in 1375; the extension features a fine net vault with bosses decorated with masks and leaves. The walls of the sacristy are covered with medieval murals, comprising a series of Apostles' heads of c 1400 and scenes of the Crucifixion and the Last Supper of c 1500.

Running alongside the southern side of the church is the Haštalská třída, where at No. 4 is an Art Nouveau house (1905) with a beautiful tree decoration on its façade; next to this is a portal of the same period incorporating an elegant rose window. Running parallel to this street to the south is the **Dlouhá Třída**, which follows the early medieval route connecting the Old Town Square with the colony of German merchants at Poříčí (see p 165). Turn left along Dlouhá, passing at No. 37 the **House At the Golden Tree** (Dům U zlatého stromu), which has a late 16C courtyard dating from the time when the house belonged to the Mayor of the Old Town, Václav Kročín. At the eastern end of Dlouhá you will come to Revoluční, where you turn right, shortly afterwards rejoining the náměstí Republiky.

2 · The Little Quarter (Malá Strana)

Across the Vltava

The Little Quarter or Malá Strana, founded in 1257 by Přemysl Otakar II in the outer bailey of Prague Castle, was known up to the early 14C as The New Town below Prague Castle. Later in the century Charles IV considerably extended this town with the creation of new fortifications incorporating the Petřín Hill to the south. Today this hill forms part of a large wooded park, the northern sides of which are fringed by lush gardens attached to Baroque palaces. Gardens and palaces, many of which now serve as embassies, are the dominant feature of the

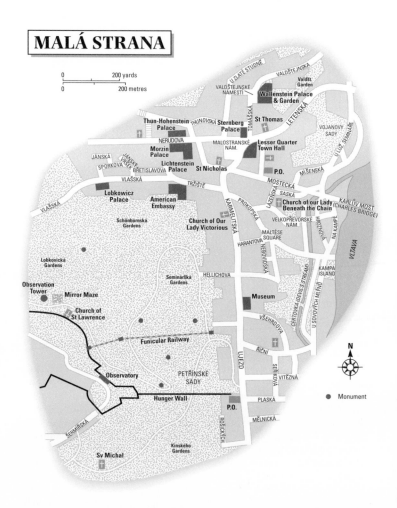

MALÁ STRANA

0   200 yards
0   200 metres

VALDŠTEJNSKÁ

U ZLATÉ STUDNĚ

Valdšt. Garden

VALDŠTEJNSKÉ NÁMĚSTÍ

Wallenstein Palace & Garden

Thun-Hohenstein Palace

TRUNOVSKÁ   Sternberg Palace

TOMÁŠSKÁ   St Thomas

LETENSKÁ

VOJANOVY SADY

U LUŽ.SEMINÁŘE

NERUDOVÁ

MALOSTRANSKÉ NÁM.

Lesser Quarter Town Hall

JÁNSKÁ   JÁNSKÝ VRŠEK   Morzin Palace

ŠPORKOVÁ   BŘETISLAVOVA

Lichtenstein Palace   St Nicholas

P.O.

MIŠEŇSKÁ

VLAŠSKÁ

TRŽIŠTĚ

MOSTECKÁ

SASKÁ

LÁZEŇSKÁ

Lobkowicz Palace

American Embassy

KARMELITSKÁ

PROKOPSKÁ

Church of our Lady Beneath the Chain

KARLŮV MOST (CHARLES BRIDGE)

Schönbornská Gardens

Church of Our Lady Victorious

VELKOPŘEVORSKÉ NÁM.

HRONOVA

NA KAMPĚ

VLTAVA

Lobkovická Gardens

Seminářská Gardens

MALTÉSE SQUARE

HARANTOVA   NEBOVIDSKÁ

HELLICHOVA

KAMPA ISLAND

Observation Tower   Mirror Maze

Church of St Lawrence

Museum

VŠEHRDOVA

ČERTOVKA (DEVIL'S STREAM)

U SOVOVÝCH MLÝNŮ

Funicular Railway

ŘÍČNÍ

N

Observatory

PETŘÍNSKÉ SADY

ÚJEZD

SEŘÍKOVÁ   VÍTĚZNÁ

Hunger Wall

P.O.

PLASKÁ

● Monument

MĚLNICKÁ

ŠERMÍŘSKÁ

ROSICKÝCH

Kinského Gardens

Sv Michal

Little Quarter, the most genuinely picturesque area of a city steeped in the picturesque, and the one which can most truly be compared to a stage set. Although overprettified in parts in recent years, and largely lacking today the romantically decayed corners of old, it has so far escaped the worst of the commercialisation now affecting the Staré Město. Furthermore, in comparison to the flat Staré Město, this steeply pitched district offers from afar an enticingly variegated profile. Despite the now almost oppressive congestion of pedestrians that can mark the Royal Route as it crosses the Charles Bridge, it is difficult not to feel an acute sense of drama and expectation while being drawn by the bridge's gesticulating statuary towards the Little Quarter's turreted entrance gate, behind which rises the massive dome of St Nicholas and, higher still, the dramatic silhouette of Prague Castle.

Charles Bridge

The Charles Bridge (Karlův most), one of Europe's most beautiful bridges, is not simply the visual centrepiece of Prague, but has also played a central role in the life and history of the city.

History of the Bridge

The first bridge to span the Vltava at this point was a wooden construction, first mentioned in 1118 and destroyed by flood in 1157. On the instigation of Queen Judith, the wife of Vladislav I, a 21-arch stone bridge was built in its place between 1158–60 but, in 1342, this too was to collapse after a flood. In 1357 Charles IV entrusted the architect Peter Parléř with the construction of a new bridge, which was to be known as the Stone or Prague Bridge up to 1870, and only thereafter as the Charles Bridge. Built out of sandstone blocks, this 16-arch structure runs a slightly irregular course due to the fact that, while the bridgeheads of the Judith's Bridge were retained, new piers were constructed in the middle of the river, just to the south of the old ones. The new structure, which was completed in the early 15C, has been damaged a number of times by floods, and two of its arches had to be rebuilt in 1890, but it has never collapsed.

As well as serving as part of the processional route of the Bohemian kings, the Charles Bridge was a place where business transactions took place, tournaments were held, custom dues collected, law suits settled, criminals executed, and delinquents punished by being dipped in the Vltava in wicker baskets. The most famous incident in its history occurred on 20 March 1393 when the future St John of Nepomuk was bound hand and foot and thrown from its parapet into the river where, according to legend, his body floated for an unnaturally long time, a group of five stars hovering above it. In 1683, at a time when the Jesuits were beginning to promote the Nepomuk cult, a statue to him by J. Brokoff was placed on the bridge, near the supposed point from where he was flung. This led to several religious orders commissioning other statues for the bridge, from J. and F.M. Brokoff, M.V. Jäckel, Matthias Braun, J.O. Mayer, and M.B. Mandl. The Baroque statues, which were all in place by 1714, were joined between 1857 and 1859 by works by Emmanuel Max; between 1908 and 1937 a number of other statues were added, and some of the more worn ones removed to the Lapidarium of the National Gallery and replaced by copies. On 9 February 1911 the bridge witnessed one of the many extravagant incidents in the life of the great hoaxer and comic writer Jaroslav Hašek. A newspaper of the time reported that 'in the small hours of this morning Jaroslav Hašek wanted to throw himself from the parapet of the Charles Bridge into the Vltava ... The theatrical hairdresser, Mr Edward Bräuer, pulled him back. The police doctor diagnosed a pronounced neurosis, and he was taken to a mental home.'

The bridge, which is closed to traffic, is overwhelmed by day by lingering tourists and street artists, and at night functions additionally as a meeting-place for singing and guitar-playing students, whose appearance and behaviour are little different to those of their hippy predecessors who gathered here in the late 1960s. The views on all sides are uninterruptedly beautiful, and the place becomes especially evocative on a winter's night when, in the dim light of lanterns, a freezing mist rises from the river, and isolated groups of pedestrians glide past and disappear into the gloom.

Another of the bridge's attractions are of course its statues, which turn the whole structure into a museum of Bohemian sculpture. On the first pier to the right immediately beyond the Tower of the Old Town Bridge (see p 98) stands the *Madonna and St Bernard* (1709) by Matěj Václav Jäckel, a sculptor who introduced to Bohemia the dynamic high-flown style of the Italian artist Bernini. This style was used to far more expressive effect in the work of Matthias Braun, an Austrian-born sculptor who first came to Bohemia in 1710, invited by the Cistercians of Plasy to execute statues for the Charles Bridge; a copy of the second statue which he did here, representing *St Ivo* (1711), can be seen on the left-hand side of the bridge, directly facing Jäckel's Madonna. The other outstanding Bohemian sculptor of this period was Ferdinand Maximillian Brokoff, an artist noted for his realism and who carried out several works for the bridge, including the sculptural group of *SS Barbara, Margaret and Elizabeth* which adorns the second pier on the left-hand side. The first monument to be placed on the bridge was a gilded bronze *Crucifix*, cast by J. Hilger in 1629, and set up on the third pier to the right in 1657; the two stone figures were executed by E. Max in 1861, while the Hebrew inscription on the cross, dating from 1696, is said to have been paid for by a Jew as a fine for mocking this Christian symbol.

Continuing to cross the bridge, you will pass between the sixth and seventh piers a relief marking the supposed spot where St John of Nepomuk was thrown into the Vltava in 1393; the bronze statue of the saint which was placed on the bridge in 1683 stands on the eighth pier to the right, and was executed by Johann Brokoff after a bozzetto by Matthias Rauchmüller. Towards its western end the bridge crosses the picturesque Kampa Island, which is separated from the left bank by a narrow canal, and is sometimes referred to as the 'Venice of Prague' (see below). Above the steps leading down to it, on the twelfth pier to the left, is a sculpture of *The Vision of St Luitgard* (1710), which was the first work which Matthias Braun made in Prague, and in many ways the most powerful and emotionally compelling on the bridge; tradition has it that the work was based on a design by Peter Brandl, and there is certainly something very painterly in its wildly agitated drapery. Two piers further along to the left is another of the sculptural masterpieces of the bridge, a group by F.M. Brokoff featuring *SS John of Matha, Felix de Valois, and Ivo*, with a Turk guarding a group of captured Christians (1714), the whole carved with Brokoff's characteristic realism (note, in particular the face of the Turk); the work was commissioned as a gesture of thanks to the Trinitarian Order for having redeemed Christians from Turkish captivity. Directly opposite this group is a statue by F.M. Brokoff of *St Vitus* (1714), the only marble work on the bridge, the other stone sculptures being all of sandstone.

The bridge ends picturesquely at a gate of 1410 flanked by two **towers**, the taller of which was built in 1466 at the behest of George of Poděbrady, and is closely similar to the tower of the bridge and the Powder Gate; the shorter tower, a survival of the Judith's Bridge fortifications, dates back to 1166 but was remodelled in 1591. Once through the Little Quarter gate the royal processional route headed west along **Mostecká**, today a busy shopping street featuring a number of fine Renaissance and Baroque palaces, most notably, at No. 15, the **Kaunic Palace**, which was built in 1773–75 by Anton Schmidt, and has a façade richly decorated with stuccoes by Ignác Platzer.

Little Quarter Square

Mostecká leads into the sloping Little Quarter Square (Malostranské náměstí), which is divided in two by the massive Church of St Nicholas and adjoining buildings.

> The square, surrounded today by buildings of largely 17C and 18C appearance, formed originally the nucleus of Prague Castle's outer bailey, and in the middle there once stood the Romanesque Rotunda of St Wenceslas. The site of a market and Town Hall for many centuries after the foundation of the Little Quarter in 1257, the square remains to this day the lively heart of this area, with an important tram junction at its lower, eastern end.

The eastern half of the square, known as the Lower Square, features on its eastern side (at No. 21) the former **Town Hall**, which was founded in the late 15C, and where in March 1575 a group of Habsburg opponents comprising neo-Utraquists, Lutherans and members of the Union of Czech Brethren formulated the so-called Czech Confession, a plea for legal recognition of Evangelical trends. This meeting is recalled in a plaque on the building's façade, the present appearance of which is due to reconstruction work carried out in 1617–22 by Giovanni Campione de Bossi. The elegant façade, divided by cornices into three main floors, is articulated by pilasters flanking paired windows crowned by broken pediments; the interior is now used for lectures, and musical and theatrical performances.

Dominating the northern side of the Lower Square is the imposing **Smiřický-Montág Palace**, which dates back to 1606 but was rebuilt in a late Baroque style by J. Jäger in around 1763; the building is

Smiřický-Montág Palace, Lower Square

famous as the place where, on 22 May 1618, Albrecht Smiřický and an invited group of leaders of the anti-Habsburg opposition hatched the plot which was to lead the following day to the 'Second Defenestration', the incident which sparked off the Thirty Years War. Adjacent to this, on the western side of the Lower Square, is the enormous and rather severe bulk of the former **Jesuit College**, which is attached to the northern side of the Church of St Nicholas,

and was built by D. di Orsi between 1674 and1691 on a site previously occupied by a group of 20 burghers' houses. In front of the east end of the church, and projecting out into the Lower Square, is the **Grömling Palace**, another late 18C work by J. Jäger. In 1874 there was installed here one of Prague's larger and more popular cafés, the *Radetzky Café*, which was later supplanted by the equally successful *Malostranská kavárna*; this celebrated institution has recently re-opened.

Walking up from the southeastern corner of the Little Quarter Square to the square's upper, western half, you will skirt to your right the southern side of the Church of St Nicholas and to your left a group of tall, narrow-fronted houses of Renaissance and medieval origin, where you will find several long-established places for eating and drinking. No. 10, **At the Golden Lion** (Dům U zlatého lva), is the only building in the whole square to have completely retained its Renaissance appearance, and houses one of Prague's better-known restaurants, *U mecenáše*; this restaurant, serving good food in intimate, Renaissance-style dining-rooms, is on the site of a tavern dating back to the reign of the Emperor Rudolph.

U mecenáše restaurant, At the Golden Lion

The upper and quieter half of the Little Quarter Square is known as the Upper or Italian Square, and has in its centre a **plague column** put up by Alliprandi in 1715 in place of a fountain. Its western side is taken up entirely by the neo-Classical façade of the **Liechtenstein Palace** (1791), while facing this is the west façade of the **Church of St Nicholas** (sv. Mikuláš), one of the outstanding Baroque buildings of central Europe, and rivalled only by Prague Castle as the dominant element in the city's skyline.

History of the Church

The present church occupies the site of a 13C three-aisled structure which was handed over to the Jesuits shortly after the Battle of the White Mountain of 1620. Later in the 17C the Jesuits built a college alongside the old church, and in 1673 laid the foundations of a new church, the construction of which was not begun until 1703, under the direction of

Christoph Dientzenhofer. The church was roofed by 1705, but work was subsequently interrupted through lack of funds, and was only continued between 1709 and 1711, when the west façade was completed and the nave vaulted. Further financial difficulties led to the east end being closed by a provisional, illusionistically painted wooden screen until 1637, when work was resumed under the direction of Dientzenhofer's son, Kilian Ignaz, who between 1737 and 1752 built the chancel and domed crossing; the tower alongside the dome was added by Anselmo Lurago in

View of St Nicholas church

1755. The finished church, the largest Jesuit church in Bohemia if not in the whole of Central Europe, was to inspire some effusive prose by the French Catholic dramatist Paul Claudel in the early 20C. In the introduction to his religious drama, *The Shoe of Satin*, Claudel referred to the building as a 'sanctuary where everything is suffused by inner life and eloquence, where the whole structure is an act of grace which immediately draws us in, where everything is peace, joy, and not simply a smile, but an outburst of laughter ...'

Despite the protracted history of its construction, the church of St Nicholas has an impressive unity, and its undulating west façade, with its remarkably rich play of concave and convex surfaces, is a powerful preparation for the dynamic interior.

Once inside the single-aisled building you are astonished by an array of pinks and pastel greens, and exhilarated by an extraordinary sense of movement. The nave walls, with their undulating balconies, and giant, obliquely set pilasters, positively ripple and create a flowing line which culminates in the enormous oval of the crossing. The originality of the nave vaulting, with its intersecting ribs as in a Gothic building, is obscured by the vast ceiling painting by Johann Lukas Kracker representing *The Apotheosis of St Nicholas* (1760–61); the dome meanwhile is covered by *The Celebration of the Holy Trinity* (1752–53) by Franz Xavier Palko, who also executed, along with Josef Hager, the wall-paintings in the chancel. The magnificent statuary was largely the work of Ignác Platzer the Elder, who was responsible for the statue of St Nicholas on the High Altar, the agitated saints along the nave, and the four overblown figures of the Church Fathers in the corners of the crossing. The remarkable pulpit (1765), a gilded Rococo confection in pink marble, is by Richard and Peter Prachner. Of the paintings, special mention should be made of the first chapel to the left, where there is an altarpiece of the Holy Rood by K. Škréta, and one of St Barbara by L. Kohl; a painting of St Michael by the Neapolitan painter F. Solimena is in the second chapel to the left, while in the third chapel to the right is *The Death of St Francis* by F.X. Palko.

After leaving the church, head to the northern end of the Upper Square, turn right, and, just before entering the Lower Square once again, turn left into the narrow **Sněmovní**. Among the old palaces and houses on this street, which lies almost in the shadow of Prague Castle, is the gabled and well-preserved Renaissance structure at No. 10 called **At the Golden Swan** (Dům U zlaté labutě), which was built by Ulrico Avostalis in 1589 for one Michal Lagrand. At its upper end the street is continued in the once picturesquely shabby cul-de-sac with the exotic name of U zlaté studně (At the Golden Well); the recently restored end house, at No. 3, is known as **At the Painters** (Dům U malíře) for it belonged to the turn-of-the-century artist Karel Klusáček, who painted on its façade a decoration featuring St Methodius.

The gardens of the Malá Strana

After turning back at the end of the street, take the first turning to the left, which leads you into the Wallenstein Square (Valdštejnské Náměstí). This narrow square is named after the **Wallenstein Palace** at No. 4 on its eastern side, which was built in 1623–30 for the great Albrecht of Wallenstein, whose family seat it was to remain until 1945.

Wallenstein's suitably imposing palace in Prague—built by Giovanni Pieroni to designs supplied first by Andrea Spezza and then by Niccolo Sebregondi— was the earliest of the many grand palaces erected in this city in the 17C and 18C. Its interior, open to the public for occasional concerts, features a splendid main hall with a stuccoed ceiling incorporating a fresco by B. Bianco representing Wallenstein himself dressed as Mars and riding in a chariot; the work was executed in 1630, only four years before Wallenstein's ignominious murder. Architecturally the finest feature of the building is the loggia overlooking the palace's wonderful gardens, the entrance to which is on Letenská (see below).

Before making your way to Letenská a number of other important palaces and gardens remain to be seen to the north of the Wallenstein Palace, beginning with the **Ledebour-Trauttmansdorf Palace**, on the northwestern corner of the Wallenstein Square. This late Baroque palace, designed by I.J. Palliardi in 1787, is remarkable above all for its gardens, which were laid out by Santini-Aichel in 1716 and rise steeply in terraces from a *sala terrena* up to a belvedere, the whole enlivened by fountains and a statue of Hercules. The gardens, recently (nad very crudely) restored thanks to help from the Prague Heritage Fund, today form part of a public park known as the **Palace Gardens Below Prague Castle** that also comprises the terraced gardens of two adjoining palaces to the north, on Valdštejnská. The first of these palaces, at No. 14, is the early 18C **Pálffy Palace** (now a music academy with an excellent and very atmospheric student-run restaurant), the gardens of which feature three terraces linked by a covered staircase and a loggia; on the middle terrace is a sundial bearing a Latin inscription and the date 1751. The entrance to all the gardens is to be found alongside

Albrecht of Wallenstein

One of the most colourful figures in Czech history, Albrecht of Wallenstein (known to the Germans as Albrecht von Waldstein, and to the Czechs as Albrecht z Valdštejna) was born in Prague on the afternoon of 14 September 1583, and was thus—according to the imperial astrologer Johannes Kepler—destined by his birth chart to be deceitful, avaricious, unloved and unloving. An opportunist of whom even Macchiavelli might have been ashamed, Wallenstein embarked on his life of dubious reputation after being expelled from his Lutheran school for the killing of a servant. Taking refuge in Italy, he married a wealthy widow and converted to Catholicism; the widow died soon afterwards, leaving him a considerable fortune, and his new-found Catholicism stood him in good stead while cultivating his friendship with the future Habsburg emperor Ferdinand II.

As a general in the imperial army, Wallenstein was able to prosper sensationally at a time when his home country was going through one of the darkest moments in its history: by appropriating the properties of the Protestant aristocrats defeated at the Battle of the White Mountain of 1620, he succeeded in amassing within five years over 50 Bohemian castles and villages. With his continuing military successes and entrepreneurial dealings, his titles and privileges multiplied, and by 1630 he had even earned the right to keep on his hat in the presence of the emperor. His increasing demands, combined with the growing resentment towards him on the part of the emperor's supporters, led him briefly to be deprived of his position as general; however, the occupation of Prague by the Saxons in 1631 forced Ferdinand to call once again on his services.

Then in 1634, amidst rumours that he had ambitions to crown himself King of Bohemia, Wallenstein openly rebelled against Ferdinand—a gesture almost certainly undertaken for purely personal gain, but which nonetheless assured his future reputation as a great Czech hero. He, and several of his loyal officers, were murdered soon afterwards at the West Bohemian town of Cheb. His megalomaniac life and inevitably tragic end have been of understandable fascination to numerous writers, most notably Schiller, whose play *Wallenstein* is one of the outstanding works of German Romantic drama.

the next palace, the **Kolowrat-Černín Palace**, situated at No. 10. The building was designed in 1784 by Ignác Jan Palliardi, who was also responsible for laying out its gardens, which are perhaps the finest of them all and comprise a luxuriant Rococo complex of staircases, terraces, fountains, loggias, balustrades and pools. The last of the great palaces along Valdštejnská is the **Fürstenberg Palace**, which was built in 1743–47 by an unknown architect clearly under the influence of K.I. Dientzenhofer; it is now the Polish Embassy, and its attractive 18C gardens are closed to the public.

Return to the Wallenstein Square and continue south along **Tomášká**, where, just before rejoining the Little Quarter Square, you will pass on the left-hand side one of Prague's best known beer-cellars, *U Schnellů*; this long-established and recently revamped tourist bar and restaurant has décor dating back to 1787. Turn left at the end of the street into **Letenská**, where you will find immediately to your left the dazzlingly restored **Church of St Thomas** (sv. Tomáše), which was founded in 1285 for the Order of Augustinian Hermits. The medieval church, partially rebuilt in the 16C and 17C, was remodelled by K.I. Dientzenhofer in 1722–31. The main façade, featuring a portal of 1617 and a sandstone statue of St Thomas by Hieronymus Kohl (1684), was given by Dientzenhofer a dramatic Borromini-inspired appearance through the addition of massive, projecting forms intended both to strengthen the structure and to make the most of the restricted site; the interior, with a presbytery retaining some of the medieval masonry, has ceiling paintings by V.V. Reiner representing scenes from the lives of SS Augustine and Thomas, and (on the dome) *The Four Continents*. In the first chapel on the right is a painting of St Thomas (1671) by K. Škréta, by whom there are two further paintings in the presbytery (an *Assumption* and a *Holy Trinity*, both of 1644). Paintings by Rubens of St Augustine and the *Martyrdom of St Thomas* were recently transferred from here to the National Gallery and replaced by copies.

The former friary attached to the church is now an old people's home, but its cellar (entered at No. 8 Letenská) continues to function as the celebrated ale house known as **U Tomáše**, which was founded here in 1348, its dark beer having originally been made by the monks. This establishment is today a tourist attraction which tends to be booked up in advance by large groups; earlier this century, however, it was the place to which the rowdy literary club known as Syrinx transferred its allegiance after tiring of the now equally spoilt *U Fleků* in the New Town (see p 172).

Across Letenská from St Thomas is the entrance to the short Josefská, on which stands the former **Church of St Joseph**, an oval structure which was built by Jean Baptiste Mathey in 1682–92 and modelled on Flemish and Roman patterns.

Continuing to walk north along Letenská, you will skirt to your left the walls of the **Wallenstein Palace Gardens** (Valdštejnská zahrada) and eventually come to the entrance. The gardens, now partly restored and open throughout the year, were laid out in the early 17C and have at their centre an avenue of bronze statues copied after works by Adriaen de Vries that were stolen from here by the Swedes in 1648 and have been standing since then outside the Swedish Royal Palace at Drottningholm. The avenue leads to a tall and magnificent loggia built by G. Pieroni in 1623–27, and decorated inside with painted scenes by B. Bianco of the Trojan Wars (1629–30), set in a stucco framework. Elsewhere in the gardens are an aviary, grottoes and a long fishpond which was used in 1816 for the testing of a model of a steamboat designed by J. Božek; the bronze of Hercules standing in the middle of the pond is an original by de Vries. On summer weekends the gardens are used by artists for the display of their works, while the former riding-school here houses occasional temporary exhibitions organised by the National Gallery.

Letenská comes to an end at the broad and busy **Klárov**, which marks the northeastern edge of the Little Quarter. Turning left here will bring you immediately to the Malostranská Metro Station, the most elegant in Prague; erected in 1978, it has a small forecourt with fountains and statuary copied from 18C models, and a vestibule containing copies both of Rococo vases and of Matthias Braun's statue of *Hope* from Kuks. In the square in front of the station there is a plaque commemorating a student, Marie Charousková, who was killed during the protests of 1968.

Turning right at the end of Letenská will bring you into U lužického semináře, which was named after a seminary (at No. 13) built in 1726–28 for Lusatian–Serbian students. To your right you will skirt the walls of the large **Vojanovy Gardens**, which were founded in the 17C and contain near their entrance (which is also on this street) a statue by I.F. Platzer of St John of Nepomuk standing on a fish. Discreetly tucked away on the opposite side of the street to the gardens (at No. 38) is the small, simple and very lively beer cellar known as *At the Two Hearts* (*U dvou srdcí*), a place as yet free of tourists and where a matronly waitress places a large glass of beer on your table almost the moment you sit down. Near the southern end of the street turn right into Míšeňská, where you will find at Nos 1 and 12 two appealing corner houses designed respectively by Kilian Ignaz Dientzenhofer and his brother Christoph.

The continuation of Míšeňská, Dražického, will bring you back to the Charles Bridge, next to the main entrance of the celebrated **The Three Ostriches** (U tří pštrosů), the exterior of which has fragments of mural decorations of ostrich feathers, as well as a house-sign with ostriches, all dating back to 1606. The building owes both its name and decoration to a merchant called Jan Fux, who rebuilt the house after 1597, and made a living partially by selling ostrich feathers, then a fashion novelty. The building was already functioning as a tavern in Fux's time, and was acquired early the following century by the Armenian coffee-salesman Deodatus Damajan (see p 96), who in 1714 opened here the first coffee-shop in the Little Quarter. Between 1972 and 1976, the place was restored and transformed into a luxury restaurant and tiny, exclusive hotel, the latter boasting the best-situated rooms in Prague; returned recently to its pre-war owner, the place is now famous principally as a hotel, with 17C paintings and other antique furnishings in the bedrooms.

The southern Little Quarter
After returning to Mostecká you should turn left immediately into **Lázeňská** to begin a tour of the southern half of the Little Quarter. On this short street were once situated the workshops of Adriaen de Vries and other foreign sculptors who came to Prague at the time of Rudolph II. Later in the 17C the street came to have a hotel, **At the Baths** (dům V lázních), at No. 6, which was to host up to the early 19C some of the most distinguished visitors to Prague, including Peter the Great of Russia in 1698, the pioneering balloonist Jean-Pierre Blanchard in 1790–91 and, in 1833, the French writer Chateaubriand; two years after the latter's visit (which is commemorated by a plaque), the hotel was rebuilt in an Empire style. In 1796 Beethoven stayed at the fine late Baroque palace **At the Golden Unicorn** (dům U zlatého je dnorožce), at No. 11.

At the southern end of the street begins a small area of town originating in plots of land that in 1169 were given over by Vladislav II to the Order of the Maltese Knights (the Johannites). The church which formerly belonged to this order, **Our Lady under the Chain** (Panny Marie pod řetězem), dominates the area, standing at the junction of Lázeňská and the narrow, connected **Square of Malta** and **Square of the Grand Priory** (Maltézské náměstí and Velkopřevorské náměstí). The original three-aisled Romanesque structure of the 12C, the oldest church in the Little Quarter, was pulled down in the middle of the 14C, and work was begun on a new building. The latter was abandoned by the end of the century, the only parts to be completed being the western vestibule and its two austere and fortress-like towers which form such an incongruous presence in the middle of this intimate part of town. The former nave of the Romanesque church serves now as a forecourt to a Baroque church built largely by Carlo Lurago in 1640–60; within the latter is a high altar of the 1660s by Karel Škréta, representing the Virgin Mary and St John the Baptist coming to the assistance of the Knights of Malta during the Battle of Lepanto of 1571.

Facing the church, at No. 11 at the northeastern end of the Maltézské náměstí, is a building dating back to 1531, and known as **At the Painter's** (Dům U malířů) after the painter Jiří Šic, who lived here in the late 16C, and whose name, when pronounced in English ('Shits'), was an unfortunate one in view of the place's later function: the building, remodelled in around 1690, and restored in the 1930s, now houses Prague's most exclusive French restaurant, with fresh produce flown in daily from France, and an entirely French wine list.

A number of fine 17C and 18C palaces line the rest of the square, at the centre of which is a sculptural group by F.M. Brokoff featuring St John the Baptist, erected as a plague memorial in 1715. On the eastern side of the square, at No. 14, is the arcaded **Straka Palace** of c 1700 (with fresco decorations inside by the early 18C Swiss painter J.R. Byss), while at No. 6 on the western side is Jäger's **Turba Palace** of 1767–68, a beautiful Rococo structure articulated with giant pilasters and serving today as the Japanese Embassy. Giant pilasters feature also on the façade of the large **Nostitz Palace** at No. 1, today the Dutch Embassy, which takes up all of the southern side of the square, and was built in 1660–70 by Francesco Caratti, who was later to perfect such an ordering of a façade in the Černín Palace on the Loreto Square (see p 152); the main portal is a Rococo addition of 1760 attributed to A. Haffenecker, while the attic was decorated in 1720 with sculpted vases and emperors by M.J. Brokoff (the originals have now been replaced by copies).

Make your way back to Our Lady under the Chain, and turn right into the Velkopřevorské náměstí. Immediately to your left on entering the square is the main façade of the **Grand Prior's Palace**, which was rebuilt to a design by Giuseppe Bartolomeo Scotti in 1726–28, and has a fine portal with vase decorations from the workshop of Matthias Braun; torchbearers and vases from the same workshop adorn the grand staircase of the richly stuccoed interior. The building, which once housed the Museum of Czech Music, was reclaimed after 1989 by the Knights of Malta, who are currently restoring it, together with the church of Our Lady under the Chain. So far they have allowed the survival of the so-called **John Lennon Wall**, an improvised multi-coloured hommage to the Beatle that was first daubed on the building's garden wall following his death in 1980, and which has now been re-done by a new generation of Beatle artists. Lennon (whose lower face in the painting has now eroded away) has enjoyed a saint-like status among the predominantly atheist Czechs, who regarded him in the Communist era as the ultimate anti-authoritarian figure and constantly resisted police attempts to remove the graffiti in this square; even today, on the anniversary of the singer's death (14 December), anachronistic crowds of long-haired guitar players gather here and on the neighbouring Kampa Island to celebrate his life.

On the southern side of the square, facing the Lennon Wall, are the late 16C **Small Buquoy Palace** at No. 3 and the adjoining **Buquoy-Valdstejn Palace** at No. 2, now the French Embassy, the present façade of which dates back to 1719. At the eastern end of the square, also on the right-hand side, is the **Hrzán Palace** at No. 1, which, despite remodelling carried out in 1760, still retains a largely Renaissance appearance, complete with extensive sgraffito decorations. Another Renaissance structure at No. 7, directly facing the palace, is the picturesquely gabled **Grand Prior's Mill** or Stepan's Mill, which was functioning up to 1936, and is one of several mills built on the narrow branch of the Vltava called the Čertovka or the Devil's Stream. This stream, separating the Little Quarter from Kampa Island, was first referred to simply as 'The Ditch', and only acquired its present, more romantic name towards the end of the 19C, when the Straka Palace on the nearby Maltese Square came to be known as 'The Devil's House' after an eccentric woman owner.

Kampa Island

Beside the Grand Prior's Mill is a bridge leading over the Čertovka stream to Kampa Island, an area once taken up entirely by vineyards, gardens and fields, and which only acquired buildings from the late 16C onwards. Successive floods have changed the shape of the island over the centuries, and the narrator of Jiří Weil's novel *Life with a Star* (1964) even recalls frequent arguments with his mistress when she 'claimed that Kampa was a peninsula and I said it was an island'. Most of the houses on this so-called Venice of Prague are concentrated in the northern half of the island, on either side of the quiet and tree-lined Na Kampě, where, at No. 11, there is a bronze plaque and bust marking the house where the composer Bohuslav Martinů lived. At its northern end the street broadens out into a picturesque square from which steps lead up to the Charles Bridge. A pottery market was regularly held here up to 1936, and this tradition has recently been revived; the square, like the Charles Bridge itself, also attracts numerous singing, guitar-playing students, who seem to have stepped straight out of the 1960s.

Walk south down Na Kampě to the southern half of the island, which largely comprises a public park. Leave the island at its southernmost point and turn right into Říční, where you will soon pass on your right the **Church of St John at the Wash-House** (sv. Jana Na prádle). The homely name of the church is entirely appropriate to this structure of rustic simplicity, which dates back to the 13C, and contains inside fragments of late 14C wall-paintings. On the opposite side of the street, at No. 11, a plaque marks the turn-of-the-century building where the brothers Josef and Karel Čapek moved to after settling in Prague in 1907.

The Čapek brothers

The brothers Čapek were to stay in their Říční house until 1925, living, according to their friend V.V. Štech, 'a simple life in an old-fashioned household, probably quite wealthy, but still very money-conscious.' An inseparable pair who kept their distance from the city's artistic community, they were described by another friend, František Langer, as invariably entering rooms together, sitting next to one another, and ordering a cup of coffee and a roll each'.

It was while living in this house that Karel wrote, in the early 1920s, the plays that were to establish his reputation as a dramatist, most notably his science fiction work *RUR* (1921) and his morality play *From the Life of the Insects* (1922), which he wrote in collaboration with his painter brother Josef. The Scottish poet and translator Edwin Muir befriended Karel at this time, and published a short memoir of him in his autobiography, *The Story and the Fable* (1940): 'We saw a great deal of Karel Čapek, who lived a few minutes' walk away from us in a rambling old house with a large garden hidden away behind it. Though he was about the same age as myself, he was already round-backed; the brightness of his eyes and the flush on his cheek showed that he was ill. He knew only a little English, and we only a little German, so we had to converse in an absurd mixture of the two. He was always busy, always merry ... Čapek seemed to be known and loved by every one, and when we walked along the street with him every second or third passer-by would shout, "Oh, Karlíčku!", the equivalent of "Hullo, Charley!", as if the mere sight of him filled them with pleasure.'

From the Church of St John at the Wash-House head northwest along Všehrdova, passing at No. 14 the **Works Mill** (Mlýn), another of the old mills on the Čertovka. The narrow and slightly run-down Všehrdova will take you to the long and busy **Újezd**, where you will find, immediately to the right at No. 40, the **Michna of Vacínov Palace**, a large complex dating back to the late 16C, and with a Baroque wing built by Francesco Caratti between 1640 and 1650. This wing, with a grimy, peeling façade overlooking Újezd, is covered both on the outside and inside with Italianate stucco decorations by Domenico Galli. The interior, which is occupied today by the sports faculty of Charles University, is also worth seeing for its small but very evocative **Sports Museum**, with old bicycles, sports trophies, photographs and other objects relating to the history of sport in Prague, all incongruously displayed under Galli's stuccoes, in rooms that appear to be as little visited as they are dusted. Open Tues–Sun 09.00–17.00.

Walk north along Újezd into its northern continuation, **Karmelitská**, on which stands, on the left-hand side, the former **Carmelite Church of St Mary the Victorious** (Panna Marie Vítězné). Built originally for the German Lutherans between 1611 and 1613, it came into the possession of the Carmelites in 1624, who subsequently had it rebuilt as a thanksgiving for the Habsburg victory at the Battle of the White Mountain. Though generally referred to as the first Baroque church in Prague, it would be better described as one of the many dreary European imitations of the Gesù in Rome, and has little of architectural interest. Its singularly dark and depressing interior, however, is much visited on account of a tiny votive image of the Infant Christ displayed in a chapel on the right of the nave.

The Bambino di Praga

The celebrated wax image of the Infant Christ lifting his arm in blessing is a Spanish work of the 16C which for some reason—perhaps confusion between the Spanish and Italian languages—is popularly known by the Italian name *Bambino di Praga* ('Child of Prague'). Brought over from Spain in the mid-16C by María Manríquez de Lara, the Spanish wife of Vratislav of Pernštejn, it was later presented by her to her daughter Polyxena on the occasion of the latter's marriage to the High Chancellor Zdeněk Popel of Lobkowitz. The widowed Polyxena gave the work to the Carmelites in 1628, since when the statue, with its numerous changes of clothing, has acquired a growing mythical status, and inspired countless reproductions in dubious taste. The absurd and kitsch qualities of the Bambino di Praga have been wittily exploited by the writer Bohumil Hrabal, whose novel *I Served the King of England* (1989) includes a fantastical tale of a successful Bolivian plot to replace the work surreptitiously with a copy and take the original back to South America, where it 'was supposed to be tremendously popular ... so popular, in fact, that millions of South American Indians wore replicas of it on chains around their necks and had a legend that Prague was the most beautiful city in the world and that the infant Jesus had gone to school there.'

Of greater artistic interest than the Bambino di Praga itself is the gilded wooden altar on which it has been placed, a Rococo structure carved by Petr Prachner in 1776; elsewhere in the church are a number of dramatic canvases of saints by Peter Brandl.

Continuing north up Karmelitská, you will pass on your left, at No. 25, the **Vrtba Palace**, which František Kaňka remodelled around 1720 and endowed with some of the most beautiful if also most hidden gardens in Prague. The **Vrtba Gardens**, reached by way of a passage running through the palace, today form a small and quiet public park at the edge of a great sweep of verdant parkland covering the Petřín Hill. After passing through a courtyard adorned with statues by Matthias Braun of Atlas and two female allegorical figures, you will come to a *sala terrena* decorated with painted mythological scenes by V.V. Reiner. Further works by Braun, of Bacchus and Ceres (c 1730) are followed by a balustraded double staircase where mythological figures alternate with Greek vases; from the highest of the gardens' terraces there are wonderful views of Prague Castle and the Church of St Nicholas.

The approach to Prague Castle

Karmelitská will bring you back at its northern end to the Little Quarter Square (Malostranské náměstí), from where you begin the steep walk up to Prague Castle, passing through what is in many ways the most attractive part of the Little Quarter. There are three main ways of climbing up to the castle from the square.

The Castle Steps

The shortest and steepest route, and the one offering the finest roof-top views, is the ascent up the Castle Steps (Zámecké schody). From the northwestern corner of the Lower Square turn right into Sněmovní, and then immediately left into Thunovská, off which stands at No. 14 the large **Thun Palace**, a building of 17C origin with a façade of 1716–27 by Antonio Giovanni Lurago; at this palace, now the seat of the British Embassy, Mozart and his wife Costanza stayed during their first visit to Prague in 1787.

Further west up Thunovská, on the right-hand side of the street, the Castle Steps begin. They pass to the left, at No. 25 Thunovská, the greyish-white and recently restored **Palace of the Lords of Hradec**, which dates back to the late 16C and is crowned by a group of small, Renaissance gables; this building, now connected to the Italian Embassy on Nerudova (see below) was from 1911 to 1928 the house of the artist Alfons Mucha, who is commemorated here by a plaque. The **Castle Steps**, which lead directly up to the Hradčany Square, were built originally in the 15C on the site of a path of 13C origin. A number of small buildings grew up alongside them, and in the 16C and 17C artists and craftsmen used to sell their wares here (the wide stone ledges of some of the windows were once used for display purposes).

The Royal Route

The tourist shops today are not to be found on the Castle Steps but are concentrated instead along **Nerudova**, which is the main and most traditional approach to the castle, and the one which was favoured by the royal coronation processions. Nerudova begins at the upper western end of the Little Quarter Square, and is lined its whole length with 16C–18C buildings, many of which have shop fronts displaying crafts products and souvenirs. The first building on the right (at No. 2) houses the once lively pub *At the Cat* (*U kocoura*), a famous haunt of the city's pre-1989 underground musicians, writers and hangers-on; it is still a good place to drink Pilsner and Purkmistr beer. Further up the street, on the left-hand side at No. 5, is the **Morzin Palace** (now the Romanian Embassy), which was built by Santini-Aichel in 1713–14, and has magnificent sculptural decoration by F.M. Brokoff on its façade: its two portals are surmounted by statues of Day and Night, while in between these is a balcony supported by figures of Moors, executed with Brokoff's customary realism. The Italian Embassy, slightly higher up Nerudova on the opposite side of the street (at No. 20), occupies another splendid Baroque building by Santini-Aichel, the **Thun-Hohenstein Palace**: built between 1716 and c 1725, its portal was decorated around 1730 with two deeply and vigorously carved eagles by Brokoff's great and dynamic rival, Matthias Braun. Santini-Aichel seems also to have been responsible for the portal of the adjoining **Church of Our Lady of Unceasing Succour at the Theatines** (Panny Marie ustavičné pomoci u kajetánů); the rest of the church, built in 1691–1717, has been attributed to J.-B. Mathey.

Further up the street at No. 34, also on the right-hand side, is the **House at the Golden Horseshoe** (Dům U zlaté podkovy), where you will find the beautifully preserved wooden interior of an early 18C pharmacy, one of the oldest surviving pharmacies in Prague. At the top of the street, at No. 47 on the left-hand side, is the **House at the Two Suns** (Dům U dvou slunců), a building of

Renaissance origin with attractive late 17C gables. Attached to its façade is a large memorial plaque—executed in 1895 by F. Houdek after a design by V. Oliva and a model by V.R. Smolík—recording that the poet and journalist after whom the street is named, Jan Neruda, lived in this house between 1845–57; the everyday life of this part of Prague provided Neruda with the subject matter of his delightful short-stories, *Tales from the Little Quarter* (1878). To complete the journey up to the castle, you should turn sharp right at the end of Nerudova and walk up the street named Ke Hradu, which means 'Towards the Castle'. Turning instead to the left you enter Úvoz, which climbs up slowly towards the Strahov Monastery and Loreta Square; the street is bordered to the right by another fine succession of 16C–18C houses, and to the left by a shaded balustrade commanding excellent views of the Petřín Park.

South of Nerudova

Another way of climbing up towards the castle and the Hradčany from the Little Quarter Square is to follow the streets running parallel to Nerudova to the south, beginning with **Tržiště**, which starts at Karmelitská, by the side of the Vrtba Palace (see above). By far the grandest palace on this dark and quiet street is the **Schönborn-Colloredo Palace** (at No. 15), which was built in the mid-17C on a site previously occupied by five houses, and remodelled in around 1715, probably by Santini-Aichel. Franz Kafka, while keeping a work-room in the Golden Lane, rented in this building from March 1917 the apartment of his dreams; unfortunately it was also here, on the night of 12–13 August, that he suffered the haemorrhage that would confirm his long-suspected tuberculosis. The palace is now the American Embassy, and its impressive gardens laid out by M. Lebsche in the late 17C—'The gardens!', exclaimed Kafka, 'When you enter the gateway of the palace you can hardly believe your eyes'—are not open to the public.

Tržiště veers to the right after the palace, and after tunnelling through a group of houses, joins up with Nerudova at a point directly in front of the Thun-Hohenstein Palace. Alternatively you could turn left at the Schönborn Palace on to Vlašská, or take the second turning to the left, and walk up the narrow street parallel to Vlašská, Břetislavova. The building at No. 2 **Břetislavova** is an early 18C structure known as **At the Child Jesus** and attributed to Santini-Aichel. However, those who visited the street in the past generally did not do so for architectural reasons.

Břetislavova

Until comparatively recently **Břetislavova** was known popularly as Corpses' Street, for it was along here that funeral prossessions would pass on their way to the now demolished cemetery on St John's Hill. This was also one of the main brothel streets of Prague, and the poet Jaroslav Seifert recalled in his charming memoirs how as a schoolboy he timidly paid a visit to the street from his faraway home district of Žižkov, his interest in the place having been excited by the report of one of his friends. The street was deserted, and the disappointed Seifert was on the point of leaving when, outside a house to be identified with At the Child Jesus, he heard a soft knock on a window, and was tempted to peer inside. 'The curtains parted, and a girl stood by the window with a dark braid hanging over her shoulder. Surprised, I remained stockstill. When she saw my frightened look she smiled and said something to me, but I did not hear her voice through the glass. The street is so narrow that two steps were enough, and I was on the other side of the street.' Yet, his curiosity now aroused, he felt compelled to return to the window, and was met this time by the sight of the smiling girl removing her blouse and beckoning him inside, a sight—his first of the naked female breast—which led him to run with heart beating all the way down to the bottom of the Little Quarter. Later he was to evoke the street in his elegaic poem, *View from Charles Bridge*: 'A few steps from the Royal Road was a dark corner,/where tousle-haired prostitutes appeared/to walkers in the evenings,/during into their dead wombs/young inexperienced boys,/as I was then./Now all is silent there./And only television aerials haunt/the ridges of the roofs.'

Břetislavova leads into Jánský vršek, where, on turning right, you will reach the upper end of Nerudova. Turning instead to the left you will come to Vlašská, at a point just below this street's most important building, the **Lobkowicz Palace** (at No. 19, now the German Embassy). Begun by G.B. Alliprandi in 1703 and completed by I.J. Palliardi in 1769, this palace took as its main inspiration Bernini's unrealised plan for the Louvre in Paris, and features an entrance hall leading to a large oval vestibule projecting out on to the palace's gardens. After 1793 these gardens, which are open to the public, were given an informal English look by J.V. Skalník, who is best known for his landscaping of the spa at Mariánské Lázně (Marienbad); the Alpinum which he created here was the first in Bohemia.

From the palace you can reach the upper end of Nerudova by walking due north along the narrow Šporkova, which curves around a picturesque group of houses before ending up at Jánský vršek (see above). Continuing instead to walk west along Vlašská you will pass to your left the northern walls of the Lobkowitz Gardens and, to your right (at No. 34), a hospital and chapel founded in the early 17C by Prague's Italian community, which was centred in this area.

Petřín Hill

At the western end of Vlašská you enter the large area of parkland covering the Petřín Hill, and can either turn right in the direction of the Strahov Monastery (see pp 153–55), or else turn left and make your way to the top of the hill, which is crowned by trees. Peering up above the summit is a slightly decrepit imitation of Paris's Eiffel Tower; this **observatory tower**, closed at present for much needed restoration, was erected for the Jubilee Exhibition of 1891 and commands a remarkably extensive panorama of the city, with particularly fine views towards the castle. Immediately to the south of this is another structure created for the Jubilee Exhibition, a crenellated neo-Gothic structure (also closed at present) containing a **hall of mirrors** and a large tableau with waxwork figures representing Czech students defending the Charles Bridge against the Swedes in 1648: the hall of mirrors is recalled in Josef Škvorecký's novel *The*

Cowards as the place where the book's hero, Danny Smiřický, asks to be kissed by the girl he loves so that 'it would be like a thousand kisses all at once'.

Just to the south of this, also among trees, is the **Church of St Lawrence**, a Romanesque structure remodelled in the 18C. Further south still is the upper station of a **funicular railway** which was built in 1891 and has recently been opened following a long period of closure; it descends down to the long Újezd Street, towards the bottom of the hill passing through the so-called **Petřín Gardens**, where there is a statue to the poet Jan Neruda.

Jan Neruda

This statue of Jan Neruda held a particular significance for the latter's great Latin American namesake, the Nobel Prize-winning poet Pablo Neruda. The real name of this Chilean poet was Ricardo Eliecer Neftalí Reyes, but he changed his name at the very start of his career, for reasons that have both mystified and irritated Czech writers (including Josef Škvorecký). The Czech satirist Erwin Kisch, whom the Chilean had befriended in Madrid in the 1930s, decided one day to ask him why he had changed his name, but he simply replied: 'My dear Kisch, you who have discovered the mystery about Colonel Redl will never clarify the mystery surrounding my being called Neruda.' The answer was in fact quite simple, as he himself admitted in his autobiography, *I Confess to Have Lived*. His father, a train-driver, was not at all happy with the idea of his son becoming a poet, and so the young man searched for another name under which to publish his first collection of verse. 'I happened upon the name Neruda in a Czech magazine without having the slightest idea that it belonged to a Czech writer, worshipped by all his people, author of the most beautiful ballads and romances, and who was commemorated by a statue in the district of the Little Quarter in Prague. As soon as I arrived in Czechoslovakia, many years later, I placed a flower at the foot of his bearded statue.'

South of the funicular the green and wooded slopes of the Petřín Hill are interrupted by the so-called **Hunger Wall** (Hladová zed´), which was erected by Charles IV in 1360–62 and marks the southeastern boundary of the Little Quarter; it derives its curious name from the fact that the poor of the city were employed in its construction, and were thus able to secure a livelihood. On the bosky slopes that stretch south of the wall into the district of Smíchov can be seen the charming, if rather neglected wooden **Church of St Michael** (sv. Michal), an 18C structure brought here in 1929 from a remote Carpathian village near the Ukranian town of Mukatchevo.

3 · Prague Castle and the Hradčany

The citadel

'A spell hangs in the air of this citadel', wrote Patrick Leigh Fermor in *A Time of Gifts* (1977), 'and I was under its thrall long before I could pronounce its name.' The enormous **Prague Castle** (Pražský Hrad) rises above the Little Quarter like a town in its own right, its elegant Classical casing holding together a veritable architectural treasury from which project the fantastical Gothic spires of St Vitus's Cathedral.

■ Grounds **open** Apr–Oct daily 05.00–midnight, Nov–Mar 05.00–23.00.

History of the citadel

The complex history of Prague's citadel goes back to around AD 870 when Count Bořivoj, founder of the Přemyslid dynasty and first count of Bohemia, erected on top of a hill a modest but strategically situated fortified settlement. This became the seat of the Přemyslid counts, later kings, replacing the previous one at Levý Hradec, further north along the Vltava. In the early 10C the Church of St George and the Rotunda of St Vitus were founded here, and in 973, when the citadel became also the seat of the Prague bishopric, Bohemia's oldest convent was established alongside St George's. A devastating fire in the early 11C led in 1041 to Count Břetislav I replacing the former earthen ramparts of the citadel with stone ones, but 26 years later the Counts of Bohemia were temporarily to abandon the citadel in favour of Vyšehrad, where they were to remain until 1139. In preparation for the return here of the Přemyslids, Soběslav I constructed a new palace and rebuilt the fortifications, the line of which is largely preserved in the citadel of today. The importance of the citadel was to reach its zenith in the 14C, during the reign of Charles IV, when the place was transformed into an imperial residence and work was begun on the great Gothic cathedral of St Vitus. Later in the century, though the citadel was to remain the seat of Bohemia's government, its role as a residence of the country's rulers was to be greatly diminished as a result of Wenceslas IV's decision to move to the Royal Court in the Old Town. King Vladislav Jagiello turned the place once more into a royal residence in 1484, and brought Benedikt Ried to Prague to rebuild and extend the castle's palace and fortifications; however, later in his reign, he and his court were to be based mainly in Budapest.

Bohemia's first Habsburg rulers, beginning with Ferdinand I, renewed the building activity in the citadel, and in the course of the 16C, the place was to become an impressive Renaissance complex, with pioneering Italianate structures such as the Summer Palace (Belvedere), and the Great Ball-Game Court. With Rudolph I, and the international group of scientific and artistic luminaries that he gathered around him, the castle was once again, if only briefly, the seat of one of Europe's most brilliant courts. His successor, Matthias, vaunted the glories of the Habsburgs through the commissioning in 1614 of the imposing triumphal arch known today as the Matthias Gateway. Yet it was only four years later that the Habsburgs were to suffer here a profound humiliation when two of their councillors were ejected from one of the palace windows. Following this incident, which sparked off the Thirty Years War, the rebelling Czech Estates made the castle the seat of their government, though they were only to remain here for two years, their cause being momentously defeated at the Battle of the White Mountain in 1620. Reduced subsequently to the status of secondary residence the castle declined, and little important work was to be carried out here until the reign of Maria Theresa, who initiated a major rebuilding campaign which was to give to the complex the late Baroque and neo-Classical framework which it has largely kept to this day.

The last important building campaign in the castle took place after 1918, when Tomáš Masaryk turned the complex into the presidential seat of the newly created Republic of Czechoslovakia. St Vitus's Cathedral was finally brought to completion, and the lively and idiosyncratic architect Josip Plečnik was entrusted with the relaying of gardens and the remodelling of courtyards and interiors. Plečnik's additions are bright and cheerful, but in the 20C the castle has acquired sinister connotations, thanks partially to the popular identification of the place with the novel of this name by Franz Kafka, who indeed worked here after 1916 in a house rented by his sister on Golden Lane. Kafka's vision of faceless tyranny and monstrous bureaucracy seems at any rate to have been prophetic of the years when the castle served as the seat of Czechoslovakia's Communist rulers.

A more human image for the whole complex has been acquired during the presidency of Václav Havel, who at one time could be seen riding around here on his scooter. The once drab costumes of the castle's guards were replaced by a colourful garb designed by a friend of Havel's whose previous most important job had been as the costume designer for Miloš Forman's film *Amadeus*. More importantly, areas of the complex once rigorously closed and guarded by machine-gun-carrying soldiers have now been opened up to the public.

There is so much to see in the castle that the better part of a day is required to begin to do justice to the complex. To conserve their energy, many people prefer to reach the castle by public transport and save the beautiful walks through the Little Quarter for the late afternoon descent. The easiest access by public transport is to take the underground to the Malostranská station, and from there catch a No. 22 bus to the junction of Mariánské hradby and U Prašného mostu, where you are left with a five-minute walk, arriving eventually in the citadel's second courtyard. If you decide to walk all the way up the hill to the castle, the quickest ascent is up the **Old Castle Steps** (Staré zámecké schody), which begin the climb at a point just to the north of the Malostranská station, and enter the citadel at its narrow eastern end.

First and Second Courtyards
Whatever route or means you choose to reach the castle, a tour of the place is best begun at its western end, which faces the Hradčany Square. Railings and a gate flanked by copies of two overblown sculptural groups of *Battling Giants* by Ignác Platzer (1786) mark the entrance to the **First Courtyard**, which is

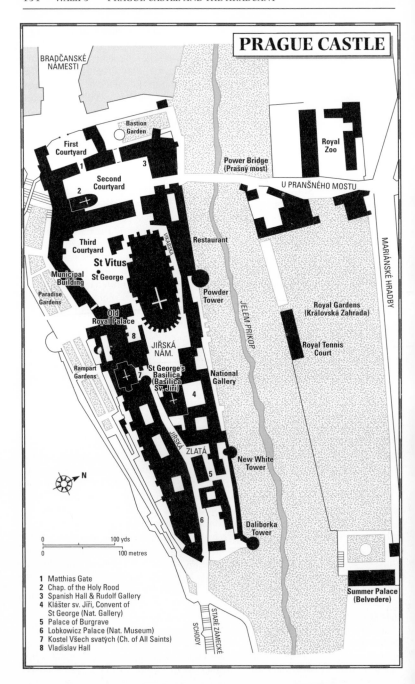

PRAGUE CASTLE

BRADČANSKÉ NÁMESTI

Bastion Garden

First Courtyard

1

3

Second Courtyard

2

Royal Zoo

Power Bridge (Prašný most)

U PRANŠNÉHO MOSTU

Third Courtyard

VIKÁŘSKÁ

Restaurant

St Vitus

St George

Municipal Building

Paradise Gardens

Old Royal Palace

8

Powder Tower

JIŘSKÁ NÁM.

Rampart Gardens

7

St George's Basilica (Basilica Sv. Jiří)

4

National Gallery

JIŘSKÁ

ZLATÁ

5

New White Tower

6

Daliborka Tower

MARIÁNSKÉ HRADBY

Royal Gardens (Královská Zahrada)

Royal Tennis Court

JELEM PRIKOP

N

0   100 yds
0   100 metres

STARÉ ZÁMECKÉ
SCHODY

Summer Palace (Belvedere)

1 Matthias Gate
2 Chap. of the Holy Rood
3 Spanish Hall & Rudolf Gallery
4 Klášter sv. Jiři, Convent of
   St George (Nat. Gallery)
5 Palace of Burgrave
6 Lobkowicz Palace (Nat. Museum)
7 Kostel Všech svatých (Ch. of All Saints)
8 Vladislav Hall

guarded by soldiers who perform a Changing of the Guard ceremony every day at 12.00 and 15.30.

On the other side of the courtyard to the gate is the **Matthias Gateway**, a large Roman-style triumphal arch inspired, if not actually designed, by the Mannerist architect Vicenzo Scamozzi and executed by Giovanni Maria Philippi in 1614. Originally a free-standing structure rising directly above the ramparts of the citadel, it was later incorporated into the palace's monumental west façade, which was built to designs by the court architect N. Pacassi in 1763–71. Further modifications to the courtyard were devised in 1920–22 by JosipPlečnik, who designed the two 25m-high flagpoles (tapering structures made out of pine trees taken, symbolically, from the Czechoslovak frontier), pierced the main block with openings on either side of the Matthias Gateway, and ingeniously planned to reduce the importance of the latter—a symbol of Habsburg dominance—by laying across the courtyard two paths of darker coloured paving stones that direct the eye to the new side entrances. To the right of the gate is a staircase climbing up to the presidential reception rooms, while to the left is a recently installed glass opening affording a view of Plečnik's greatest work for the castle—an enormous hall built in 1927–31 and named today after the architect: featuring a ceiling of copper panels and walls articulated by three superimposed rows of Ionic columns, this room looks ahead to many of the 'Post-Modernist' structures of the 1970s and 1980s. Havel, as befitting a true follower of Masaryk, is a great enthusiast of Plečnik's work, and is anxious to make as much of it as possible accessible to visitors.

To enter the castle's Second Courtyard you can go through either the Matthias Gateway or else the arch just to the left of the First Courtyard; adjacent to the latter, at the northern end of the castle's west façade is a small **Bastion Garden** laid out by Plečnik in 1927, and arranged on two levels that are joined by an ingenious circular stairway.

The **Second Courtyard**, dating back to the late 16C, and given its present unified appearance in the late 18C, is centred around a Baroque fountain adorned with statues by Jeronym Kohl (1686). The southern side of the courtyard comprises the western end of a long building known as the **Municipal Building**, which extends all the way up to the Old Palace in the Third Courtyard; its monotonous, uniform façade shields a series of rooms (closed to the public) dating back to 1534. Attached to the southeastern corner of the Second Courtyard is the **Chapel of the Holy Rood** which was built in 1756–63 by Anselmo Lurago after a plan by Pacassi, and remodelled in 1852–56. Now brashly transformed into the castle's ticket office, it previously housed for many years the greater part of the treasury of St Vitus's Cathedral.

The main rooms on the northern side of the Second Courtyard comprise the **Spanish Hall** and the **Rudolph Gallery**, two mirrored and richly stuccoed halls dating back to the late 16C but remodelled in a neo-Baroque style by Heinrich von Ferstel in 1866; generally closed to the public (except for the occasional concert) they are used today mainly for governmental meetings and receptions. The Rudolph Gallery originally housed the extraordinary art collection belonging to Rudolph II, the sorry remnants of which can once again be seen in the ground-floor rooms below, which were formerly the imperial stables: these rooms, comprising what is now the Prague Castle Gallery, were closed for many years after a couple of visitors brazenly walked off with one of the paintings.

History of the collection
Rudolph II ranked with his cousin Philip II of Spain as one of the greatest of the Habsburg collectors, but many of his pictures were transferred after his death to Vienna, and others were seized by the Swedes in 1648. In the mid-17C Ferdinand III built up a new collection at Prague, the nucleus of which was made up of works acquired from the collection of the Duke of Buckingham, which was auctioned at Antwerp in 1648–49. The new gallery remained intact until 1721, when Charles IV began removing many of the better works to Vienna; later in the century Maria Theresa sold off many more of the paintings, as did her son Joseph II in 1782. The dispersal of the collection continued throughout the 19C, and by the end of the First World War it was thought that all the paintings had gone from Prague. Investigations carried out in 1962–64 by the art historian Jaromír Neumann revealed that in fact much had remained in the city, and in 1965 the surviving works were brought together to form the Prague Castle Gallery.

The **Prague Castle Gallery** occupies a series of beautifully modernised rooms, and there are few other collections in the Czech Republic that are quite so well displayed. The works on show, however, are largely minor ones, and a panel of photographs reconstructing Rudolph II's original collection only emphasises the general mediocrity of what has survived. Works by artists of Rudolph's time include paintings by Bartolomaeus Spranger, Hans von Aachen, Cornelisz von Harlem, and an excellent wooden relief of the *Adoration of the Kings* by Adriaen de Vries. There are works by the Bohemian artists Peter Brandl and Jan Kupecký, and a painting by Rubens of the *Council of the Gods*, executed probably in Mantua in 1602. The bulk of the collection is of the Italian 16C and 17C, including a *Flagellation* by Tintoretto, a *Young Woman at her Toilet* by Titian (a version of a painting in the Louvre), *St Catherine and the Angel* and *Christ washing the Feet of His Disciples* by Veronese, *The Centaur Nessus and Deianeira* by Guido Reni, and a peculiarly erotic *St Sebastian* by Saraceni, with a single arrow placed directly in the groin; among the other Italian paintings are works by Bernardo Monsú, Viviano Codazzi, Orazio Gentileschi, and Leandro, Jacopo and Francesco Bassano. **Open** Apr–Oct daily 09. 00–17.00, Nov–Mar 09.00–16.00.

Third Courtyard ~ the Cathedral of St Vitus
Entering the third and principal castle courtyard you find yourself directly in front of the west front of the Cathedral of St Vitus, one of the finest and most richly endowed in central Europe.

■ **Open** Apr–Oct daily 09.00–17.00, Nov–Mar daily 09.00–16.00. Tower open daily 10.00–16.00.

History of the cathedral
The cathedral of St Vitus has its origins in a rotunda founded by Prince Wenceslas c 925, and transformed in 973 into the cathedral church of the Prague bishops; in 1060 this was replaced by a three-aisled Romanesque basilica. On the occasion of Prague's elevation from bishopric to archbishopric in 1344, Charles IV ordered the construction of the present Gothic building, for which he summoned from the papal court at Avignon the

architect Matthew of Arras. Matthew had laid the foundations of the building and completed its east end up to the triforium level by the time of his death in 1352. In search of an architect to complete Matthew's work, Charles IV turned this time to Germany, and found there Peter Parléř, who had been born in about 1330 to a family of Cologne builders and whose father had been responsible for the great town church at Schwäbisch-Gmund. From 1353 up to his own death in 1399 Parler was to be engaged on the building, completing the east end, doubling the chapel of St Wenceslas on the southwestern corner of the ambulatory, constructing the south portal and its adjoining open staircase, and beginning the nave; his work was to be continued by his sons Václav and Jan, who began work on the south tower. When the Hussites occupied the castle in 1421 the cathedral was greatly damaged and many of its furnishings destroyed; building activity was subsequently suspended for many years, the completed east end being closed off by a temporary wall.

Work on the cathedral was only to be resumed towards the end of the 15C, during the reign of Vladislav Jagiello: the strange Royal Oratory was put up on the south side of the ambulatory in the 1480s, the upper walls of the Wenceslas Chapel were painted in 1504, and the foundations of the north tower were laid in 1509–11. At the same time Vladislav Jagiello's principal architect, the great Benedikt Ried, formulated grandiose plans for the completion of the nave but, sadly, lack of funds led to their having to be abandoned in 1511. The main additions to the cathedral later in the century were the work of Bonifác Wohlmut, who was responsible in the 1560s for the Renaissance organ loft in the north transept and for crowning the Gothic south tower with a Renaissance gallery and bulbous domes (the top part of the tower was later destroyed by fire and rebuilt by N. Pacassi after 1770). A new attempt to complete the nave was made by Domenico Orsi in 1675, but this too was thwarted, and it was not until after the formation in 1861 of the 'Union for the completion of the Cathedral' that work was begun in earnest to try and finish the building. This new campaign was begun by Josef Kranner, and taken over by Josef Mocker, who was Czechoslovakia's answer to Viollet-le-Duc and someone responsible for the 'restoration' and pseudo-Gothic remodelling of many of Prague's other medieval monuments, such as the Powder Gate. The last architect at work on the cathedral was Kamil Hilbert, who finally completed the fabric of the building in 1929.

The most recent and dullest part of the cathedral is the twin-towered west façade, which features a large rosette window with stained-glass by F. Kysela and three portals with tympana containing carved reliefs executed between 1948 and 1952 to designs by K. Dvořák and L. Pícha. The high point of the exterior is undoubtedly the **south façade**, thanks to Peter Parléř, who wanted to give particular emphasis to the side of the building which both housed St Wenceslas's tomb and faced the city. This façade is dominated by its 96m-high **tower**, the tapering Gothic part of which was begun by Parléř's sons in the early 15C and has a main window protected by a wonderfully intricate Renaissance grille; the arcaded gallery above this is a mid-16C addition by Bonifác Wohlmut, while the crowning steeple was designed by Palassi in 1770.

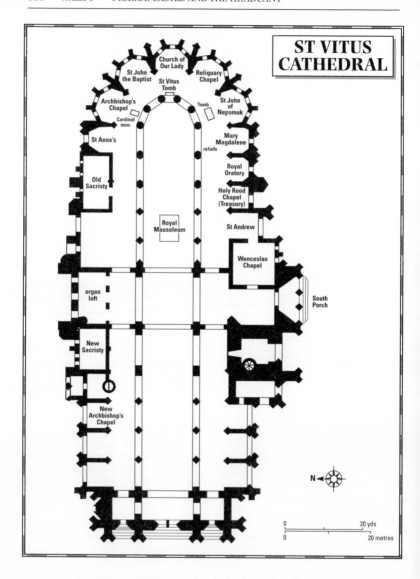

ST VITUS CATHEDRAL

Church of Our Lady

St John the Baptist

St Vitus Tomb

Reliquary Chapel

Archbishop's Chapel

Tomb

St John of Nepomuk

Cardinal mon.

St Anne's

Mary Magdalene

reliefs

Royal Oratory

Old Sacristy

Holy Rood Chapel (Treasury)

Royal Mausoleum

St Andrew

Wenceslas Chapel

organ loft

South Porch

New Sacristy

New Archbishop's Chapel

N

0   20 yds
0   20 metres

Immediately to the right of the tower are the three arches of Peter Parléř's South Porch or **Golden Portal**, which is decorated on the outside with a much-restored mosaic decoration of the Last Judgement executed in the late 14C by Venetian artists; in the spandrels of the central arch are the work's donors, Charles IV and his wife Eliška Pomořanská. One of Peter Parléř's main contributions to the cathedral was his inventive vaulting, as can be seen inside the porch, where a skeletal system of ribs is spread out like a fan. Above the porch is a further example of Parléř's structural daring—a complex, openwork staircase which was to be imitated in the cathedrals at Ulm and Strasbourg.

Entering the church through the south porch you should note how Parléř creates an ingenious progression from three arches to a double doorway, and, finally, to a single portal. Once inside you will find yourself in the south transept, from where one of the best views of the interior can be had. The plan and proportions of the building clearly reflect the work of a French architect, and indeed the arrangement of the east end, with its radiating chapels, seems to have been inspired by that of Narbonne Cathedral, which was completed early in the 14C by Jean Deschamps. Peter Parléř provided the choir with its elegant vaulting system of parallel diagonal ribs, and also began the triforium, which runs round the whole building and has inside it a celebrated series of **portrait heads** representing all those involved in the building of the cathedral, including Parléř himself and members of Charles IV's family. Twenty-one of these busts— which are so high up that they can scarcely be seen—were executed by members of Parléř's workshop, but the rest (mainly in the nave) are modern works portraying recent figures such as the sculptors Bohumil Kafka and J. Štursa. The whole west end of the nave is a lifeless imitation of the east end, and bears little relation to the ambitious structure which Benedikt Ried would have created. The finest of the modern contributions to the building are the **stained-glass windows**, executed mainly by F. Kysela, K. Svolinský and Max Švabinský, the latter's largest work here being the *Last Judgement* window in the south transept.

To your right, immediately on entering the church from the south portal, is the **Wenceslas Chapel**, which Parléř enlarged by pushing out its southern and western walls, the latter at the expense of the transept. Visitors today are no longer allowed inside the chapel, and have to content themselves with the views from the railings. The chapel, containing the much-restored 14C tomb of St Wenceslas (d. 929 or 935), has a door of 1370 incorporating a Romanesque lion's-head knocker to which Wenceslas is said to have clung when he was attacked and murdered by his brother Boleslav. The interior, reflecting perhaps Charles IV's love of jewellery, is studded on its lower level with c 1372 precious stones, one of which was later thought to resemble the head of Napoleon (the French poet Apollinaire, on being shown this particular agate in 1902, was shocked to recognise his own features in the stone, and began fearing for his sanity).

On this same level are also to be found a series of paintings of the Passion by an anonymous Czech artist of 1372 (identified variously as Master Theodoric and Master Oswald). The story of St Wenceslas is portrayed above these, in elaborately detailed works of 1504 generally attributed to the Master of the Litoměřice Altarpiece; the room is further enhanced by Parléř's splendid ceiling, comprising parallel diagonal ribs springing from eight corbels to form a star-shaped dome.

The Bohemian Crown Jewels (shown to the public only on special occasions) are kept in a room above the chapel, and constitute the main survival of the extraordinary **treasury** founded by Charles IV. One of the most important cathedral treasuries in Europe, this contained numerous objects that had been brought by Charles to Prague from the court of France, and many others that were given to him as gifts by the leading dignitaries of his time. Others still were commissioned from his own jewellers and goldsmiths, including the dazzling Royal Crown of Bohemia, which was made in 1346 out of pure gold, 91 precious stones and 20 pearls; a copy of this work can be seen today in the Historical Museum installed in the Lobkowicz Palace (see below).

In the middle of the long east end of the cathedral stands the **Royal Mausoleum**, a large memorial in white marble, executed in 1571–89 by the Netherlandish sculptor Alexander Collin, and surrounded by a Renaissance grille by J. Schmidthammer: on its upper slab are reliefs of the Emperor Ferdinand I, his consort Anne of Jagiello, and his son Maximilan II, while on the sides are shown Charles IV and his four consorts, and the kings Wenceslas IV, Ladislav Pohrobek and George of Poděbrady. The actual tombs of these monarchs, as well as those of Rudolph II and members of the Přemyslids, can be seen in the **Royal Crypt**, the entrance to which lies just to the right of the mausoleum; within the crypt are also displayed the excavated remains of the cathedral's foundations, including masonry of the 10C and 11C. Behind the mausoleum is the uninspired High Altar, a neo-Gothic work of 1868–73, designed by J. Kranner and later altered by J. Mocker.

Walking around the ambulatory from its southwestern end, you will find next to the Wenceslas Chapel the Chapel of St Andrew, containing the tombstone (to the left, under the window) of Jaroslav von Martinic (d. 1649), one of the two Habsburg councillors thrown out of the Old Royal Palace window in 1618 (see below). The subsequent Chapel of the Holy Rood, with fragments of 14C murals, is followed by one of the more remarkable additions to the ambulatory, the **Royal Oratory**—a balcony decorated with characteristic late Gothic fantasy and naturalism, the architectural members imitating the branches of a tree; this highly entertaining work, dating back to the early years of Vladislav Jagiello's reign, is sometimes attributed to the Frankfurt sculptor Hans Spiess.

Next comes the Chapel of the Mary Magdalene, containing the wall tombs of the cathedral's two main architects, Matthew of Arras and Peter Parléř; fragments of late 14C wall-paintings can be seen here, as they can in the following Chapel of St John of Nepomuk, which also contains the marble tomb of Jan Očko of Vlašim, a work of 1370 from the Parléř workshop. The actual **tomb of St John of Nepomuk** stands in the ambulatory passage in front of the last chapel, and is unquestionably the finest of the Baroque furnishings in the cathedral: an elaborate silver structure under a canopy hung with draperies supported by angels, the tomb was made in Vienna between 1733–36 to the designs of the great J.B. Fischer von Erlach.

Tombs from the Parléř workshop (1370s) of prominent members of the Přemyslid family are to be found in the next three chapels: the tombs of Kings Přemysl I (d. 1230) and Přemysl Otakar II (d. 1278) are in the Reliquary Chapel; those of Counts Břetislav I (d. 1055) and Spytihněv II (d. 1061) are in the Chapel of Our Lady (the chapel where work on the cathedral was probably begun in 1344); and those of Counts Břetislav II (d. 1100) and Bořivoj II (d. 1124) are in the Chapel of St John the Baptist, where there can also be seen a statue by J.V. Mylsbek of St Method (1869–70) and the so-called Jerusalem candelabrum, a fine example of Rhenish craftsmanship of the early 12C. Behind the High Altar, and directly in front of the Chapel of Our Lady, is the **tomb of St Vitus**, with a statue of the saint by J. Max of 1840. The northernmost of the five radiating chapels of the apse is the Archbishops' Chapel, featuring the plain brown marble tomb of Vratislav of Pernštejn, a work of the late 16C by J. Vredemann de Vries.

In the ambulatory passage in front of this chapel is J.V. Myslbek's over life-size bronze statue of the kneeling Cardinal Bedřich Schwarzenberg (1891–95), the most important of the 19C sculptures in the cathedral. South of this is St Anne's Chapel, displaying on its altar a silver reliquary of 1266, decorated with enamels and precious stones. Further south you come to the **Old Sacristy**, the vaulting of which (begun in 1356) shows Peter Parléř at his most daring, featuring a dramatically suspended boss supported by four skeletal ribs.

Attached to the north wall of the north transept is Bonifác Wohlmut's **Organ Gallery** (1557–61), which curiously combines a harmonious Renaissance front taken from the pages of Serlio with Gothic vaulting inside; the stained-glass window above this is the work of Max Švabinský and contains scenes of *The Holy Trinity*, *The Madonna with Count Spytihněv II*, and *St Wenceslas with Charles IV* (1939–49). The finest of the chapels in the nave is the third on the left-hand side, the **New Archbishop's Chapel**, which has been the burial place of Prague's archbishops since 1909, and also houses the tomb of the art historian bishop Antonín Podlaha, whose researches played an important part in the last phase of the cathedral's construction. The chapel is adorned with a vivid stained-glass window by Alfons Mucha of the *Lives of SS Cyril and Methodius*, and has next to it a powerful wooden sculpture of the *Crucifixion* (1899) by F. Bílek.

Leave the cathedral by its western door and turn right, touring the rest of the castle complex in a clockwise direction. Skirting the northern side of the cathedral is the narrow Vikářská, where at No. 2 is the former Deanery, which was remodelled after 1705 by Santini-Aichel. The congested tourist eateries crammed into this street have replaced a famous beer-cellar in which the 19C writer Svatopluk Čech set his very popular tale about Mr Brouček—a man who, under the influence of beer, goes on a series of imaginative adventures, including to the moon and back to the 15C.

A nearby alley leads from the street to the castle's northern bastions, which were renewed by Benedikt Ried in 1485 and include the round tower known as the **Powder Tower** (Mihulka). A small exhibition relating to the castle's fortifications is housed in the ground floor of this building, while on the upper floors (from where there are good views north towards the Summer Palace) are exhibits relating to the scientific and cultural life at the Renaissance court of Prague: the emphasis is on the time of Rudolph II, of whom there is an elaborately detailed bronze bust by Adriaen de Vries.

Vikářská leads to **George's Square** (Jiřské náměstí), which faces the apse of the cathedral and is named after the former Basilica of St George and its adjoining convent. The **Convent of St George** (Klášter sv. Jiří), in the northeastern corner of the square, was founded in 937 by Count Boleslav II and his sister Princess Mlada, who became its first abbess; rebuilt several times—including, most recently, between 1657 and 1680—it was turned into a barracks after its dissolution in 1782 and then converted in 1962–72 into the branch of the **National Gallery** containing Czech art from the medieval to Baroque periods. The plain white rooms arranged around the convent's simple cloister provide a perfect setting for the paintings and sculptures, through which you are directed chronologically by arrows. **Open** Tues–Sun 10.00–18.00.

Early Czech art at the Convent of St George

The basement and the ground floor contain the early holdings (up to around 1530), the first important sculpture being the bronze equestrian statue of *St George and the Dragon* (1373) by the brothers George and Martin of Kolosvar, a copy of which stands in the Castle's Third Courtyard. An adjoining room is dedicated to the first major Bohemian painter, the anonymous Master of the Vyšší Brod Altarpiece. This altarpiece of the mid-14C, originating from the former Cistercian monastery at Vyšší Brod in southern Bohemia, was probably commissioned by Petr I of Rožmberk; it comprises nine panels of scenes from the life of Christ and the Virgin.

A more distinctive personality of slightly late date, and one of the earliest Bohemian artists known by name, was Master Theodoric, who is best known for his panels and murals painted in the Holy Rood Chapel at Karlštejn Castle in 1357–65; he is represented here by six large and luminously modelled heads of saints. A work of great historical interest is the votive picture of John Očko of Vlasim, which portrays the enthroned Madonna flanked by what are sometimes considered as the earliest examples of Bohemian portraiture—remarkably realistic representations of Charles IV, Wenceslas IV and the panel's donor, John Očko, Archbishop of Prague, himself. The main sculpture from this period in the gallery is the tympanum of the Crucifixion, which was taken from the north portal of the Týn Church in Prague.

The last years of the 14C are dominated by the Master of the Třeboň Altarpiece, whose principal work, from which he derives his name, is to be found here. Only three panels of this work—which was painted c 1380 for the former Augustinian church of St Giles in the southern Bohemian town of Třeboň—have survived: these panels, painted on both sides with the most vivid colours and charming naturalistic detail, represent Christ on the Mount of Olives, SS Catherine, Mary Magdalene and Margaret, SS Augustine, Giles and Jerome, the Resurrection, and SS James, Bartholomew and Philip. Of the many anonymous sweetly smiling Madonnas of the early 15C the finest is the famous Vyšší Brod Madonna of 1420.

The last of the outstanding Bohemian painters represented in the lower rooms of the gallery is the anonymous Master of the Litoměřice Altarpiece. The altarpiece itself is in the North Bohemian Gallery at Litoměřice (though it seems originally to have come from St Vitus's Cathedral in Prague), but the National Gallery has a number of other impressive works associated with him, most notably a series of panels from the Strahov Monastery in Prague (c 1505) and a triptych of *The Holy Trinity* of 1515–20. Of the later sculptures, special mention should be made of the expressive relief of the *Lamentation of Žebrák* (early 16C) and a series of five intricately carved reliefs by the artist known as the Monogramist IP, who seems to have come from the Passau or Salzburg region.

The collections of Renaissance and Baroque art on the first floor begin with works by artists of the Rudolph Circle, including a bronze of Hercules (1625–26) by Adriaen de Vries and an outstanding painting by Bartolomaeus Spranger of the *Risen Christ* (c 1590), which was intended for the tomb of the artist's father-in-law, the Prague goldsmith Nicholas Müller (who appears, together with other members of his family, at the bottom of the work). The 17C collections feature an especially large number of paintings by Karel Škréta, of which the most striking are the portraits, in particular a bust of the French painter Nicolas Poussin (whom Škréta met in Rome in 1634–35), an informal group portrait of the gem-carver *Dionysio Miseroni and his Family* (1653), and a delightful full-length portrait of *Maria Maximiliana of Sternberg dressed as a Shepherdess* (1665).

Among the later paintings of the 17C are the very Rubenesque *Liberation of St Andromeda* (1695) by M. Willmann, and a number of rapid oil sketches by Jan Liška. Baroque sculpture is represented most notably by J.G. Bendl's *Archangel Raphael* of c 1650, which was taken from the demolished plague column on the Old Town Square; several works by F.M. Brokoff, in partic-ular two *Moors* of 1718–19 from the gates of the Mansion at Kounice, and a polychromed statue of *St John of Bohemia*; and Matthias Braun's hysteri-cally posed *St Jude Thaddeus* (1712), originally forming part of an altarpiece from the now demolished Church of Our Lady in Prague's Old Town. From the latter dismantled altarpiece there is also a painting of St Jude Thaddeus by Peter Bendl, one of the most successful and prolific Bohemian artists of the early 18C: in addition to this and numerous other religious works by him, the gallery has an extensive collection of his portraits, including two self-portraits dating from 1697 and 1703.

A more remarkable portraitist than Bendl was Jan Kupecký, who is repre-sented here by two of his greatest works, a seated portrait of the ostenta-tiously dressed miniaturist Karl Bruni and a portrait of *The Artist with his Wife*: the latter, a work of uncompromising realism, was painted, unusually, as a token of reconciliation with his wife, whom he had found to be unfaithful and whom he portrayed here in the guise of a penitent. Among the other 18C works are V.V. Reiner's *Orpheus with Animals in a Landscape* (before 1720), A. Kern's *St Augustine* (c 1735), N. Grund's *Gallant Scene with a Lady on a Swing* (c 1760) and oil sketches for frescoes by F.A. Maulbertsch.

The **Basilica of St George** (Basilika sv. Jiří), attached to the southern side of the convent, is the oldest church in the citadel, having been founded in 905. Transformed into a three-aisled structure in 973, it was rebuilt following a fire in 1142, and then again in 1657–80; restoration campaigns undertaken in 1897–1907 and 1959–62 brought back many of the building's 10C–12C features, making the church one of the best-preserved Romanesque structures in Bohemia. The main Baroque survival is the vivid ochre west façade (facing George Square) and the adjoining **Chapel of St John of Nepomuk** (sv. Jan Nepomucký), which was built by F.M. Kaňka and the Dientzenhofer brothers in 1718–22, and is adorned on the outside with a statue of the saint by F.M. Brokoff. The south portal of the basilica, facing Jiřská, is an early 16C coffered Classical structure by Benedikt Ried incorporating in the tympanum a late Gothic relief of *St George and the Dragon*, the original of which is in the National Gallery. The principal Romanesque features of the basilica's exterior are the twin white towers rising up at the eastern end of the church.

The cold and heavily restored interior, which is now deconsecrated and used only for the occasional concert, retains in its nave the original arcades of the 10C and 11C. At the end of the nave, in front of the raised choir, are the tombs of Count Boleslav II (encased by a Baroque grille of 1730), and Count Vratislav I (in painted wood), the founder of the church. In between the two flights of the Baroque staircase which leads up to the choir is the entrance to the remarkable **crypt** of 1142, featuring columns with cubic capitals, and a particularly grim and realistic sculpture of a decomposing female corpse (executed in 1726). The vault of the choir has scant fragments of wall-paintings of c 1200 representing the Celestial Jerusalem; fragments of 16C painting decorate the vault of the adjoining **Chapel of St Ludmila**, which was added in the late 14C and houses the tomb (from Peter Parléř's workshop) of the murdered St Ludmila, one of Bohemia's patron saints.

The eastern citadel

Jiřská or George's Street, which runs due east of the basilica and slowly descends through the tapering eastern half of the citadel, is the main and oldest street of the complex, and is lined with a number of Renaissance and Baroque buildings. Before reaching the finest of these, you should take the first turning to the left to visit the celebrated Zlatá ulička (**Golden Lane**). This row of tiny houses dating from the end of the 16C runs directly underneath the north-eastern ramparts of the citadel, in between the New White Tower and the Daliborka Tower, both of which formed part of the new fortifications designed by Benedikt Ried for Vladislav Jagiello. The name of the lane is sometimes romantically connected with the alchemists at Rudolph's court, though in fact it derives from the gold-smiths who once lived here alongside the castle's guards. In the 18C and 19C the dwellings here were inhabited by the very poor, and it was only after 1960 that they were to receive their cheerfully-coloured doll's-house appearance and become tiny shops selling artefacts for the thousands of tourists who daily throng this restricted area.

The **New White Tower** (Bílá Věž), at the western end of the lane, served after

Residents of Golden Lane

In the summer of 1916, Kafka, looking for some quiet place to write, went on a flat-hunt with his favourite sister Ottla, and asked 'just for fun' if there was any place available in the lane; to their surprise they were able to rent from November the house at No. 22, which they kept for nearly a year, Kafka reputedly drawing inspiration here for his novel, *The Castle*.

The lane is also associated with the Nobel Prize-winning poet Jaroslav Seifert, who lived in a house (now gone) between the eastern end of the lane and the Daliborka Tower in the late 1920s and early 1930s, writing here his two collections of poems, *Eight Days* and *Bathed in Light*. The latter tower, another former prison, is named after the first person to be incarcerated here, Knight Dalibor of Kozojedy, whose life was to inspire Bedřich Smetana in his opera *Dalibor* (1868); a later prisoner was the aristocratic eccentric Count František Antonín Špork, the founder of the hospital and spa at Kuks in eastern Bohemia.

1584 as a prison, among its most famous inmates being the English alchemist Edward Kelley and the leaders of the anti-Habsburg uprising of 1618.

Returning to Jiřská and continuing to walk east you will pass to your left, at No. 4, the former Palace of the Burgrave of Prague Castle, which was built in 1541 by Giovanni Ventura and adapted in the early 1960s to serve as the House of Czechoslovak Children; today, it maintains its association with children by housing the deeply disappointing **Toy Museum**, an unimaginative display of objects such as toy robots, cars, and even Barbie dolls (not even the most undemanding of today's children could possibly enjoy this). **Open** Tues–Sun 09.30–17.30.

More interesting (at least for its setting) is the hotch-potch of drably arranged objects making up the **Historical Museum**, on the other side of the street. This documents the history of Bohemia from the arrival of the Slavs up to 1848–49, and occupies the **Lobkowicz Palace**, which was rebuilt in 1651–68 to the designs of the Italian architect Anselmo Lurago, and retains several 17C and 18C ceilings, including, in Room 19, a heavily stuccoed 17C ceiling incorporating a clumsy if amusing painted panel of the *Triumph of Caesar*. **Open** Tues–Sun 09.00–17.00.

A little below the palace Jiřská reaches the citadel's eastern gate, on the other side of which you will come out at the top of the Old Town Steps (Staré Zámecké schody; see above).

Old Royal Palace and gardens

Make your way back to George Square and bear left, passing to your left immediately on re-entering the square the **Church of All Saints** (Všech svatých), which was rebuilt after a fire at the end of the 16C and attached after 1755 to the adjoining Theresian Convent for Noblewomen.

On the western side of the Church of All Saints is the **Old Royal Palace**, which has parts dating back to the 12C but owes its present appearance largely to the rebuilding campaign undertaken by Benedikt Ried in the late 15C for Vladislav Jagiello.

History of the Old Royal Palace
Occupying the site of the 9C palace of the Princes of Bohemia, it served from the 13C to the 16C as the palace of the Kings of Bohemia. After the Habsburgs moved their quarters to the western end of the citadel and up to the end of the 18C the building functioned as the central offices of the Bohemian state. Thereafter it was neglected and partially used as storage space until 1924, when it was thoroughly restored and taken over for governmental purposes; its main rooms, which have only been open to the public since the 1960s, are still the scene of the occasional important political assembly.

The palace is entered from the castle's Third Courtyard, and as you make your way there from the Church of All Saints you will pass to your left a parapet overlooking the palace courtyard, above which rises the **Vladislav Hall**, which is adorned on the outside by elegant Renaissance windows that give no hint of the late Gothic fantasies to be found within. When you eventually enter the hall after crossing a dark and austere antechamber adjoining the palace's main entrance, you are confronted with what is architecturally one of the most exciting spaces to be seen in Europe. The vast hall—so vast that jousting touraments had once been held here—was built by Benedikt Ried in 1493–1502 and is dominated by vaulting of breathtaking elaboration: the ribs, likened frequently to the intertwined branches of a forest, have largely ceased to play a structural role, but snake their way around the ceiling in an essentially decorative way, drawing the visitor into the room through their powerful movements, and creating dynamic effects that look ahead to the Baroque period. The vaulting, representing an extreme development of the late Gothic style, contrasts markedly with the innovatory Renaissance windows, yet even when handling Classical forms, Ried often did so in a highly idiosyncratic fashion, as can be seen in his famous door at the northeastern end of the room, where a Renaissance arch is supported by twisted pilasters which are almost a mockery of all that the Renaissance stood for.

Before crossing to the eastern end of the hall, you should go through the door in its southwestern corner to visit the room of the **Bohemian Chancellery**, which is famous as the place where the 'Second Defenestration' took place in 1618.

The Second Defenestration

Early on the morning of 23 May 1618, a group of Protestants led by Count Thurn burst into the Chancellery determined to punish the two Catholic councillors Martinic and Slavata, who had been appointed by Ferdinand over their heads. Following a violent row, the councillors, accused of being traitors and worthless followers of the Jesuits, were thrown out of the window. They managed to grab on to the ledge, but Thurn beat their knuckles with the hilt of his sword until they fell. Surprisingly they were not killed; thanks to the unhygienic conditions then prevailing at the castle, the ditch which at that time ran below the whole complex was piled high with sewage which broke the two councillors' fall. This excremental intervention in the course of history was later attributed by Catholics to a miracle.

After returning to the hall walk across to its southeastern corner, where there is a door leading to a **terrace** offering a magnificent view of Prague; the helical staircase which descends from here to the gardens below was built by Otto Rothmayer in 1951. Back once more in the hall, and crossing over to its northeastern corner, you will pass to your right a balcony looking down into the Church of All Saints (see above), which has mainly 17C and 18C furnishings. The extraordinary door with twisted pillars at the northeastern corner of the hall leads into the **Diet Hall**, which is covered with another late Gothic vault of fascinating complexity. The room, built by Ried in 1500, was destroyed by fire in 1541, and reconstructed nine years later by Bonifác Wohlmut, who provided it with the Renaissance tribune once used by the Supreme Scribe.

Returning to the Vladislav Hall, and turning right, you will come immediately to a double Renaissance portal. Through the arch on the left is a spiral staircase climbing up to the rooms of the **New Land Rolls**, where there is a ceiling decorated with the heraldic shields of the clerks of the Land Rolls; the right-hand arch leads directly to the **Riders' Staircase**, which horses had once climbed on their way to joust in the Vladislav Hall. Built by Ried in around 1500 it is vaulted in a way which almost surpasses in complexity this architect's achievement in the Vladislav Hall, with ribs that intersect, interrupt and are suddenly truncated, the overall effect being one of suspended movement, a sense of playful abandon controlled by a rigorous geometrical discipline in a way which would have impressed the Baroque architect Borromini.

Patrick Leigh Fermor, in *A Time of Gifts* (1977), wrote of the vaults that 'they were impossible to describe', and promptly went on to describe them at great length in prose which is almost as difficult to follow as the ribs themselves. To Leigh Fermor 'the marvellous strangeness of the late Gothic vaults enclosing this flight must have germinated in an atmosphere like the English mood which coaxed fan-tracery into bloom.'

Walking down the Riders' Staircase you reach the palace's northern door, where you can either leave the building or else continue your visit by going first to the ground-floor rooms of Charles IV's palace, and then to the gloomy cellar below, a survival of the 12C palace of Count Soběslav; these Romanesque and Gothic chambers are largely bare, but there are copies of some of Parléř's triforium sculptures from St Vitus's Cathedral in the large **Charles Hall**—a space currently ear-marked to house the cathedral's famous treasury. **Open** Apr–Sept daily 09.00–17.00, Oct–Mar daily 09.00–16.00.

After walking back to the western end of the palace, you should take a closer look at the southern half of the Third Courtyard, in the middle of which stands the famous bronze statue of *St George and the Dragon* by the brothers George and Martin of Kolosvar (the original is in the National Gallery at the Convent of St George). Between 1928 and 1932 the whole courtyard, which at one time was slightly sloping, was relaid and straightened by Josip Plečnik, who also designed for it a granite monolith commemorating the dead of the First World War.

At the same time Plečnik pierced the eastern end of the monotonous Municipal Building on the southern side of the courtyard with a portal and ingenious staircase leading down to gardens which had been laid out originally in the late 17C over the notorious ditch into which the two councillors had been thrown in 1618. The gardens, commanding a magnificent panorama of Prague, were also relaid by Plečnik, who divided them into the **Rampart Garden** and the **Paradise Garden**, thus breaking up the monotony of the original formal plan. One of the more welcome recent changes to the castle has been the opening of these gardens to visitors, who might well find them a refreshingly quiet place to get away for a while from the crowds of fellow sightseers. From the Paradise Garden, where Plečnik placed a 40-ton granite basin on two small blocks, there is also a monumental staircase leading back to Hradčany Square. **Open** Apr–Sept Tues–Sun 10.00–18.00.

North of the citadel
From the Third Courtyard you should make your way back to the Second Courtyard, which you should leave through the arch on its northern side. This will take you to the **Powder Bridge** (Prašný most), which spans the so-called **Stag Moat** (Jelení příkop), where red deer were kept from the 16C to 18C. After

crossing the bridge and continuing to walk north, you will pass on the left an elegantly simple building designed by J.-B. Mathey in 1694 as the **Royal Riding-School** (Jízdárna), and then restored by Pavel Janák in 1948–54. On the other side of the path are the gates to the beautifully maintained and azalea-laden **Royal Gardens** (Královská zahrada), which have been largely re-opened to the public following years of closure during the Communist period.

Walking east inside the garden you will come shortly to the much-restored **Great Ball-Game Court** (Míčovna), an harmonious Renaissance structure built by Bonifác Wohlmut and Ulrico Avostalis in 1565–69, and covered all over with Renaissance sgrafitto work. More impressive still is the **Summer Palace** (Letohrádek královny Anny) at the gardens' eastern end, which touched the heart of Chateaubriand on his visit to Prague in 1833: 'Not far from the shape-less masses [of the Hradčin]', wrote the famous French author and politician, 'there stands against the sky a pretty building decked with one of the graceful porticoes of the cinquecento: this architecture has the drawback of being out of harmony with the climate. If at least one could, during the Bohemian winter, put these Italian palaces in the hot-house, with the palm trees? I was almost preoccupied with the thought of the cold which they must feel at night.' Popularly and wrongly known as the Belvedere, the Summer Palace is indeed one of the purest examples in central Europe of the Italian Renaissance style, the proportions of its arcaded lower level strongly recalling the architecture of Brunelleschi. Begun in 1537 to a design by Paolo della Stella (who executed as well the exquisite mythological and ornamental reliefs on the arcade), it was completed in 1552–69 by Bonifác Wohlmut, who provided it with the one feature which reveals it as a work situated in Central Europe rather than Italy— the curious copper roof shaped like the inverted hull of a ship. The interior, remodelled in the mid-19C, was restored after the Second World War by Pavel Janák, and again in recent years. The tiny Renaissance garden on its western side contains a celebrated bronze fountain known as the **Singing Fountain** on account of the sounds made by the water dropping from its two basins: the finely detailed work was designed in 1563 by Francesco Terzio.

■ The Royal Gardens are **open** May–Oct Tues–Sun 10.00–17.45; Belvedere open May–Oct Tues–Sun 10.00–18.00.

On the eastern side of the palace is the small **Chotěk Park**, which was founded in 1833 by the Supreme Burgrave K. Chotěk, and was Prague's first public park; in an overgrown bosky setting at its eastern end stands a delightful memorial by Josef Maudr to the 19C poet Julius Zeyer, whose bronze bust is placed on top of a grotto enclosing a group of white marble figures from his poems.

North of the Royal Gardens, on the opposite side of the parallel Mariánské hrady, is a small residential area comprising the northernmost extremity of the Hradčany municipal district: this area was developed after 1910 following the purchase of military land by the Prague community; the architects responsible for the overall plan, Vlatislav Hofman and Vladimír Zákrejs, laid out the streets along the Hradčany's half-filled Baroque fortifications. The main surviving military monument in the area is the **Písek Gate** (on U Písecké Brány, a few minutes walk northeast of the Summer Palace), which was built by Charles VI in 1721. Just to the east of this is Mickiewiczova, on which stand a number of interesting early 20C buildings, including at No. 239 a house designed in 1911 by Jan Kotěra for T.G. Masaryck, who lived there from 1911 onwards. At the eastern end of the street (at No. 1) is the former house and studio of the sculptor František Bílek: designed and built by Bílek himself in 1911–12, this large and curious brick structure, partially inspired by Egyptian architecture, has been kept to a certain extent as it was in Bílek's day; the garden and studio, both filled with his expressive carvings, are open to the public during the summer months. But perhaps the most impressive of this area's houses is Josef Gočár's Cubist double villa at 4–6 Tychonova, just to the west of the Písek Gate. Built in 1912–13, the **Hofmann and Stach Twin House** has the overall appearance of an Empire mansion, complete with mansard roof. What makes the exterior so exciting is the powerful frontispiece featuring giant Cubist columns framing an oval stairwell and a futuristic portal; the garden has a delightful wooden summer house in a Cubist style.

West of Prague Castle

Return to the castle's Second Courtyard, and from there make your way back to the Hradčany Square to begin a tour of the former township that grew up to the west of the castle's walls. Made a township in 1320, and enlarged 40 years later by the construction of the Hunger Wall (see p 131), after 1541 this area became the scene of intensive rebuilding work; the place was raised to the status of royal town in 1598, and remained as such until the creation of a unified Prague in 1784.

The district covers a relatively small area, but is crowded with important monuments, beginning with those on the **Hradčany Square** (Hradčanské naměstí) itself. This sloping, wedge-shaped square, lined with imposing palaces, features at its centre a **Marian column** of 1726 ringed by eight statues of saints by F.M. Brokoff. Adjacent to the western façade of the castle, behind a fine ironwork lampholder, is the **Archbishop's Palace** (No. 16), which dates back to a building of Wohlmut's of 1562, but was rebuilt by J.-B. Mathey at the end of the 17C and given an Italianate Baroque façade, with a crowning pediment and statuary by J.J. Wirch, in 1763–65; the interior, closed to the public, is rich in 18C furnishings, including a set of eight Gobelin tapestries of 1753–56.

Šternberg Palace

On the left-hand side of the palace is an alley descending to the Šternberg Palace (No. 15), a gloomy but impressive structure which is completely hidden from the square. Designed by D. Martinelli, and executed between 1698 and 1707 by G.B. Alliprandi and J.B. Santini-Aichel, it is particularly remarkable for its courtyard, which is dominated on its western side by a large oval pavilion. However, the building is visited less for its architecture than for its paintings, for it houses the pre-modern Foreign School holdings of the **National Gallery** (the modern ones have now been transfered to the Trade Fair Palace in Holešovice; see pp 196–202). **Open** Tues–Sun 10.00–18.00.

The rooms of the Šternberg Palace, featuring a number of fine stuccoed and painted ceilings of the early 18C, make an elegant setting for the old master Foreign School paintings (which have been housed here since 1945), but the display is crammed, old-fashioned and poorly lit. The dingy main staircase adjoining the ticket-office leads up to where the bulk of the collection is shown.

On the first floor are the Italian 14C to 16C paintings, which include among the primitives works by **Nardo di Cione** and **Bernardo Daddi** and an expressive *Lamentation* by **Lorenzo di Monaco**; the quattrocento is represented only by four works, the finest of which are by **Benozzo Gozzoli** and **Pasqualino Veneto**.

It is on the second floor that the true quality of the gallery is felt, beginning with an excellent group of German 15C–16C paintings, including **Hans Schücklin**'s *Beheading of St Barbara* (1470), monochrome fragments of an altarpiece of 1509 by **Hans Holbein the Elder**, a portrait by his son of Elizabeth Vaux, **Altdorfer**'s *Martyrdom of St Florian*, **Baldung Grien**'s *Beheading of St Dorothy* (1516), and a variety of works by **Lucas Cranach** the Elder, most notably a delightful *Adam and Eve* of 1537, a *Judith and Holofernes* of 1550, and fragments from an altarpiece in St Vitus's Cathedral which was taken down by Protestants in 1619 (the main survival is a panel of the Assumption surrounded by angels and saints). Especially powerful are two large panels by **Hans Süss** of Kulmbach which originally decorated the organ loft of the Church of Our Lady in the Snows in Prague's New Town; they are vigorous and near life-sized representations of the Emperor Henry II and the Empress Chunegunda.

Süss was an artist greatly influenced by **Albrecht Dürer**, who is represented here by one of his most famous works, *The Feast of the Rose Gardens*. Painted in Venice in 1506 for the church of San Bartolomeo (the church of Venice's merchant colony), this work shows the great influence on the artist of the brilliant colouring of Venetian painters such as Giovanni Bellini; in turn the painting made an enormous impact on the Venetian public, and indeed was their first main contact with contemporary German art. Among the many contemporary personalities that Dürer vividly portrayed on either side of the enthroned Virgin are Pope Julius II, Emperor Maximilian I, Domenico Grimani, Jakob Fugger and Hieronymus of Augsburg; the artist himself, a man not known for his modesty, also included himself among this distinguished company, standing under a tree and holding his signature. The painting was acquired by Rudolph II in 1606, and is the most important of his pictures to have remained in Prague.

A small room, tucked away behind the room with the Dürer, contains the small and unimpressive holdings of 17C and 18C French and Spanish art, featuring works by **Bourdon**, **Charles le Brun**, **Boucher** and **Mignard**, and an indifferent portrait by **Goya** of *Don Miguel de Lardizabal* (1815). The best of the French paintings—a dramatically coloured *Suicide of Lucretia* (1625/6) by **Simon Vouet**—was painted in Rome under the influence of Caravaggio and is thus displayed in the rooms devoted to the 16C–18C Italian School.

The Italian cinquecento section contains good portraits by **Lotto** and **Bronzino**, and the so-called *Madonna of the Veil*, a Holy Family group painted c 1519 by **Sebastiano del Piombo**, and on loan from the cathedral at Olomouc. The 17C and 18C Italian paintings include **Domenico Fetti**'s *Christ in the Garden of Gethsemane*, **Magnasco**'s *Mary Magdalene in a Landscape*, **Piazetta**'s *St Joseph and Child*, an enormous view of London by **Canaletto**, a head of an old man by **G.D. Tiepolo** (erroneously attributed to his father Giambattista), a St Jerome by Ribera, and small oils by **Pittoni** and **Sebastiano Ricci**.

Of the Netherlandish holdings of the 15C and 16C, **Jan Gossaert**'s *St Luke* *drawing the Virgin and Child* (1513–16) and **Pieter Brueghel** the Elder's *Haymaking* (1565) stand out; the former was hung on the main altar of St Vitus's Cathedral from 1618 up to the end of the 19C, while the latter formed part of a famous series of panels of the months painted for the artist's Antwerp friend Nicolaes Jonghelinck (the other surviving panels from this series are in the Kunsthistorisches Institut in Vienna).

Among the 17C Flemish paintings are a **Van Dyck** of St Bruno (1615) and several works by **Rubens**, including a *Cleopatra* of c 1615, and two large canvases, one of St Augustine and the other *The Martyrdom of St Thomas*, which the artist painted between 1637 and 1639 for the former Augustinian Church of St Thomas in Prague's Little Quarter.

The Dutch 17C holdings are extensive and feature genre scenes by **Dou**, **Ter Borch**, **Ochtervelt**, **Metsu** and **David Teniers**, still-lifes by **Pieter Klaesz** and **Willem Kalf**, and landscapes by **Jan van Goyen**, **Salamon Ruisdael** and **Aert von der Meer**; the two outstanding works in this section are **Rembrandt**'s *Scholar in his Study* of 1634 and the half-length portrait by **Frans Hals** of the rather cocksure Jasper Schahde van Westrum (c 1645).

Leaving the gallery and continuing to tour the Hradčany Square, you will find on the southern side of the square, at No. 2, the **Schwarzenberg-Lobkowicz Palace**. This large, gabled palace, built by Augustín Vlach for Jan of Lobkowicz in 1543–63, is one of the finest examples in Prague of Bohemian Renaissance architecture, and is covered with restored sgraffito decorations, including on its wide projecting cornice; the interior, featuring 16C painted ceilings on the second floor, now houses a beautifully displayed **Military Museum**, with exhibits relating to early military history throughout the world. **Open** May–Oct Tues–Sun 09.30–16.30.

The wide, western end of the square is largely taken up by the Thun-Hohenstein Palace (No. 5); though known sometimes as the 'Tuscan Palace' (the Duke of Tuscany owned it after 1718), this is in fact a Roman-inspired building, built by J.-B. Mathey in 1689–91, and with an upper balustrade crowned by statues by F.M. Brokoff. At the northwestern corner of the square, overlooking Kanovnická Street, is the gabled Martinic Palace of 1618–24, its façade sgraffitoed with biblical and mythological scenes.

Walking north along **Kanovnická** you will come at the end of this street to the **Church of St John of Nepomuk** (sv. Jana Nepomuckého), which was built by K.I. Dientzenhofer in 1720–28 and is the first known church by this architect; its newly repainted exterior is unremarkable, but the Greek Cross interior, with ceiling paintings of the life of the saint by V.V. Reiner (1728), is richly decorated and stuccoed, and full of movement.

Turning right at the end of Kanovnická, and then immediately left, you will come to the top of what is perhaps the most picturesque of the Hradčany's street **Nový Svět** or 'The New World' (a name which is also applied to this whole corner of town). This narrow, cobbled street, originating in a path leading from Prague to Střešovice, was lined at the end of the 16C with a number of modest houses; the latter, crumbling away over the centuries, came to be occupied by the very poor, but have now become some of Prague's most exclusive addresses. At No. 1, on the left-hand side, is the house which belonged first to the astronomer Tycho Brahe and then, after 1600, to his successor as court astronomer, Johann Kepler; at No. 25, further down on this same side, is a memorial plaque by O. Španiel commemorating the house where the violinist František Ondříček was born in 1857.

After turning around at the last house and retracing your steps for a few metres, take the first turning to your right, Černínská, and climb up to the quiet and sloping **Loreto Square** (Loretánské náměstí), which was a major source of inspiration early this century to the bizarre and idiosyncratic painter Jan Zrzavý, who described it as one of Prague's 'overpowering' places: 'This is the home of the poor', he continued, 'a nook inhabited by the people deserted in this world, so simple and primitive that even a child could paint it. How well I lived in this area, nowhere else in Prague did I ever feel so good.' Not only did Zrzavý paint the square repeatedly, but also conceived here many of his most famous works, including his *Obsession (Lovers)* of 1914 (now in the Modern Art Gallery in the Trade Fair Palace).

At the narrow northern end of the square, immediately to your right, is the former **Capuchin Church of Our Lady**, the monastery of which is the oldest Capuchin institution in Bohemia and was founded in 1600; the mid-17C church is very plain in its architecture and decoration, in accordance with the ideals of this order, but is worth visiting during the Christmas period to see the famous crib which is assembled here.

Rising above a terrace, and occupying the whole western side of the square, is the **Černín Palace**, which was designed and begun by Francesco Caratti in 1669 for Humprecht Jan Černín of Chudenice, the imperial ambassador to Venice. Domenico Rossi, G.B. Alliprandi and F.M. Kaňka were among the later architects to play a part in the construction of the palace, which would fall seriously into disrepair by the beginning of the 19C. The American diplomat and future author of *Tales from the Alhambra*, Washington Irving, saw the palace in 1822 and found there a scene of desolation even greater than that which he would discover in the Alhambra several years later. Deserted apparently by its owners, the main portal was boarded up, and there were rags and old clothes hanging out to dry from a main façade whose broken windows were patched up with paper; a side door led into a courtyard taken over by cackling geese, ruined statuary, and impoverished old women washing and drawing water from a well.

In 1928–34 the whole palace was extensively restored and remodelled by Pavel Janák. However, the main façade overlooking the Loreto Square remains, in its overall conception if not in its detailing, essentially as Caratti planned it, and is not only one of the most monumental façades in Prague, but also the first truly Baroque structure in the city, being articulated the whole of its great length (150m) by a giant order of Corinthian columns. Since 1918 the building has served as the Ministry of Foreign Affairs, and in 1948 was the scene of a notorious incident when one of Beneš' ministers, Jan Masaryk (the son of Czechoslovakia's first president), experienced the peculiarly Czech fate of falling out of the window. This incident, proved only in 1991 as a suicide, was the subject of intense speculation, and the Catalan exile Teresa Pamiés related how even years afterwards she was unable to pass 'the beautiful Loreto Square without thinking of the bloody corpse of Jan Masaryk stretched out on the old pavement'.

Sanctuary of Our Lady of Loreto

Facing the Černín Palace on the eastern side of the square is the Sanctuary of Our Lady of Loreto (Loreta), an important place of pilgrimage as well as one of the Hradčany's main tourist attractions. The sanctuary dates back to 1626 when Benigna Kateřina of Lobkowicz, anxious to revive the Marian cult, commissioned a replica of the Virgin's House at the Italian town of Loreto, a house which, according to a 15C tradition, had been transported there miraculously from the Holy Land; at least 50 other copies of this house have been made, but the one in Prague remains the most famous. The Virgin's House is encased by a Baroque complex, the main, western façade of which was begun by Christoph Dientzenhofer in 1716 and completed by his son Kilian Ignaz in 1722; in front of it is a balustrade decorated with statues of cherubs by O. Quittainer. The elegant tripartite façade has a frontispiece crowned by a tall tower enclosing an elaborate **carillon** which was made by Petr Neumann in 1694 and plays various melodies by means of a keyboard, including—at the stroke of every hour—the Marian hymn, *We Greet Thee a Thousand Times*.

After passing through the main portal you come to the cloisters, in the middle of which stands the **Virgin's House**, which was built by G.B. Orsi in 1626–31 and shrouded in 1664 with a heavy stuccoed decoration featuring Old Testament figures and scenes from the Life of the Virgin; the simple, barrel-vaulted interior in unfaced brick has traces of 17C frescoes. The cloisters themselves date back to 1661 but were raised by a storey by K.I. Dientzenhofer in the 1740s. They are surrounded by small and elaborately decorated 18C chapels, and feature off their eastern side the **Church of the Nativity**, which was designed by J.J. Aichbaurer in 1734 and has a sumptuously gilded interior with ceiling paintings by V.V. Reiner and J.V. Schöpf. **Open** Tues–Sun 09.00–12.15 and 13.00–16.30.

After having walked around the cloisters in a clockwise direction you complete your tour of the sanctuary by climbing up to a room off the cloister's western side, where you will find—displayed under a modern ceiling hung with a glass decoration in questionable taste—a **treasury** comprising chalices, monstrances and other liturgical objects from the 16C to 18C. Among these is a work so outstanding as to make all the other pieces, fine though they are, dull and pedestrian. This, the so-called Diamond Monstrance (known also as 'the Prague Son'), was designed by the great Viennese architect J.B. Fischer von Erlach and executed in 1699 by the Viennese court jewellers Matthias Stegner and Johann Kanischbauer. A gift from Ludmilla Eva Franziska of Kolovrat (who donated to the sanctuary her entire estate), it incorporates within its 12kg of silver gilt 6222 out of the 6500 diamonds that had been used for Ludmilla's wedding dress (the remaining ones being the draughtsmen's fee). One of the more delightful touches of this spectacular piece of fantasy is the tiny enamel dove floating serenely within the explosion of rays.

Stravhov Monastery

At the foot of the Sanctuary's main entrance is a flight of steps leading up to the southern end of the Loreto Square. Turn right at the top of the square and you will come almost immediately to **Pohořelec**, a square which has its origins in a suburb of the Hradčany founded in 1375; it is lined today with 17C and 18C buildings that, after long years of grime and decay, now sparkle under their pastel coats of paint. Climbing up the dark and narrow passage through the house at No. 8 (on the southern side of the square) will lead you into the peaceful and newly restored courtyard of the **Strahov Monastery** (Strahovský klášter); alternatively you could reach this courtyard by walking to the south-western corner of the square, and then turning left, entering the monastery through its elegant gate of 1742, and passing on your left the early 17C Church of St Roch (now a private art gallery).

History of the monastery

The former Premonstratensian Monastery of Strahov was founded by Vladislav II in 1140 on the instigation of the Bishop of Olomouc, Jindřich Zdík, who had first come into contact with the Premonstratensian Order on a visit to Palestine. The monastery, endowed with a formidable library, soon became one of the great centres of learning in Bohemia, and many of the leading personages of the day were educated here. Devastated and plundered by the Swedes in 1648, the place prospered once again after the subsequent Treaty of Westphalia, and acquired so many more books that in 1671 G.D. Orsi began building a new library hall, known today as the Theological Hall. Between 1682 and 1689 the rest of the monastery was remodelled and extended by J.-B. Mathey, and towards the end of the following century a further library hall, the Philosophical Hall, was commissioned from I.J. Palliardi by the enlightened abbot Václav Mayer (1734–1800). Mayer was also responsible for the founding of the abbey's Cabinet of Curiosities, and it was during his abbacy that the man known as the 'patriarch of Slavic philology', J. Dobrovský, used to stay here. In deference to the monastery's literary traditions, a Museum of Czech Literature was established in the monastery buildings in 1953. Archaeological investigations carried out here during this same decade uncovered extensive remains of the 12C monastery. Since 1989 the place has become occupied again by monks (there are currently 32 of them), and they have made the complex more commercially viable than it was during the Communist period: the monastery's brewing traditions have been revived, two of its buildings have been profitably leased out, and the place's tourist potential has been exploited to the full.

On the southern side of the courtyard is the functioning **Monastery Church of Our Lady** (Kostel Nanebevzetí Panny Marie). This church, which retains its 12C Romanesque basilica plan, was remodelled in the early 17C and again in the middle of the following century; the mid-18C interior has a ceiling decorated with stucco cartouches designed by J. Palliardi, and an organ on which Mozart played. The finest of the Baroque additions to the monastery are its two library halls, the entrance to which is adjacent to the church's west façade. The grander of the two is the first one you come to, the **Philosophical Hall**, which was built at the end of the 18C around richly gilded and carved walnut furnishings by J. Lahofer that were brought here from the dissolved Premonstratensian monastery at Louka outside the South Moravian town of Znojmo. In 1794 one of the greatest fresco painters of central Europe, the Austrian F.A. Maulbertsch, covered the entire vault of this hall with a vast ceiling-painting representing the modest theme of *The Struggle of Mankind to Know True Wisdom*.

The **Theological Hall** has kept its original wooden shelving and is adorned in its centre with 17C and 18C globes as well as tables displaying a select few of the library's incomparable collection of illuminated manuscripts and incunabula, among which is the Strahov New Testament, an Ottonian work of the 9C–10C constituting one of the oldest written documents surviving in the Czech Republic; the magnificent ceiling is decorated with late 17C stucco cartouches by Silvestro Carlone framing frescoes by Siard Nosecký also celebrating human knowledge. In the short corridor in between the two libraries are glass cabinets displaying some of the natural history 'curiosities' (including a whale's penis) amassed by Abbot Mayer and others.

The once rambling and delightfully chaotic **Museum of Czech Literature** (of interest largely to Czech speakers) has now been streamlined and relegated to some ground-floor rooms off the church's adjoining cloisters. Above them is the small and recently opened **Strahov Art Gallery**, which features some of the works of art acquired by the monks over the centuries and now returned to them after being confiscated by the Communists (a few of these works were hung until 1989 in the Šternberg Palace; see above). The paintings range from an excellent small group of medieval paintings—including the chubbily-featured mid 14C Strahov Madonna, and some marvelously realistic late 15C works attributed to the Master of Litoměřice—to a number of fine Baroque and Rococo oils Skřeta, Brabdl, Sebastiano Ricci, Maulbertsch and Antonín Kern; in between are some striking works of the Rudolphine period, notably Spranger's *Resurrection of Christ* (c 1576), Hans von Aachen's portrait of Rudolph II (1604–12) and, more interesting still, Dirck de Quade van Ravesteyn's *Allegory of the Reign of Rudolph II* (1603), a good example of the erotic use of allegorical figures. **Open** Tues–Sun 09.00–17.00.

A gate through the monastery's eastern wall brings you out into the extensive parkland covering the Petřín Hill, and an enjoyable short walk, with beautiful views towards Prague Castle, can be made from here to the observatory tower at the top of the hill (see p 130). To return instead to the Hradčany Square, go back to Pohořelec and from there head east down Loretánská, which has a number of fine palaces at its eastern end, including, at No. 4, the **Martinic Palace**, which was built by G.B. Scotti in 1700–05 for Jiří Adam II of Martinic—the imperial ambassador to Rome—and was closely modelled on the buildings of the Roman architect Carlo Fontana. At No. 1 is the former Hradčany Town Hall (Hradčanská radnice), which dates back to shortly after the raising of the Hradčany to the status of a Royal Town in 1598, and has early 17C sgraffito decorations by Marian de Marianis.

4 · The New Town (Nové Město)

The New Town, which was founded by Charles IV in 1348, lies to the south and east of the Old Town. Formed by the construction of a great line of outer fortifications stretching from the foot of the Vyšehrad hill in the south all the way to the Vltava in the north, it constituted one of the most ambitious examples of town planning in 14C Europe. The largest of the four original townships of

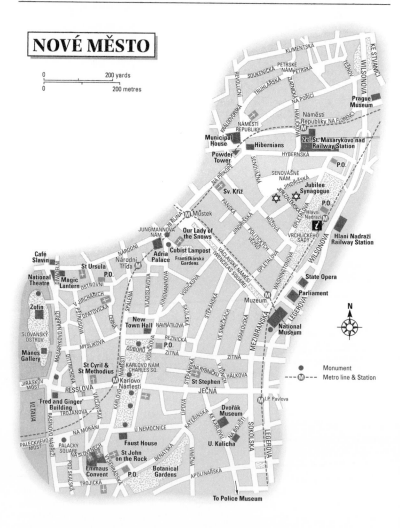

NOVÉ MĚSTO

0 ————— 200 yards
0 ————— 200 metres

KLIMENTSKÁ
KE STVANIC
PETRSKÉ NÁM.
SOUKENICKÁ PETRSKÁ
REVOLUČNÍ
TĚŠNOV
WILSONOVA
TRUHLÁŘSKÁ
ZLATNICKÁ
NA POŘÍČÍ
Prague Museum
KLOMOVÁRSKÁ
HAVLÍČKOVA
Náměstí Republiky NA FLORENCI
NÁMĚSTÍ REPUBLIKY
Municipal House
Hibernians
Zel St. Masarykovo nád Railway Station
Powder Tower
HYBERNSKÁ
P.O.
NA PŘÍKOPĚ
SENOVÁŽNÁ
SENOVÁŽNÉ NÁM.
Sv. Kříž
JERUZALÉMSKÁ
Jubilee Synagogue
JINDŘIŠSKÁ
Můstek
PANSKÁ
POLITICKÝCH
JINDŘIŠSKÁ
P.O.
ŘÍJNÁ
RŮŽOVÁ
OPLETALOVA
Hlavní Nadraží
JUNGMANNOVA NÁM.
Our Lady of the Snows
VRCHLICKÉHO SADY
Hlani Nadraži Railway Station
Café Slavin
NÁRODNÍ
Cubist Lampost
Adria Palace
Františkárská Gardens
VÁCLAVSKÉ NÁMĚSTÍ WENCESLAS SQUARE
VĚZNÍ
WILSONOVA
St Ursula
Národní Třída
P.O.
OPLETALOVA
State Opera
National Theatre
Magic Lantern
OSTROVNÍ
SPÁLENÁ
VODIČKOVA
JUNGMANNOVA
VLADISLAVOVA
WASHINGTONOVA
Parliament
Muzeum
JIRCHÁŘÍCH
ŠKOLSKÁ
ŠTĚPÁNSKÁ
Zofín
PŠTROSSOVA
OPATOVICKÁ
ČERNÁ
New Town Hall
NAVRÁTILOVA
VE SMEČKÁCH
MEZIBRÁNSKÁ
National Museum
N
SLOVANSKÝ OSTROV
MASARYKOVO NÁBŘEŽÍ
MYSLÍKOVA
ŘEZNICKÁ
KRAKOVSKÁ
Manes Gallery
DITTRICHOVA
P.O.
ODBORŮ
VODIČKOVA
ZITNÁ
ZITNÁ
LEGEROVA
Monument
JIRÁSKŮV MOST
St Cyril & St Methodius
KARLOVO NÁM. CHARLES SQ.
ŠTĚPÁNSKÁ RYBNÍČKU
HÁLKOVA
---M--- Metro line & Station
VLTAVA
RAŠÍNOVO NÁBŘEŽÍ
'Fred and Ginger' Building
TROJANOVA
KARLOVO NÁM.
Karlovo Náměstí
St Stephen
JEČNÁ
SOKOLSKÁ
NA MORÁNI
VÁCLAVSKÁ
U NEMOCNICE
KATEŘINSKÁ
KE KARLOVU
Dvořák Museum
NA BOJIŠTI
I.P. Pavlova
LEGEROVA
PALECKÉHO NÁBŘEŽÍ
PALACKÝ SQUARE
NA SLUPI
Faust House
BENÁTSKÁ
U. Kalicha
St John on the Rock
PALECKÉHO MOST
POD SKALSKÁ
Emmaus Convent
P.O.
VINIČNÁ
Botanical Gardens
APOLINÁŘSKÁ
TROJICKÁ
To Police Museum

● Monument
---Ⓜ--- Metro line & Station

Prague, it was to begin with the main home of the city's craftsmen and poor, and was later to emerge as the commercial, administrative and social centre of Prague. The medieval street plan has been largely retained to this day, but rapid urban development from the late 19C onwards led to the pulling down of the fortifications in 1875, and the demolition of most of the surviving old houses to make way for large apartment blocks and imposing civic buildings. There are a number of medieval churches to be seen in the district, and numerous Baroque monuments; but the appeal of the New Town to the sightseer lies essentially in its great range of exciting monuments from the late 19C and early 20C.

Wenceslas Square

The heart of the New Town, and indeed the bustling centre of the whole city, is the Wenceslas Square (Václavské náměstí), a thoroughfare 60m wide and 750m long, which slopes down from the National Theatre to the long boulevards marking the boundary of the Old Town.

History of Wenceslas Square

Originally a place where horse markets were held, the Wenceslas Square was known as the Horse Market (Koňský trh) up to as late as 1848, when it acquired its present name. The principal thoroughfare of Prague, the square has also been since 1848 the stage of some of the key historic moments in Czech history. A national mass held here in 1848 heralded the revolutionary disturbances of that year, while in 1918 crowds gathered here to celebrate the downfall of the Habsburgs.

On 25 February 1948, a popular demonstration in support of the Communist Party of Czechoslovakia took place in the square, and on 16 January 1969 the student Jan Palach set fire to himself near here to draw world attention to the plight of the Czech people. The square also played a major role in the great events of November 1989, beginning on the 17th of that month, when a group of students, officially commemorating the 50th anniversary of a Czech student's murder by the Nazis, made their way here from Prague's second district, their numbers greatly swollen in the course of the journey. Greeted by riot police, they burst into chants of 'Freedom' and began singing the Czech version of 'We Shall Overcome', but the police reaction was brutal, and one person was killed and many more injured. This was to spark the whole country into action, and over the next few days crowds gathered in their thousands at the square, chanting 'Freedom', 'Resign' and 'Now is the time'; the statue of Wenceslas was papered with posters and protest leaflets, and in front of it flowers and candles were placed in commemoration of Jan Palach. To the utter disbelief of the crowd, on 24 November, Alexander Dubček, followed by Václav Havel, appeared on the balcony of the Socialist Publishing House to proclaim the imminent success of the 'Velvet Revolution'.

The present-day character and appearance of the Wenceslas Square belie its glorious history, the whole place having something of the tackiness and seediness of London's Leicester Square, or Berlin's Kurfürstendamm. Shopping-arcades, hotels, cinemas, cheap eating establishments and bars and nightclubs with a distinctly dated look surround the square, and at night the place teems with drunken tourists and other more sinister types; muggings have greatly increased here since the 'Revolution', and many Czechs now like to warn you of the dangers of the square late at night, though these dangers remain slight in comparison with those of many Western cities.

The balcony of the free word

It was to the balcony of the Melantrich House that Alexander Dubček and Václav Havel made their way from the nearby Magic Lantern building to address a vast protesting crowd in the Wenceslas Square on Friday 24 November 1989. One of those accompanying the two men was the English historian and writer Timothy Garton Ash , who gave a vivid account of this triumphant occasion in his short book, *We the People: The Revolution of '89* (1990): 'Protected by Havel's bodyguards ... we emerge from the belly of the Lantern, Dubček and Havel side by side, and scuttle through covered shopping arcades and tortuous back passages to reach the balcony of the Socialist Party publishing house and the offices of *Svobodné slovo*: the balcony of the free word. Along the arcades people simply gape. They can't believe it. Dubček! It is as if the ghost of Winston Churchill were to be seen striding down the Burlington Arcade ... But when he steps out on to the balcony in the frosty evening air, illuminated by television spotlights, the crowds give such a roar as I have never heard. "DUBČEK! DUBČEK!" echoes off the tall houses up and down the long, narrow square.'

National Museum

Tall buildings dating from the late 19C onwards line the whole length of this long thoroughfare and flank a central row of gardens which were laid out in the 1980s and lead up to the vast National Museum (Národní muzeum), a pompous neo-Renaissance structure rising on ramps at the very top of the square, and dominating the whole vista. **Open** Mon, Fri 09.00–16.00, Wed, Thur, Sat, Sun 09.00–17.00.

History of the National Museum

The National Museum was founded in 1818 by a group of Czech intellectuals headed by the botanist, geologist and palaeontologist Count Kašpar Šternberg and including Josef Dobrovský, the pioneer of modern Slavonic studies. Thanks largely to the particular interests of Šternberg, the emphasis of the collections was largely on science, but the museum was greatly broadened in its scope from the 1830s onwards, when it became the increasing focus of Czech cultural life and national endeavours; a very important role in developing the scope of the museum was played by the celebrated historian František Palacký, who became the museum's secretary in 1841, and envisaged a place which would reflect every aspect of his country. The involvement of the institution in nationalist political movements, culminating in the insurrections of 1848–49, inspired a growing hostility towards the place on the part of the Austrian authorities, yet the museum was soon to occupy one of the most prominent sites in Prague. The collections were housed at first in the refectory of the Minorite monastery attached to the Church of St James, but the demolition of the New Town fortifications in 1875 and the consequent removal of the Horse Gate led to a site becoming available at the top of the Wenceslas Square. The opportunity to use a site of such patriotic associations was immediately seized upon by the museum authorities, and in 1883–84 a competition was held for the design of the museum building to be erected here. The competition was won by Josef Schulz, and work on the structure was completed in 1890; its extensive sculptural embellishment involved most of the prominent academic sculptors of the day.

The main façade of the museum features a tall rusticated basement supporting a giant order of Corinthian columns, in the middle of which is a pedimented frontispiece crowned by a gilded dome. The sculptural decoration, like the architecture itself, is very conventional and includes, at the top of the double ramp which climbs up to the main entrance, a dull group by Anton Wagner representing Bohemia between the Rivers Labe and Vltava.

The principal component of the dauntingly large, red marbled interior is the Pantheon, a room decorated all over with ambitious historical and allegorical murals by Václav Brožík, František Ženíšek and Vojtěch Hynais; in the centre of the room are six statues and 42 busts—mainly executed between 1898 and 1901—of distinguished Czechs from the 14C onwards, the work of A. Popp. A. Procházka, J.V. Myslbek, M. Havlíček, B. Vlček, L. Šaloun, J. Štursa and K. Dvořák.

The National Museum's collections have now been shared out between various buildings throughout Prague, the ones on show in this building comprising those devoted to geology, archaeology, prehistory and coins and medals (all of which are to be found on the first floor), and to zoology and palaeontology (on the second floor). The display is gloomy and unimaginative, and the layman might well agree with the writer Stephen Brook's assessment (voiced in his book, *The Double Eagle*) that the main emotion which the museum inspires is a sense of awe at the sight 'of so many display cases exclusively devoted to the cockroach'.

Walking down the Wenceslas Square from the National Museum, the first monument you come to, in the middle of the thoroughfare, is the **St Wenceslas Monument**, the masterpiece of J.V. Myslbek and comprising an equestrian statue of Wenceslas surrounded by four other patron saints of Bohemia—SS Ludmilla, Procopius and Adalbert and the Blessed Agnes. Originally conceived in 1887, the work was to occupy much of Myslbek's life up to his death in 1922; in the course of the monument's long gestation, the artist's vision of the saint significantly changed, so that the initial romantic representation of a spiritual and temporal leader of the Slavic people became transformed into a sturdy, tightly modelled portrayal of a man embodying the power and authority of the Czech state.

The buildings at this end of the square are modern and of little architectural interest, and there is no longer even the gastronomical attraction of the once wonderfully well-stocked House of Food (at No. 59), which has now been turned into a giant McDonalds Further down the square on the right-hand side, at No. 45, is the Jalta Hotel, another building of the 1950s, this one exemplifying the drab uniformity of so much Czech architecture of this period.

On the opposite side of the square to the hotel begins a dark street, Ve Smečkách, where you will find at No. 6 one of the Czech Republic's better-known small theatres, the **Činoherní Klub**; emerging to prominence in the 1960s, this theatre has maintained its reputation through its long association with Jiří Menzel, who is best known outside the Czech Republic as a leading protagonist of Czech New Wave cinema.

The next street off the left-hand side of the square is **Štěpánská**, at the entrance to which is a corner building centred around a tall, imposing rotunda; this building, with entrances at No. 63 Štěpánská and at Nos 40/38 Václavské náměstí, was erected by Matěj Blecha in 1912–16, and was originally the headquarters of the Moravian Bank. Adjoining it on Štěpánská is the **Lucerna Palace**, an ugly block of 1907–10 featuring a gallery with shops, a cinema, and sleazy restaurants and, in the basement, a large hall used for concerts and dances; Václav Havel's grandfather, also called Václav, was one of its architects and owners, and the family later joined this establishment to their restaurant at Barrandov to form the lucrative Barrandov-Lucerna Enterprises. Continuing to walk down the Wenceslas Square, the next building on the left-hand side after the former Moravian Bank is the **Melantrich House** (No. 36), the headquarters of the Melantrich Publishing House and the editorial offices of the newspaper *Svobodné slovo* ('Free Word').

The adjoining building at No. 34 is a gabled structure in a Bohemian Renaissance style designed by A. Wiehl in 1896 and covered with restored sgraffito decorations by Mikoláš Aleš. Facing this, on the other side of the square (at No. 25/27) is a far more remarkable turn-of-the-century building, the **Grand Hotel Europa**. Built in 1903–06 by Bedřich Bendelmayer and Alois Dryák, it features a beautifully ornamented façade crowned by a large ceramic lunette; but its great joy is its perfectly preserved interior, above all that of its bar and restaurant, both boasting stained-glass windows and elegant panelling.

Further down on this same side, at No. 19, is a neo-Baroque building of 1895–96 now housing the Polish Cultural Centre but originally the Prague headquarters of the Trieste-based insurance company, **Assecurazioni generali**. This is famous as the place where the 24-year-old Franz Kafka began his first job, in October 1907; a medical certificate attesting to 'nervousness and cardiac excitability' allowed him to leave the company the following year, but he continued a career in insurance by joining in July 1908 the Workmen's Accident Insurance Institute, where he was to remain for the rest of his life.

Most of the square's remaining buildings of architectural interest are to be found on the left-hand side, beginning at No. 28, the Alfa Palace, a large Functionalist apartment block with shops and a cinema, designed by L. Kysela and J. Jarolím in the late 1920s and featuring shop-windows of Cubist inspiration. The adjoining Hotel Adria at No. 26 is housed in the oldest surviving building on the square, dating back to the late 18C; just below it, at No. 22, is a hotel of radically different character, the Hotel Juliš, a Functionalist work of 1931–32 by Pavel Janák. Further down, at No. 12, is the Peterka House, an Art Nouveau former bank built by Jan Kotěra between 1898 and 1910, when greatly under the influence of the Viennese architect Otto Wagner; the façade is adorned with stucco decorations by J. Pekárek and S. Sucharda. Below an Art Nouveau building at No. 8 is the recently restored **Báťa Department Store** at No. 6, which was built by Ludvík Kysela in 1926–28 for the visionary shoe-manufacturer Tomáš Báťa.

> ## Báta shoes
>
> The shoe empire of Tomáš Báta (1876–1932) was initiated in 1894 with the founding of a factory in the Moravian town of Zlín. After prospering with the provision of army boots during the First World War, Báta went on to become an internationally known name, with outlets all over Europe; by the time of his death in a plane crash in 1932, Báta was employing 16,000 people to produce 150,000 shoes a day. The success of the company went hand in hand with the founder's avant-garde approach to both shoe-manufacture and architecture. Not only did he turn Zlín into a model city for his workers, but he also commissioned the most revolutionary architects of his day to build stores that would display his goods with a startling modernity in keeping with the company's progressive spirit.

The Báta store on the Wenceslas Square, a Functionalist building of striking simplicity, comprises a reinforced concrete frame with minimum numbers of corridors in the sales areas, floor slab zones covered with translucent white glass (once used for advertising), and some of the earliest bands of continuous glazing uninterrupted by architectural supports to be seen in Europe. Restoration work carried out in 1990–92 removed later unattractive additions but also substituted the original tubular steel furniture and fittings with some half-hearted modern imitations; the place is at its best at night, when it is turned into a glowing apparition dominated by the neon sign promoting the name of Báta. The store's architect, Kysela, was also responsible for the adjoining and slightly fussier Lindt's House at No. 4, which was built two years earlier and was indeed one of the first examples of Functionalism in Prague.

Immediately north of here the square broadens to form a large pedestrian area featuring the Metro Station Můstek and extending into the adjacent boulevards of 28. října and Na příkopě. The last building on the right-hand side (at No. 1) is the **Koruna Palace**, a fine Art Nouveau structure by Antonín Pfeiffer of 1910–14 with a futuristic corner tower and decorative detailing which looks ahead to the Art Deco period.

The northern and eastern New Town

The southern façade of the Koruna Palace overlooks the busy pedestrian thoroughfare of **Na příkopě**, which is lined with banks, bookshops and department stores, including the British stores Marks & Spencer, Mothercare and Next. Turning into this boulevard from the Wenceslas Square you will pass immediately to your left, at No. 1, one of the better examples of recent architecture in Prague: built by Jan Šrámek and Alena Šrámková in 1974–83, it is crowned by a glass-and-steel gable incorporating the clock of the department store which once stood here. Also to your left, at No. 3, is the former Wiener Bankverein (now the Czech National Bank), which was built by Josef Zasche in 1906–08 and is faced with polished granite. Prague's oldest department store, known originally as Haas, is on the opposite side of the street at No. 4 and was built in a North Italian Renaissance style by the Viennese architect T. Hansen in 1869–71.

The oldest surviving building on the street, and one of the most elegant Baroque palaces in the New Town, is further down on the right-hand side at No.

10. This, the **Sylva-Taroucca Palace** (1743–51), was built for Prince Ottavio Piccolomini by K.I. Dientzenhofer with the assistance of A. Lurago, and is a pedimented structure with a rusticated basement and a main floor articulated by giant order pilasters; the attic is decorated with sculptures of mythological figures and vases by F.I. Platzer, who was also responsible for the putti and vases on the balustrade of the staircase inside. Despite the atmospheric potential of the setting, the Swedish-run café-restaurant that can now be found here (*Segafredo*) is disappointingly lacking in character. On the building at No. 14—the Česká obchodní banka (1930)—a bust and plaque by B. Neužil records the site of the house where the writer Bozena Němcová died in 1862. Facing this, across the narrow Panská, is the **Church of the Holy Rood** (sv. Kříže), a massively built neo-Classical structure designed by G. Fischer in 1816.

A short detour down Panská should be made to see Prague's latest attraction, the **Mucha Museum** at No. 7, which opened in 1998 in the late 19C Kaunický Palace.

Born in 1860 in the Moravian town of Ivancice, Mucha showed a prodigiously early talent for draughtsmanship that none the less failed to get him accepted into the Prague Academy of Fine Arts. Apprenticed later as a theatrical scene painter in Vienna, he stayed there until the burning down of the Ring Theatre in 1880, soon after which he attracted the attention of the Moravian landowner Count Khuen Belasi, who arranged for Mucha to continue his artistic training in Munich and then in Paris. Settling in Paris, he embarked on a varied artistic career that included oil painting, jewellery and furniture design. However, his popular reputation was established above all with his sinuously decorative poster designs, the fame of which was due initially to a chance commission from the actress Sarah Bernhardt, who therafter contracted him to produce posters for all her theatrical work. After Mucha's return to Bohemia in 1910 he devoted much of his energy to an epic cycle of patriotic canvases now displayed in the Moravian town of Moravské Krumlov. He died in 1939, at a time when his art nouveau whimsicality and over blown historicism must have seemed ridiculously old-fashioned.

Though Mucha's popular appeal has been almost continuous since his death (his richly decorative posters were indeed to have an especial resonance during the psychodelic 60s), his critical reputation declined considerably, and indeed only began to revive with a large retrospective of his work held in the Grand Palais in Paris in 1980.

Sadly the much-awaited Mucha Museum in Prague is unlikely to further any serious interest in his art: it is a souless institution that seems aimed essentially at promoting the ersatz art nouveau spirit currently sweeping through this city. Mucha lived in a world of decorative exuberance (one need only look at photographs of the still intact Mucha family home at No. 6 Hradcanské námestí to be aware of this); but the small suite of sparsely hung rooms constituting his museum gives barely any hint of such a world. Apart from a large collection of his much reproduced posters (the main reason for visiting the place), there are examples of his decorative designs, a handful of appalling oil paintings, a group of pastels and figurative drawings, and an empoverished attempt—with the aid of photographs and the artist's chair and easel—'to recreate some of the atmosphere of *fin de siècle* Paris and of Mucha's studio at Rue Val de Grace'. A significantly large amount of space is taken up by a shop selling Mucha-inspired merchandise. **Open** daily 10.00–18.00

The Slavonic House restaurant

In the early 1950s the restaurant of the Slavonic House became a great meeting-place for Spanish political exiles in Prague, thanks to its cook at that time, a Catalan exile called Josep Esquerré who learnt how to adapt Czech and Slovakian food to Spanish tastes. Teresa Pamiès, another exile from Catalonia, fondly remembered his cooking in her nostalgic book on Prague (1987): 'To please our particular (Spanish) palates he would cook succulent beans with pieces of pigs' ears, prepare stupendous rice dishes with Russian crab in place of Mediterranean sea-food, and make some memorable stews that would leave us bloated and fuel our aversion to Czech "knedlíky" (dumplings), potato soup ("bramboračka"), greasy goose with cherries, the ubiquitous bitter cauliflower known as "kyselé" and the equally ubiquitous "párky", grilled sausages that were sold in the street ... as soon as Autumn came.'

Continuing northeast down Na příkopě, you will pass at No. 18 the former Provincial Bank (now the headquarters of Čedok), an Art Nouveau building of 1911–12 by O. Polívka, attractively decorated on the outside with mosaics by J. Preisler and sculptures by C. Klouček and L. Šaloun. The same architect and sculptors collaborated on the adjoining former Savings Bank (No. 20; now the Živnostenská), a building of 1894–96 in a Czech Renaissance style and incorporating a Baroque portal from a palace of 1757; the entrance vestibule is covered with wall-paintings of 1896 by Max Švabinský. The late 18C palace at No. 22 was converted in 1945 into the **Slavonic House** (Dům Slovanský), a cultural centre with a restaurant that would soon become a gastronomic Mecca to the city's Spanish community.

Next to the Slavonic House, at No. 24, is the Czech State Bank, which was put up in 1929–38 on a site that was occupied in the 19C by two hotels, *At the Blue Star* and *At the Black Horse*; a number of distinguished people were guests at these hotels, including the Russian anarchist Mikhail Bakunin, and the composers Chopin (to whom there is a plaque) and Liszt. Across the street, in a site now occupied by the grim 1930s administrative building at No. 33, there once stood Prague's most elegant café, the *Café Français*, where Liszt was frequently to be seen.

Na příkopě comes to an end at the Powder Gate and the náměstí Republiky (see p 80), where you should turn right into **Hybernská**, a narrow but busy street of 18C and 19C buildings, many in a decrepit condition, and others covered permanently in scaffolding. The first building to your right, at No. 20, was formerly a hotel where Tchaikovsky stayed in 1888 when he came to conduct the Prague première of his opera *Eugene Onegin*. Further down on the right-hand side, at No. 10, is the former and newly restored **Hotel Central** (now a theatre), a narrow-fronted but lavishly ornamented Art Nouveau structure built by F. Ohmann, B. Bendelmayer and A. Dryák in 1899–1902.

On the other side of the street the late 18C Sweerts-Špork Palace (at Nos 3/5) is followed by the beautiful and recently restored **Kinský Palace**, which was designed by Carlo Lurago after 1651 and given a new façade at the end of the 18C. This building, which until recently housed a Lenin Museum, played an important part in the history of the Czech Communist Party, and was the scene in 1912 of the 16th All-Russian Conference of the Social-Democratic Party of Russia (the so-called Prague Conference), chaired by V.I. Lenin. In 1920, after the building had been forcibly occupied by right-wing leaders of the Social-Democratic Party, the left-wing leadership of the party declared a general strike, during which there were violent clashes between workers and police on Hybernská; this conflict led to the formation in 1921 of the Communist Party of Czechoslovakia.

Further down the street Hybernská reaches an intersection formed by Havlíčkova to the north and Diážděná to the south; at No. 15 on the corner of Hybernská and Dlážděná is the **Café Arco**, latterly a down-market and unremarkable-looking establishment (and currently closed), but at one time one of Prague's famed literary meeting-places, and with an elegant interior designed by Jan Kotěra and decorated with paintings by Kysela.

Café Arco

The *Café Arco* on Hybernská came into being at the end of the 19C when the headwaiter of a staid café bearing the same name but in a far more fashionable part of town quarrelled with his employer and spitefully opened his own *Café Arco* in the rather less salubrious neighbourhood of Prague Central Railway Station. This new establishment, which was to reach the height of its notoriety in the years immediately preceding the First World War, soon attracted most of Prague's artistic and literary élite. Its regulars, who came to be known as the 'Arconauts', included a large proportion of German-Jewish writers, most notably Franz Werfel, Max Brod, Franz Kafka and Egon Erwin Kisch. The writer Karl Kraus, believing that this Jewish group at the Café Arco represented a cabal which besmirched the purity of the German language, penned a violent attack on the café, writing of the place the untranslatable line: 'Es werfelt und brodet und kafkat und kischt'.

The **Masaryck Railway Station** (Nádraží Praha-střed), at the corner of Hybernská and Havlíčkova, was Prague's first railway station, and was opened on 20 August 1845. The building, which has a main hall covered with an interesting roof in iron, wood and glass, is in a most depressing condition and attracts numerous loiterers of seedy and sinister appearance. Walk to the northern end of Havlíčkova, and turn right into Na poříčí, where you will find immediately to your right at No. 24 the former **Legio Bank** (now the Ministry of Consumer Goods), an extraordinary structure of Cubist inspiration built by Josef Gočár in 1922–25. In this highly sculptural building, featuring a heavy, projecting attic and a giant order of cubic columns crossed by deeply cut bands, Gočár enjoyed a most successful collaboration with the sculptors Jan Štursa and Otto Gutfreund; above the shop-front Jan Štursa placed four enormous consoles of workers (1922–23) to support a long frieze by Gutfreund (*The Return of the Legionaries*, 1921), a work of great stateliness and power which is considered by many to be one of the key landmarks in 20C Czech sculpture.

Further along the street, at No. 40, is the Hotel Axa, a fine Constructivist building of 1935 by V. Pilec. Just before the hotel, you should cross the street and head north along the short Biskupská, which was where the Merchants' Court of Poříčí's German community was situated up to 1235. At the end of the street is the late Gothic tower belonging to the former German church of **St Peter na Poříčí**. This building, just to the north of the tower, is a triple-aisled structure which dates back to the mid-12C and was originally the parish church of the German Poříčí district; in 1235 the church and surrounding area fell into the hands of the Knights of the Cross. Fragments of the original Romanesque church survive in the west façade and south wall of the main nave, but the rest of the building was much altered over the centuries, and was subject to neo-Gothic remodelling by Josef Mocker in the 1870s.

Running behind the church is Petrská: walking west along this street you will come to the small Petrské náměstí, off which runs Soukenická. There you will find on the house at No. 13 a plaque marking the site of the birthplace of the topographical artist Wenceslas Hollar, who is best known for his views of London, where he died in 1677. Walking instead east along Petrská and then taking the first turning to the right you will rejoin Na poříčí at the point where it disappears under the large flyover which marks Wilsonova, the eastern boundary of the New Town.

On the other side of the flyover is the tiny and unpromisingly situated **Šverma Park** (Švermovy sady), which was founded in 1875 on the site of the recently demolished New Town fortifications. On this park's southern side, adjoining today a noisy area occupied by tacky market stalls, stands a grand neo-Renaissance structure built by A. Balšánek in 1896–98 to house the newly formed **Museum of the City of Prague** (Muzeum hlavní města Prahy). On the ground floor of this slightly run-down museum is a fine display of artefacts and works of art from the 6C onwards relating to the early history of Prague, and including Slavonic pots, fragments of 13C frescoes, old Bohemian glass, and Renaissance and Baroque furnish-ings; the second floor, at present being rearranged to take in recent developments in the city's history, is reached by a grand oval staircase and features an enormous plaster model of Prague made by Antonín Langweil between 1826 and 1834. **Open** Tues–Sun 10.00–18.00.

Only a short distance south of the museum along the Wilsonova is the magnif-icent Art Nouveau **Central Station** (Hlavní nádraží), but the journey is complicated on foot and best undertaken by taking the metro from the Florenc station on Sokolovská (directly in front of the museum) to the following stop, Hlavní nádraží. The metro will take you to the station's modern extension, which dates from the 1970s and is built underneath the Wilsonova února and the narrow Vrchlického Park to the west. The original station (once called the Franz Josef Station) stands

Central Station, by Josef Fanta

above the eastern side of the wide Wilsonova, and was built by Josef Fanta between 1901 and 1909; its most exciting feature is its twin-towered façade, featuring an ironwork central canopy and large-scale carvings of nudes and other allegorical figures by S. Sucharda, H. Folkmann and Č. Vosmík.

Further south along the Wilsonova in the direction of the nearby National Museum are the reconstructed late 19C Smetana Theatre (originally the main German theatre in Prague), today the State Opera, and the modern glass building of the **Federal Assembly**. At the southwestern corner of the Vrchlického Park is another of the old luxury hotels of Prague, the Hotel Esplanade (with a neo-Baroque gilded interior), while directly across the park from the Central Station begins Jeruzalémská. Walking down the latter street, you will pass at No. 5 to your right the Jubilee Synagogue, a neo-Moorish building of 1906 with a vividly coloured façade.

At the end of the street turn left on to Jindřiská, where you will find to your left the **Church of St Henry** (sv. Jindřicha), which was founded in 1350 but much altered in later periods and given a neo-Gothic exterior by Josef Mocker in 1879; Mocker was also responsible for the neo-Gothic remodelling of the late 15C **belfry tower** on the other side of the street. Continuing to walk down Jindřišská you will soon reach its intersection with Panská and Politických vezňů. At the corner of Panská is the Palace Hotel, a lavishly refurbished hotel dating back to the turn of the century; on Politických vězňů meanwhile, you will find at No. 20 the notorious Petschek Palace, a neo-Renaissance building of 1923–25 which served as the Gestapo headquarters during the last war, and was the place where numerous Czechs, including Julius Fučík, were tortured and executed. At the end of Jindřišská you will come back to the lower end of the Wenceslas Square.

The southern and western New Town

You can begin a tour of the southern half of the New Town from the northern end of Wenceslas Square, where you should turn left into the quiet **Jungmann Square** (Jungmannovo náměstí), which runs parallel to the pedestrian thoroughfare of 28. října. The square epitomises the city's architectural richness, featuring as it does the back façade of the pioneering Bátă Building (see above), a gabled late 14C Gothic gateway, and—as its centrepiece—a beautiful and highly eccentric **Cubist lamp-post** of 1913; this last monument, though recently re-attributed to the minor architect Emil Králíček (it was previously thought to be by the much better known Vratislav Hofman), is a work of great originality anticipating by many years Brancusi's *Endless Column*. The Gothic gateway, at the square's southeastern corner, opens out on to a courtyard leading to the former **Carmelite Church of Our Lady of the Snows** (Panny Marie Sněžné).

History of the church

Founded by Charles IV in 1347 on the occasion of his coronation as King of Bohemia, the church of St Mary of the Snows was intended as a vast triple-aisled structure which would have extended right into the present Jungmann Square. However, work on the building was interrupted during the Hussite wars, in which this church played an important role. The radical Hussite speaker Jan Želivský preached here between 1419 and 1422, and it was from here that on 30 July 1419 a procession set out to the

New Town Hall to carry out the 'First Defenestration' in Prague. Želivský was buried in the church in 1422, but the building was later left to decay and its steeple demolished. The abandoned church and convent came in 1603 into the hands of the Franciscans, who embarked on a campaign of restoration and rebuilding.

On entering the church you are immediately struck by its great height and size, though in fact what you are seeing constitutes only the chancel of the triple-aisled structure which was originally conceived. The furnishings are Baroque, but the building has otherwise a completely Gothic look despite the fact that the net-vaulting and much of the masonry dates back only to the time of the Franciscan restoration. The former monastery gardens on the south side of the building were relaid in the 1950s and form today a pleasant public park, shaded by trees.

At its western end the Jungmann Square leads to the busy junction of 28. října, Jungmannova třída and Národní třída. The white corner building at the end of 28. října, at No. 1, is a fine Functionalist department store of 1927–31, while at No. 30 Jungmannova třída (almost immediately to your left on reaching the street from the square) is one of the earliest Modernist buildings in Prague, the **Urbánek House** (1912–13). The latter, with its large triangular gable and grid of brickwork squares encased within a deep rectangular frame, is a structure of great geometrical

Cubist lamp-post in Jungmann Square

purity that reveals the architect J. Kotěra's debt to his master Otto Wagner. Built for the music and arts publisher Mojmír Urbánek, it was intended to house apartments, offices, a small concert hall (the Mozarteum) and, on the ground floor (flanked by caryatid figures by Jan Štursa), an art gallery. This gallery, the Havel Gallery, was an important if brief-lived centre of the avant-garde, and organised as its inaugural show an exhibition of Futurist art that divided the Prague Cubists.

The corner of Jungmannova třída and Národní třída is taken up by the bizarre and colossal **Adria Palace**, a heavily ornamented structure built by Pavel Janák and Josef Zasch in 1923–25 and featuring an attic level made up of square, crenellated towers that give the whole building the look of some futuristic urban fortress; the sculptural decoration on the façades was carried out by J. Štursa, Otto Gutfreund and K. Dvořák. This fantastical building appropriately hosted for many years the theatrical spectacle known as the Magic Lantern, which has recently transferred to a specially built venue next to the National Theatre (see below). Performances of the Magic Lantern were still taking place here in November 1989, when its theatre became the meeting-place of the newly formed Civic Forum, which in a matter of days succeeded in ousting the Communist Government of Czechoslovakia and hoisting Havel to the presidency of the country.

The Magic Lantern

The critical discussions that took place in the Magic Lantern were held not only in the dressing and smoking rooms but also on the stage, against the absurd background of a set for a production of the *Minotaurus*. The only foreigner present for most of the meetings was the Englishman Timothy Garton Ash, who wrote that for nearly two weeks he was 'privileged to watch history being made inside the Magic Lantern'. His short book, *We The People: The Revolution of '89* (1990), includes a long and vivid account of these days, days when 'in a sense, all of Prague became a Magic Lantern'.

Národní třída (National Street) is Prague's most important street; it is vibrant with cars and people, and lined its whole length with department stores and monumental civic buildings. As you walk down it in the direction of the Vltava the first major building which you will pass to your right is the **Platýs House** at No. 37, which was rebuilt and enlarged by Henri Hausknecht after 1813 and turned into the first tenement building in Prague; the main wing contains a hall where concerts were once held, one of the musicians who performed here being Franz Liszt in 1840 and 1846 (a marble bust of the composer has been placed on the building's back entrance). On the other side of the street, at No. 26 (at the junction with Spálená), is Prague's main department store, former Máj (now Tesco's), a light structure in glass and aluminium built in the 1970s by the Liberec architectural firm SIAL 02.

A short detour down Spálená can be made to see the first Constructivist building in Prague, the former **Olympic Department Store**, which is situated on the left-hand side of the street, at No. 16. This eight-storey reinforced concrete structure, with elements derived from transatlantic steamers, was built in 1923–27 by Jaromír Krejcar, who married shortly afterwards the journalist and former mistress of Kafka, Milena Jesenská; the building houses today one of the most interesting of Prague's small theatres, the Studio Ypsilon.

Back on the Národní třída and continuing west, you could cast a nostalgic glance towards the other side of this street where, at No. 29 at the junction with Spálená's northern continuation, Na Perštýně, there stood until 1950 one of Prague's most celebrated artistic and literary cafés of old, the *Café Union*: situated in a late 18C palace (pulled down in 1950 to make way for the Albatross Publishing House), this experienced its heyday in the first two decades of the 20C, when its series of small interconnected rooms were individually appropriated by the city's various literary and intellectual coteries, such as T.G. Masaryk and his university colleagues, Hašek and his Bohemian friends, and all the leading Czech Cubists from Janák to Kubista (who were able to benefit from the café's large collection of specialist art books and magazines).

Continuing to walk west, you will pass almost immediately on the left-hand side at No. 20 the **Reduta**, a famous and tourist-loved jazz club, which has photographs and a bronze plaque recording its most recent moment of glory: the visit in 1994 of President Clinton, who played his saxophone here. The novelist and jazz enthusiast Josef Škvorecký, who was present at this historical occasion, remembered less the details of the president's performance than his own general happiness at being there, 'with the president of a great democracy that I had always sworn by, and the Czech president, surrounded by jazzmen, who had triumphed so magnificently over forty years of an obscurantism that had once even tried to ban the saxaphone.'

Just after crossing Voršiliská you will come to the late 17C former **Convent church of St Ursula** (sv. Voršily), which was designed by Marcantonio Canevale. Facing this on the other side of the Národní třída are two remarkable and adjoining Art Nouveau buildings, both designed by Osvald Polívka. The first of these, at No. 9, is the former Topic Publishing House (1910), a richly stuccoed building which is now used by the Union of Czech Writers; the second building, at No. 7, is the former headquarters of the Praha Assurance (1905–07) and, though a less decorative structure than its neighbour, has superlative reliefs on its façade by Ladislav Šaloun. Much of the remaining right-hand side of the street is taken up by the Czech Academy of Sciences (at Nos 5 and 3), a grimly impressive neo-Renaissance structure built by V.I. Ullmann in 1858–61 as the headquarters of a bank. The last building on the right, at No. 1, is the recently reopened **Café Slavia**, a popular tourist haunt which is also one of the oldest of Prague's surviving literary cafés.

Café Slavia

The German poet Rainer Maria Rilke was one of the many artists and writers who frequented the *Café Slavia* in the early years of the 20C, and he used the place as the setting of his evocative short stories, *Tales of Prague*. A later habitué was the poet Jaroslav Seifert, who was one of the stalwarts of Prague's coffee-house culture from the 1920s right up to the 1960s; he evoked the place in his *Slavia Poems*, in which he dreamt up imaginary encounters with the likes of Apollinaire. Another, more recent writer to feature the café in his works is Michal Ajvaz (born 1949), whose short story, *The Past* (1991) opens with the words, 'I'm sitting at the Slavia, people-watching.'

Since the 1960s the place has held regular jazz concerts, which used to attract many of the city's political dissidents, including Václav Havel, who protested vigrously when the café closed down in 1991 for restoration that was endlessly protracted as a result of a leasing dispute between a group of Boston investors and the next-door film-school. When the latter eventually won, and the café re-opened in January 1998, Havel was reported in the world press as saying that a national institution had been saved.

The two end buildings on the left-hand side of the street are the **New National Theatre** (Nová scéna) at No. 4 and the National Theatre at No. 2. The former, one of the boldest and most distinguished examples of recent Czech architecture, is arranged around a small square and comprises three shaped blocks coated in glass, the one facing the street resembling a translucent honeycomb; the complex was built in 1977–83 by Karel Prager. The building is used almost exclusively for drama productions organised by the National Theatre Company, the present director of which is Otomar Krejča, who achieved international fame as an actor and director in the 1960s, when he ran The Theatre Beyond the

The Magic Lantern ~ a history

The Magic Lantern was created for the Brussels World Exhibition of 1958 by Alfréd Radok, who, together with the brilliant stage designer Josef Svoboda and up-and-coming talents such as the film director Miloš Forman, devised a brilliant illusionistic spectacle involving stage-sets, actors and film. Such was its success in Brussels, where it did much to draw world attention to the cultural life of Czechoslovakia, that it was decided afterwards to turn it into a permanent cultural institution in Prague. However, Radok and his collaborators were soon to fall victims to the political situation of the time, and were ousted and replaced by lesser talents.

The Magic Lantern has survived to this day as an anodine and at times embarassingly bad tourist attraction booked up weeks in advance by large groups, and virtually impossible to get into on your own without recourse to bribery at the door. That it should now be so prominently placed next to the National Theatre is truly a national disgrace.

Gate (Divadlo Za Branou). The southern block has now been taken over by the Magic Lantern.

National Theatre

As a result of recent privatisation Prague opera is now divided between the more innovative State Opera and the National Opera, the latter having as its premises the superb National Theatre (Národní divadlo), one of the great landmarks of Prague and by far the most eloquent architectural expression of Czech nationalist aspirations in the late 19C.

History of the National Theatre

In 1845 a group of prominent Czech patriots, including František Palacký Josef Jungmann, Josef Kajetán Tyl and Jan Evagelista Purkyně, sent a petition to the Emperor Ferdinand V asking for permission to build an independent Czech theatre in Prague. The proposal was also supported by the writers Jan Neruda, Vítězslav Hálek and Karel Havlíček Borovský, the latter making the practical suggestion that the money for the building should be raised through voluntary contributions. A fund-raising campaign with the slogan 'the Nation for Itself' was subsequently begun, but it was not until 1868 that the foundation stone of the building was laid. The architect chosen was Josef Zítek, who was supervising the final details of his work in 1881 when a fire broke out, destroying the auditorium and much of the building's decorations. Within the remarkably short space of six weeks enough money had been raised to rebuild the theatre, a task which was given to Josef Schulz. The theatre was finally opened on 18 November 1883 with a production of Bedřich Smetana's opera Libuše.

The painters and sculptors involved in the decoration of the building include almost all the leading Czech artists of the late 19C, a generation which is in fact referred to as 'The Generation of the National Theatre'; among these artists were the sculptors J.V. Mylsbek, Bohuslav Schnirch and Anton Wagner, and the painters Mikoláš Aleš, Václav Brožík, Vojtěch

Hynais, Josef Tulka and František Ženíšek. In 1977–83 the building was extensively restored by Karel Prager, and can be appreciated today at its resplendent best.

The grand exterior of the building, which has echoes of the Vienna Opera House and rather more distant ones of Renaissance Italy, is crowned by a Palladian-style roof highlighted by gilding. Some of the finest **statuary** of the main façade is concentrated on the attic level where there is a row of statues of Apollo and the Muses by B. Schnirch, who also modelled the flanking bronze chariot groups; on the side façade overlooking the Masaryk Embankment is a portal decorated with reclining figures of Opera and Drama by J.V. Myslbek.

A bronze figure by Myslbek representing Music presides over the profusely embellished main foyer, where can be seen allegorical ceiling paintings by Ženíšek, fourteen lunette paintings by M. Aleš of scenes from Smetana's symphonic poem, *My Country* (*Má Vlast*) and a gallery of bronze busts by different artists of the leading figures in the history of Czech theatre and opera. Of the many other decorations in the building special mention must be made of the works of Vojtěch Hynais. He decorated the stairs leading up to the presidential box with a painted allegorical frieze, painted vivid representations of the Four Seasons for the ladies' boudoir of the presidential box (note in particular the female figure floating over a snow-covered landscape), and provided the stage with its superlative and celebrated **back-cloth**; the latter, portraying the unpromising theme of *The Origin of the National Theatre*, is full of references to Raphael and Renaissance painting and yet is saved from the absurder excesses of academic art through the sheer energy of the composition and execution.

The Národní třída comes to an end by the Vltava river, where you should head south down the **Masaryk Embankment** passing alongside the **Slavonic Island** (Slovanský ostrov). This island, formed by alluvial deposits in the 18C, was strengthened by container walls in 1784, and partially built upon. In 1830 a restaurant was erected in its southern half, and this soon became one of the main centres of Prague's social and political life. Concerts were held in the building—including ones given by H. Berlioz and F. Liszt—and in 1848 the place hosted the inaugural session of the Slavonic Congress. Memorial plaques commemorating both this congress and the distinguished Slovak writer Ludovít Štúr, one of its participants, are to be seen on the walls of the present restaurant, which was built in 1884 and is now the home of the National Folk Song and Dance Company. The rest of the island is taken up by a wooded public park laid out in 1931 and containing at its northern end a bronze memorial by K. Pokorný to the writer Božena Němcová.

Straddling the narrow stretch of water between the island and the southern end of the Masaryk Embankment is the **Mánes Gallery**, the seat of the Mánes Society of Artists, which was founded in 1898 in opposition to the Czech Academy of Arts. Their present headquarters, a simple, white Functionalist building erected by Otakar Novotný in 1923–25, is curiously but picturesquely linked to a Renaissance water tower which once formed part of the Sitka Mills; the gallery puts on exhibitions by contemporary artists.

The Mánes Gallery is a favourite building of Václav Havel, despite the one-time presence there of agents from the Czech Secret Service, who used to spy on him from the top of its water tower when he was living at No. 78 Rašínovo nábřeží, immediately to the south of the Masaryck embankment. His riverside apartment there, designed by his grandfather, adjoins today a controversial new building that has proved especially popular with the city's foreign tourists. Popularly known as the '**Fred and Ginger**', on account of its vague resemblance to a dancing couple, this was built in 1993–94 by the American architect Frank Gehry, currently at the height of his international fame following the opening in 1997 of his Guggenheim Museum in Bilbao. Although this gloriously topsy-turvy, inebriated-looking structure is intentionally at variance with its sombre neighbouring buildings, it seems perfectly in tune with the more expressionistic and fantastical side to the Central European spirit. The interior, sadly, is rather less interesting than the exterior, and is partly occupied by the singularly unfriendly French-run café and restaurant pretentiously calling itself *La Perle de Prague*. The restaurant, on the top floor, is none the less worth a visit simply to climb out on to its terrace, which enjoys perhaps the most overwhelmingly beautiful views in the whole city; there are occasional group visits to the building for those who do not want either to eat here or try and gain entry through their powers of persuasion (a largely futile task).

Retrace your steps towards the Mánes Gallery and then head east down Myslíkova, turning off on to the third street to the left, Křemencova, to visit at No. 11 on the left-hand side Prague's most famous beer-cellar, **U Fleků**.

History of U Fleků

The origins of U Fleků go back to at least 1499 when the brewer Vít Skřemenec acquired the house which stood on the site of the present building and founded the beer-cellar and small brewery which came to be known for the next 250 years as *Na Skřemenici* (hence the name of the street). The name *U Fleků* dates back to after 1762, when the establishment was bought by the Flekovsky family from Počenice, who, during the short time that they owned the place, became celebrated throughout Prague for the quality of their beer. The present neo-Gothic appearance of the interior is due to renovations carried out in 1898–1905, under the direction of the architect F. Sander; the pseudo-medieval wall-paintings were the work of L. Novák. The newly restored ale-house soon became a popular literary haunt, and for years afterwards there would always be a section reserved for writers.

In the early years of the 20C the place served as the meeting-place for the literary club known as Syrinx,

Prague's most famous beer cellar, U Fleků

whose members included a number of future leading Czech writers and dramatists, including K.H. Hilar (later to become director of the Prague National Theatre under the Republic), the poet Opočensky, the playwright Jiří Mahen, and Rudolf Těsnohlídek, who wote the story of Janáček's opera, *The Cunning Little Vixen*. Another of its members, then experiencing his first taste of Bohemian life, was the future author of the *Good Soldier Švejk*, Jaroslav Hašek, who doubtless enjoyed the rowdiness of many of their meetings, the tone of which can be judged from what one of its sculptor members once told him: 'Come here, you hairy bastard, and let me tear all those lice off you!' Later the club changed its allegiance to the St Thomas' Tavern in the Little Quarter, but Hašek himself was soon to tire of the group, finding it not too silly but too intellectual, and having no interest in its occasional serious discussions about 'modern art'.

A picturesque old clock, hung like a tavern sign, marks the entrance to U Fleků, which has a number of attractively panelled rooms, with wooden tables, and neo-Gothic vaulting; the dark beer which they make and serve here is excellent. Unfortunately, however, the place today has mainly been taken over by loud-mouthed carousing tourists, and this is not an establishment where many Czechs would be proud to be seen.

Returning to Myslíkova turn left until you reach the lower end of Spálená, where, on turning left again, you will find shortly on the right-hand side the wonderful Cubist corner building known as the **Diamond House** (Diamant), which was built in 1910–12 by Ladislav Skřivánek and Matěj Blecha; an amusing feature is the Cubist arch (designed perhaps by Antonín Pfeiffer) which joins the building to the neighbouring 18C Church of the Holy Trinity and frames a statue of St John of Nepomuk by M.J. Brokoff (1717).

Retracing your footsteps and heading south down Spálená you will soon reach the northern end of the long **Charles Square** (Karlovo naměstí), a square which is even larger than that of Wenceslas, but with a much more sober and less energetic character. Originally Prague's biggest market square, and known as the Cattle Market until 1848, it was transformed in the middle of the 19C into a wooded public park, complete with statues to famous Czechs such as the poet Vítězslav Hálek and the botanist Benedikt Roezl; the buildings that surround the park are set back from it by wide and busy streets and have largely a stately but unremarkable 19C character.

The main building at the square's northern end is the **New Town Hall** (Novoměstská radnice), which dates back to 1367 but has kept little of its medieval structure apart from the tower of 1425–26, the cellars and the double-aisled entrance hall (now used for marriages); the gabled façade overlooking the square is a reconstruction of 1905 of the building as it appeared in the 16C. The town hall is famous as the place where on 30 July 1419 an irate mob led by the reformist preacher J. Želivský were greeted by stones as they stood outside demanding the release of certain reformist prisoners; in anger they stormed the building, and flung the mayor and several of his councillors out of the window and onto the square, where they were torn limb from limb, thus sparking off the Hussite revolution and inaugurating a long Czech tradition of 'defenestration'.

Adjacent to the Town Hall, on the northeastern corner of the square at No.

24, is the late 18C **Salm House**, which marks the site of a Renaissance home (of which the portal has survived) owned in the early 18C by the leading Baroque sculptor Matthias Braun, who died here in 1738.

Cross over to the western side of the square and walk half-way down it to **Resslova**, where you turn right, heading back in the direction of the river. On the right-hand side of the street at No. 9 is a former priest's home designed in 1736 by K.I. Dientzenhofer, who was also responsible for the adjoining **Church of SS Cyril and Methodius** (sv. Cyrila a Metoděje) to which this institution was attached. This impressive church, built in 1730–36 and originally dedicated to St Charles Borromeo, is a tightly-composed structure with symmetrically treated pedimented façades and a powerful entablature tying the whole building together; the interior is stuccoed by M.I. Palliardi and decorated with frescoes by K. Schöpf depicting the life of St Charles Borromeo. In 1942 the parachutists responsible for the assassination of the German Protector of Bohemia R. Heydrich, took refuge in the church's crypt but were killed here while making a last stand against the Nazis. Crypt **open** Mon–Sat 09.00–11.00.

Further down the street, on the left-hand side, is the **Church of St Wenceslas** (sv. Václava), which was founded in 1170 but rebuilt at the end of the 14C, during the reign of King Wenceslas IV. The building has been much altered over the centuries though fragments of the medieval masonry are to be seen in the façade, and there survives inside a late Gothic vault of 1586–87; the distinguished Art Nouveau sculptor F. Bílek executed the pews and the altar of the *Crucifixion* (1930).

At the end of the street head south down the Rašínovo nábřeží until you come to the **Palacký Square** (Palackého náměstí). The late 19C **Palacký Bridge**, which spans the river at this point, was once crowned at its corners by large and imposing sculptural groups by J.V. Myslbek representing mythical figures from Prague's early history, but these were transferred in 1945 to the park at Vyšehrad. Their absence is amply compensated for by the presence in the middle of the square of the **Palacký Monument**, one of the most exciting examples of public statuary in Prague, and the masterpiece of Stanislav Sucharda, assisted by the architect Alois Dryák. As with the near contemporary Hus Monument in the Old Town Square, its gestation was a long one, being first planned in 1898 and not unveiled until 1912, by which time it was to seem rather dated and its outstanding qualities not fully appreciated; a romantic and deeply poetic work, it shows an ingenious use of different materials, the real world—including the heavy, seated figure of Palacký himself—being depicted in stone, the allegorical one in bronze, the whole composition culminating in a magnificent, asymmetrically placed bronze group soaring up above the central stone plinth.

From the square head east up Na Moráni, which will bring you back to the Charles Square, at its lower end. The southern side of the square is taken up by a hospital wing of the Charles University, the large building at its western corner being romantically known as the **Faust House**. This late 18C structure marks the site of a house where Edward Kelley—the English adventurer at the court of Rudolph II—carried out his alchemical experiments in the hope of producing gold; later alchemists also worked here, and in the 18C, when a chemist occupied the building, the legend was born that the imaginary Doctor Faust had been another of its occupants until he was carried off through its laboratory ceiling after having sold his soul to the devil. Whether out of a sense of humour or in respect of the building's tradition, the Medical Faculty of Charles University has installed here its own pharmacy.

Walking south from the Faust House down **Vyšehradská** you will soon see, picturesquely rising above a great double-ramp staircase on the left-hand side of the street, the **Church of St John on the Rock** (sv. Jana Na skalce), which was built between 1729 and 1739 and is one of the more remarkable buildings by K.I. Dientzenhofer. Extracting the maximum dramatic potential from the restricted site, the architect canted the twin towers of the west façade to create a powerful sense of movement which is continued in the interior, the nave of which comprises an octagon with concave sides. Floating above the white walls inside are ceiling frescoes by K. Kovář depicting the *Glorification of St John of Nepomuk* (1745), while on the high altar has been placed a wooden statue of the saint by J. Brokoff (1682), a work which served as the model for the bronze of this subject on the Charles Bridge.

On the other side of the street to the church is the former Na Slovanech Monastery (popularly known as the **Emmaus Monastery**), which was founded by Charles IV in 1347 for the Croatian Benedictines. Extensively remodelled and rebuilt during the 18C and 19C, the whole complex was heavily damaged by bombing in 1945, and thereafter restored for the use of the Czechoslovak Academy of Sciences. The finest medieval survival, though heavily restored after 1960, are the frescoes of 1370–75 preserved in the vaulted monastery cloister and representing scenes from the Old and New Testaments; these were the work of three painters, M. Wurmser, Master Osvald and the painter known as the Master of the Emmaus Cycle. The Gothic walls of the monastery church now support a daring but very elegant modern superstructure built by František Černý in 1965–68 and comprising two interlaced sail-like forms soaring up into the sky.

The southern continuation of Vyšehradská, Na slupi, skirts the **University Botanical Garden** (Botanická zahrada; open Apr–Aug daily 10.00–18.00, Sept–Oct and Jan–Mar 10.00–17.00, Nov, Dec 10.00–16.00) and passes to the left, as it nears the Vyšehrad Hill, the **Church of Our Lady Na Slupi** (Panna Maria na Slupi), a building of late 14C origin which was restored by Bern Grueber in 1858–63; a notable feature of the interior is the way the 15C vault is supported by a single pillar. Immediately south of the church turn left into Horská and head east until you reach the large monastic complex known simply as the **Karlov**. This former Augustinian monastery was founded by Charles IV in 1351 and has a most exciting church, the nave of which is octagonal in emulation of Charlemagne's burial chapel at Aachen.

The church was completed in 1377, but its nave was covered by Bonifác Wohlmut in 1575 with an astonishingly bold star-shaped vault. The furnishings and other elements of the building are additions of the Baroque period, including the steep triple-flighted staircase which leads up to the Chapel of the Holy Steps on the southern side of the church; this Scala Santa, up which pilgrims are meant to climb on their knees, was built in 1708–09 and is often attributed to Santini-Aichel.

A visit to the church is completed by descending into the crypt, where you will be surprised and delighted to find yourself in an early 18C grotto imitating the cave in Bethlehem where Christ was born; the walls are covered with pastel-coloured stucco decorations by R. Beier, representing Classical buildings and giving you the impression that you have taken a wrong turning and stumbled from the Holy Land into Arcadia. **Open** Sun 14.00–17.15.

The fantasy of the whole experience will soon disappear as you walk from the church to the adjoining monastic buildings (dating from the late 17C), for you will find here a museum dedicated to the now not very fascinating subject of the Czech Police Force: the **Police Museum**, dating back to the 1970s, but completely changed since 1989, is today full of displays relating not to 'spies and agents' but to such pedestrian topics as traffic offences and crime prevention. What has happened, you might wistfully ask, to the place's most popular exhibit of old—the stuffed carcass of Brek (an Alsatian hound famous for capturing an exceptionally large number of fugitives trying to escape from Communist Czechoslovakia)? 'Ne Brek', the attendant replies with a sad shake of the head. **Open** Tues–Sun 10.00–17.00.

Heading north from the Karlov up **Ke Karlovu**, the third street which you will pass to your right is Na Bojišti, where, at No. 12, is a large beer-house that owes its fame to being mentioned in Jaroslav Hašek's book *The Good Soldier Švejk*. To this establishment, known as **U kalicha** (The Chalice), the congenital idiot Švejk decides to come on the day that the Sarajevo assassination is announced in Prague. He soon enters into an unwise conversation with the only client then present in the bar, a plain-clothes police-officer, and thus unwittingly embarks on his inglorious career in the Austrian army. The landlord described in the book is one Mr Palivec, a notoriously rude man whose every other word is 'arse' or 'shit'. The present-day establishment is scarcely more prepossessing than the place known to Hašek, but with the difference that it is constantly booked up by tour groups. It exploits to the full its Hašek connections, with representations of people from the book covering the walls of its large dining-room, and numerous Švejk souvenirs being sold in its vestibule; the usual drab Czech dishes which it serves are given exotic 'Švejkian' names such as 'Mrs Müller's dumplings' or 'Mr Palivec's stew'.

Returning to Ke Karlovu and continuing north, you will come almost immediately to the elegant summer pavilion which was built by K.I. Dientzenhofer in 1715–20 for Jan Václav Michna (at No. 20 on the right-hand side), and is generally known as the **Villa America** on account of a hotel which existed nearby. This jewel-like building, painted outside a vivid red, is set in a small garden adorned with sculptures from the workshop of Matthias Braun; the main room on the first floor is covered with a delightful illusionistic ceiling painting (c 1730) by J.F. Schors. Since 1934 the building has housed the **Dvořák Museum**; the composer lived in the vicinity (see below) and his writing-desk, piano and other personal belongings are exhibited here. **Open** Tues–Sun 10.00–17.00.

On the other side of the street is a small and rather neglected wooded park, off which stands the former Augustinian **Church of St Catherine** (sv. Kateřiny). This building and its adjoining convent were founded by Charles IV in 1354 in thanksgiving for his victory at the battle of San Felice in Italy. Destroyed by the Hussites in 1420, the church was rebuilt in 1518–22, and then again by K.I. Dientzenhofer and F.M. Kaňka in 1737–41. The one survival of the medieval church is its enormously tall tower, which, thanks to its octagonal upper floors, is sometimes known as 'the Minaret of Prague'. The outside of the building is remarkably dilapidated, but the magnificent Baroque interior, with ceiling frescoes by V.V. Reiner, has been given added magic and drama through housing the sculpture collections of the Museum of the City of Prague, including works by J. Platzer and Matthias Braun, and J.J. Bendl's wonderful statue in polychromed wood of the *Archangel Rafael* (c 1650).

At its northern end Ke Karlovu emerges at the wide and busy Ječná, which you should cross, then turn left and enter the first street to your right **Štěpánská**. Walking north up Štěpánská you will pass to your right Na Rybníčku, on which stands the much restored and altered **Rotunda of St Longinus**, which dates back to the beginning of the 12C and is the smallest of Prague's Romanesque rotundas. Further north Štěpánská joins **Žitná**, another busy thoroughfare, where, if you turn left, you will find on the left-hand side at No. 14 the building where the the composer Antonín Dvořák lived from 1877 up to his death in 1901; he stayed at first in a now ruinous house in the courtyard, but later moved to a more salubrious location at the front of the building (where a plaque to him has been placed high up on the façade). On the opposite side of the street begins Školská, where at No. 16 you will find a plaque recording the house where the writer Jaroslav Hašek was born on 30 April 1883; ironically for the birthplace of the future *enfant terrible* the house belonged at that time to a respected advocate and Prague alderman, Dr Jakub Škarda, a family relative. Near the eastern end of Žitná you will come to the Wilsonova, where, on turning left, you will soon return to the National Museum and the Wenceslas Square.

5 · Vyšehrad and Southern Prague

Vyšehrad citadel

Below the southern end of the New Town is a great wooded outcrop of rock rising directly and steeply above the Vltava river and supporting the citadel of Vyšehrad ('The Castle on the Heights'), the history of which is tied to the mythical origins of Prague.

History of the Citadel

According to legend the castle at Vyšehrad was the home of Countess Libuše, who foresaw from this site the future glories of Prague, and married here the ploughman founder of the Přemyslid dynasty. The truth, however, was that this was not the first seat of the Czech princes, and was preceded both by Prague Castle and Levý Hradec. Founded probably in the early 10C, at the end of the century it became briefly the seat of Boleslav II. In the late 11C the Přemyslid princes once again abandoned Prague Castle in favour of the Vyšehrad, and founded here in 1070 a Collegiate Chapter. The latter, headed by a dean whose role came to be analogous to that of Chancellor of Bohemia, was to remain here for centuries afterwards, but the princes themselves returned permanently to Prague Castle in 1140. The importance of the Vyšehrad declined, though it was to be renewed once more during the reign of Charles IV, who rebuilt the royal palace, erected new fortifications, and established the castle as the starting-point of the Czech coronation processions. In 1420, during the Hussite Wars, almost all the buildings on the Vyšehrad were destroyed, and in their place there was

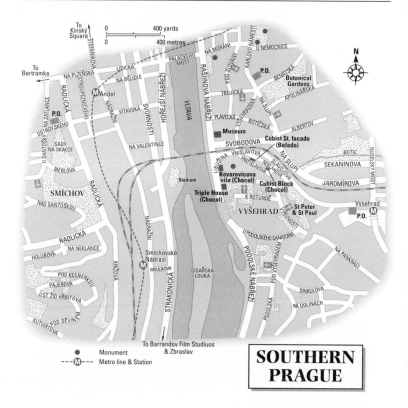

SOUTHERN
PRAGUE

subsequently built up a small town of craftsmen and tradesmen. This town, known as the Town of Mount Vyšehrad, was destroyed in the mid-17C to make way for a Baroque fortress, which was to be abolished in 1866, just under 20 years before the Vyšehrad was to be incorporated into the city of Prague.

The Vyšehrad's mythical early history, its nationalist associations and, not least, the romantic beauty of its site, combined to make the place a great source of inspiration to 19C artists, writers and musicians, and not only to those of Czech blood but also to a number of Germans as well. The German works referring to the rock and its history include C. Kreutzer's opera *Libussa*, Mendelssohn's sonata, *Libussa's Prophecy*, K.E. Ebert's poem, *Vision from the Vyšehrad* and Grillparzer's drama, *Libussa*. M. Aleš, J. Döbler, K. Postl, E.G. Buquoy and K. Pluth were among the many Czech painters to feature the place in their works, while their compatriot J. Zeyer wrote an enormously popular series of poems entitled 'Vyšehrad' (1879–80). But the Czech who did most to establish the place and its legends in the national consciousness was B. Smetana, whose opera *Libuše* (with a libretto by J. Wenzig) was chosen appropriately for the inauguration of the Prague National Theatre in 1883. At the height of all this romantic adulation of Vyšehrad, two deans, V. Šulc and M. Karlach, proposed to convert the original parish cemetery of the Chapter into a national cemetery, a scheme which took root in the 1880s and culminated in the building between 1889 and 1893 of a great pantheon of celebrated Czechs, the Slavín. The rest of the citadel was laid out in 1927 as a public park.

The easiest approach to the Vyšehrad from the centre of Prague is to take the metro to the Vyšehrad station, where you will find yourself on the southern side of a long bridge—a masterly piece of engineering of the late 1960s—which connects the hill with the New Town and the Vinohrady. On the eastern side of the station stands one of Prague's most recent luxury hotels, the bland, American-style Hotel Forum (opened in 1989), which overlooks a large prison, the courtyard of which had to be roofed over so that the hotel guests would not be offended by the sight of exercising prisoners. On the other side of the bridge is the similarly characterless **Palace of Culture** (1969–81), which none the less enjoys a wide terrace with extensive views to the north, a panorama dominated by the Karlov church (see p 175).

Walking west along this terrace you will come to Na Bučance, a quiet street which will take you to the eastern entrance of the Vyšehrad citadel in a few minutes. You enter through the mid-17C **Tábor Gate**, and, after passing to your right the scant ruins of part of the 14C fortifications erected by Charles IV, reach the monumental **Leopold Gate**, the most impressive survival of the 17C citadel, and protected by a deep ditch once spanned by a drawbridge; it was built before 1678 by C. Lurago. On the other side of this gate you will see to your right the oldest surviving structure in the Vyšehrad, the **Rotunda of St Martin** (sv. Martina), which dates back to the late 11C, but was heavily restored in 1878–80: the earliest of Prague's Romanesque rotundas, it is also the only one to have kept its original shape. Walking west from here along the lane called K. rotundě, you will pass to your left the former late 18C **Deanery**, which was built on the site of the Romanesque basilica of St Lawrence; the foundations of this church (which was destroyed by the Hussites in 1421) can be seen at the back of the building, while inside is a small display relating to the history of the Vyšehrad.

Further west on the right-hand side of the road is the **Church of SS Peter and Paul** (sv. Petra a Pavla), which, though founded by Vratislav II in 1070 in conjunction with the Collegiate Chapter, owes its present appearance to neo-Gothic rebuilding carried out by J. Mocker and F. Mikeš between 1885 and 1903. Beside the twin-towered western façade of the church is the entrance to the **Vyšehrad Cemetery**, which is surrounded by a neo-Renaissance arcade designed by A. Wiehl in

Rotunda of St Mrtin

1887, shortly after it was decided to convert the former parish cemetery into the resting-place of great and famous Czechs. **Open** May–Sept daily 08.00–19.00; Mar, Apr, Oct daily 08.00–18.00; Nov–Feb daily 09.00–16.00.

Apart from its historical and sentimental interest the cemetery constitutes a major gallery of sculpture, many of the tombs being executed by leading sculptors who themselves lie buried here, such as J.V. Myslbek, O. Španiel and B. Kafka. Among the tombs to be found in the main part of the cemetery are those of the artists Mikoláš Aleš, Antonín Chitusi, Julius Mařák, Karel Purkyně, Otakar Spaniel and Václav Levý; the musicians Antonín Dvořák, Bedřich Smetana, František Ondříček, Josef Slavík and Zdeněk Fibich; the scientists Jan E. Purkyně and Josef Heyrovský; and the writers Karel Čapek, Karel Hynek Mácha, Jan Neruda, Vítězslav Nezval and Božena Němcová. Particularly touching is the grave

Vyšehrad Cemetery

of Němcová, who was treated better in death than she was in life (she died neglected and in poverty), and given a tombstone carved with scenes from her best known work, *The Grandmother*. A special part of the cemetery (on the eastern side) is taken up by the Pantheon or Slavín, which was built by Wiehl in 1889–93 and is dominated by statues by F. Maudr representing the *Rejoicing Homeland* and the *Mourning Homeland*. Over 50 people have been buried here to date including the artists Vojtěch Hynais, Bohumil Kafka, Ladislav Šaloun, Jan Lauda, Alfons Mucha, Jan Stursa, J.V. Myslbek, and Václav Špála; the architects Josef Gočár, Kamil Hilbert and Jaroslav Fragner; the writers Julius Zeyer, Josef Hora and Jaroslav Vrchlický; the musicians Jan Kubelík, Jan Heřman, Zdeněk Otava and Vílem Zítek; and the actors Zdeněk Štěpánek and Eduard Kohout.

To the south of the church is a shady **park** entered through a Baroque gate taken from a 17C armoury; standing forlorn and neglected in the middle of this area are J.V. Myslbek's large sculptural groups of mythical Czech figures such as Libuše and Přemysl which once proudly stood on the corners of the Palacký Bridge in the New Town. The most enjoyable feature of the park is the dramatic view down to the Vltava from the western ramparts, from where you will also see, clinging to the rock face, the ruins of an early 15C watch-tower which was given in the 19C the romantic name of Libuše's Baths. After leaving the park turn right down K rotundě, and then immediately left, skirting the eastern wall of the cemetery. You will soon reach the citadel's 19C northern gate, from where you begin the sharp descent to the heavily built area comprising the former outer bailey of the castle.

Most of the buildings are apartment blocks of the 19C and 20C, and at the bottom of the first street to the right, Přemyslova, you will find at No. 98 (on the corner with Neklanova) a tall, angular and exceedingly graceful building artic-ulated by prismatic forms. This remarkable apartment building of 1911–13 is the earliest and largest of three **Cubist buildings** erected by Josef Chochol at the foot of the Vyšehrad. Turning left at Neklanova, and walking around the hill in an anti-clockwise direction you will come after Vnislavova to Libušina, on which stands, at No. 3, a building by Chochol of 1912–13 intended for single family occupancy and featuring a beautiful façade built up of diamond shapes. At its southern end the short Libušina joins the Rašínovo nábřeží (the former Engels Embankment), where, on turning left, you will shortly find on the left-hand side of the street at No. 6 the third of Chochol's buildings in the area, a house intended for three families, also dating from 1912–13.

The southern districts
South of the Vyšehrad extends a vast area of suburbs with little of architectural or scenic interest until you reach the outlying district of Zbraslav, which lies on the other side of the Vltava and was not incorporated into Prague until 1974. From the Rašínovo nábřeží you could take trams No. 3, 17 or 21, which go under the Vyšehrad Tunnel of 1902–03 and follow the right bank of the Vltava all the way south to Prague-Braník Station; a No. 245 bus runs from there to Zbraslav.

Zbraslav
Zbraslav, 12km from the centre of Prague, will give you a first taste of the Czech countryside. It continues to be a popular place for weekend excursionists, being accessible in the summer months by a pleasure boat departing from below the Palacký Bridge: it was on a boat outing to Zbraslav organised by the Mánes Association of Artists in 1926 that Kafka's former mistress, Milena Jesenská, met and fell in love with the man who was to become her first husband, the architect Jaromír Krejcar. The beauty of the place lies essentially in the wooded riverside parkland attached to its former **Cistercian Monastery**, one of the best views of which is to be had from the bridge which the No. 245 bus crosses.

The monastery, founded in 1292 on the site of a royal hunting-lodge, was entirely rebuilt in the early 18C, first under the direction of Santini-Aichel (from about 1700) and later under that of F.M. Kaňka (from 1724–32). The elegant buildings, with their white-washed rooms and large ceiling paintings by V.V. Reiner and F.X. Palko, once made a most beautiful and restful setting for the National Gallery's remarkable Czech sculptures of the 19C and 20C, many of which are now in the Trade Fair Palace at Holešovice (see p 196), and many others in storage while awaiting the possible setting up of a museum of 19C Czech sculpture. A scattering of sculptures can still be seen in the the monastery garden; but the building itself was re-opened in October 1998 to show off the National Gallery's extensive and outstanding **Collection of Asian art**, which contains some 12,000 pieces that had not been seen by the general public for forty-six years.

The relative remoteness of Zbraslav (in fact it is only a fifteen minutes bus journey from the Smíchovské nádraží metro station) should not deter anyone from visiting the new Asian museum, which is surely one of the finest of its kind in Europe, not simply for the high quality of the exhibits but also for the sensational nature of the actual display. Information panels of exemplary clarity and informativeness in both Czech and English guide you through a museum that can also be enjoyed as a purely aesthetic and, at times, theatrical experience: imaginative lighting, and coloured timbers arranged to suggest bridges, temples, tea-rooms and so on, convey an oriental context and atmosphere with the most stunningly simple of means.

The **ground floor** rooms are taken up almost entirely by the Japanese holdings, which range mainly from the 16C–19C, and feature superlative examples of laquerwork, enamelling, sword hilts, porcelain, metalwork and Buddhist sculptures, as well a regularly changing selection of screens, prints and painted scrolls. But the museum's greatest strength are the Chinese works on the **first floor**: largely amassed by Czech archaeologists and collectors travelling in China between the wars. These objects had an enormous influence on leading Czech artists of those years such as Emil Filla and Ludvík Kuba, who is represented here by a self-portrait in front of Chinese porcelain. The Chinese holdings, dating from the Bronze Age right up to the 19C, comprise works in a great variety of media (with even some wonderful fragments of 6C AD wall painting), and reveal the extraordinary degree of naturalism attained by Chinese artists during Europe's Dark Age; for instance, in the funerary ceramics of animals and other figures from the Six and Tang dynasties. A highpoint of the collection is the darkened room showing a series of 11C–14C Buddhas against a dark blue ramp, which gives the viewer a strong sense of being inside in a cave temple. Moving on from the Chinese collection to the relatively small holdings of Islamic and South-East Asian art comes inevitably as a slight disappointment, but there is the consolation of a large and dramatically-lit group of painted Tibetan scrolls from the 17C.

Hlubočepy and Barrandov

Several buses (Nos 129, 241, 243 and 245) head back north from Zbraslav along the left bank of the river, following a dual carriageway which in its later stages runs directly alongside a train line and other roads to create a polluted thoroughfare of inhuman proportions. To your left, as you enter the suburb of Hlubočepy, there rises above all this a wooded hill crowned by the spacious residential district of Barrandov, which was laid out by Max Urban, Václav Havel and Josef Barek in 1927–37. To walk up to this district you should descend from the bus just before the Antonín Zápotocký Bridge, and bravely make your way across the road and train line until you reach the pleasant path which ascends to the **Barrandov Tower**, at the northern end of the narrow Barrandov.

This fine Constructivist building, surrounded by trees and with a terrace commanding an excellent panorama of the Vltava, was created by the father of President Havel (with the assistance of Max Urban); originally a restaurant forming part of Havel's Lucerna-Barrandov Enterprises, it is now a nightclub.

Numerous Functionalist villas built for the wealthy and enlightened middle classes of the 1930s can be seen in the course of a walk to the upper southern end of Barrandov, three particularly interesting ones being situated at the junction of Skalní (No. 10), Barrandovská (No. 60) and Lumiérů (No. 41). Lumiérů, a straight street running along the top of the ridge, leads at its southern end to the greying buildings of the **Barrandov Film Studios**, which were founded by President Havel's uncle Miloš in 1933. Now privately owned, and producing far fewer and less original films than they did during their '60s heyday, they have frequently been used in recent years for international co-productions, such as Steven Soderbergh's critically mauled *Kafka* (1992). Outside the studios you can catch a No. 248 bus, which will allow you to rejoin your route north along the river.

Smíchov

North of the great 'spaghetti junction' which surrounds the Barrandov Bridge (Barrandovský most) you will reach one of Prague's most heavily industrialised areas, Smíchov. Most of the buses stop at the Smíchov Station, which though modernised and enlarged after the Second World War, is one of the oldest of Prague's main railway stations, being founded in the 1860s. The actual district of Smíchov, despite its largely bleak look, has several places of interest, but these are all to the north of its station, from where it would be best to take the underground to the following stop, Anděl, which is in itself worth a visit, at least if you are a lover of Soviet kitsch: formerly known as Moskevská (there is an identical station in Moscow called Prashkaya or Prague Station), Anděl might have lost its Russian name but it has kept its Utopian murals of Soviet workers marching into a future in which thrusting towerblocks rise up alongside St Basil's Cathedral.

From Anděl, walk west along the busy **Plzeňská** for about 1.5km, and then turn left on to Mozartova, where you will find, at No. 169 at its upper end, the main tourist attraction of Smíchov, the **Bertramka**. This modest and recently restored 18C villa, with a wooden gallery and a quiet, bosky garden, was the home in the late 18C of the composer F.X. Dušek and his wife J. Dušková, a famous singer. They were close friends of Mozart, who stayed with them on his visits to Prague in 1786, 1787 and 1791. The house has now been done up as a delightful small **Mozart Museum**, with appropriate 18C furnishings, unobtrusive background music, and several mementoes of the composer's stay in Prague: these include a piano on which he allegedly played, and a curious German painting of c 1800 showing the interior of a former beer-cellar near the Powder Gate, and bearing the inscription: 'This is where Mozart ate, drank and composed *Don Giovanni* in 1787.' Casanova, who was also staying in Prague at this time, later claimed responsibility for forcing Mozart to write this opera. **Open Tues–Sun 09.30–18.00.**

On your way back to Anděl metro station you could make a short detour to your left at the bottom of Mozartova to visit the house at No. 2 Duškova where the Communist journalist and Nazi victim Julius Fučík was born in 1903.

Back at Anděl metro station head north along Štefáníkova (the former S.M. Kirova), where you will shortly pass to your right a large and dark neo-Renaissance church by Antonín Barvitius (1881–85). In the decayed garden on its northern side is the **Portheimka**, a small summer villa built by K.I. Dientzenhofer for his own family, but now in a crumbling condition; this toy-like building, with a first-floor room covered with a ceiling painting by V.V. Reiner, is used today for avant-garde art exhibitions that often clash violently with the faded setting. Due east of here is the small Lesnická, where a plaque at No. 7 marks the house where the physicist Albert Einstein lived while teaching at the German university in Prague from 1911–12.

Continuing north along the busy shopping street of Štefánikova you will pass to your left **The Realistic Theatre**, the drab appearance of which belies the lively nature of its productions (a liveliness which dates back to the 1920s, when J. Čapek was a director) and the important part which it has played in Czechoslovakia's recent history. For it was here, following a strike of actors and students on 19 November 1989, that a hastily convened late-night meeting led to the creation of the Civic Forum Party, which was soon to replace the Communist regime. Just to the north of the theatre the street emerges at the **Kinský Square** (náměstí Kinských), which, until only a few years ago, was named náměstí Sovětských Tankistů, and had at its centre a plinth supporting one of the first Soviet tanks to reach Prague in May 1945.

Černý's tank

The presence here of this Russian tank after 1989 was the subject of much controversy, but suggestions that it should be removed were turned down on the grounds that it was one of the more familiar of Prague's landmarks, as well as being a popular meeting-place. ('See you at the tank' was a remark often to be heard here.) As a compromise solution, a 'situationist artist' called David Černý gave the tank a more friendly and human aspect by painting it a vivid pink early in 1991; but this 'unlawful' artistic act led to protests from the Soviet Embassy, with whom the Czech government was then engaged in sensitive negotiations about the removal of their military presence from Czechoslovak territory. The paint was subsequently removed, and Černý was arrested; protests then followed, the paint was reapplied, and Černý released. The tank remained pink for a while before being removed for good.

On the western side of the square is the entrance to the **Kinský Gardens**, which form part of a vast area of parkland stretching up the Petřín Hill and into the Little Quarter (see pp 130–31). Turning left immediately on entering the gardens and following the path parallel to Holečkova, you will reach the early 19C **Kinský Villa**, where you will find the ethnographic collections of the National Museum, with costumes, pottery and other exhibits relating to Czech and Slavonic folk culture.

6 · Eastern Prague

Vinohrady

East of the Wenceslas Square extends the district of Vinohrady, a large area of long, straight streets lined with dirty 19C and 20C apartment blocks and offices, some with a decayed splendour. The places of specific interest here, as throughout eastern Prague, are widely scattered, making a walking tour practicable only to the most dedicated sightseer. The main civic buildings of Vinohrady are around the large **Náměstí míru**, which lies one metro stop away from the southern end of the Wenceslas Square. In the middle of the square stands the brick neo-Gothic **Church of St Ludmila** (sv. Ludmily), which was built by Josef

EASTERN PRAGUE

● Monument

---Ⓜ--- Metro line & Station

Mocker in 1888–93 and has a west tympanum decorated with a relief by J.V. Myslbek of *Christ with SS Wenceslas and Ludmila*. The northern side of the square is dominated by the grand façade of the recently restored **Vinohrady Theatre**, a neo-Baroque building with Art Nouveau elements, built in 1903–06 and crowned by winged allegorical groups by M. Havlíček.

East of here begins one of the longest streets of Vinohrady, **Slezská**, where, on the left-hand side at No. 7, is an interesting red-brick building by Josef Gočár, built in 1924–26 as an Agricultural College. Nearby, on the parallel **Vinohradská**, stands the former School of Commerce, which is decorated around its entrance by four sculptural groups of workers by Karel Dvořák (1925), a very lively example of so-called Objective Realism.

Further east down Vinohradská, adjoining the Jiřího z Poděbrad metro station (one stop east from náměstí Míru) is one of the greatest and most original monuments erected in Czechoslovakia between the wars. This, the **Church of**

Church of the Sacred Heart

the **Sacred Heart** (Nej-světějšího Srdce Páně), was built by Josip Plečnik in 1929–33, and looms massively over the bleak gardens that have been laid out in the middle of George of Poděbrady Square (Náměstí Jiřího z Poděbrad). Inspired by a combination of an Early Christian basilica and an Egyptian temple, it handles its eclectic borrowings with a bold-ness which is uncompromis-ingly modern. Its glazed brick exterior, studded all over with what seem to be overblown guttae, has walls that project diagonally near the top to form a massive cornice; a great pedi-mented clock tower, as wide as the building itself, rises high above the east end of the building and supports an enor-mous clock, glass-fronted on both sides and resembling a rose window.

The wide single-aisled interior, with coffered ceiling, unfaced brick walls and marble floors, has an altar made with marble from the Šumava mountains and impressive statuary at its east end by D. Pešan. The whole building, which acquires a particular magic when spot-lit at night, looks ahead to 'post-Modernist' architecture of the 1960s and 1970s, but has a grandeur and indi-viduality which is quite unique to Plečnik. There are few other modern churches in Europe which are quite as powerful as this one.

The other attraction in the vicinity of the square is of a rather different kind: at No. 21 Jagellonská (turn left at the western end of the square, and then take the first turning to the right) is Prague's longest established game restaurant, *Myslivna*, a place where you can eat one of the best meals to be had in the Czech Republic, served in intimate surroundings that have yet to be taken over by tourists. Just to the north of this restaurant, on the Mahler Park (Mahlerovy sady), soars Prague's futuristic television tower of the late 1980s.

At its bleak, easternmost end, Vinohradská passes next to three of Prague's largest cemeteries. Beyond the Flora metro station the street skirts the southern side of the **Olšany Cemetery**, which was founded during the big plague in 1680, and soon became the main burial place serving the communities on the right bank of the Vltava. Besides the main entrance gates on the náměstí Jiřího z Lobkovic are photographs of the tombs of some of the famous Czechs who are buried here, among whom are the writers Josef Jungmann, Pavel Šafařík and Jan Kollár; the philosopher Bernard Bolzano; the architects Antonín Barvitius and Josef Fanta; the sculptors Josef Max, Bohumil Schnirch and Josef Mařatka; and the painters Josef Mánes, August Pipenhagen, Josef Navrátil and Antonín Slavíček. The tombs are adorned with works by many of the leading Czech sculptors, including Myslbek, Mařatka, Max, Bílek and Kafka, but perhaps the most endearing is that of the illustrator to *Švejk*, Josef Lada, who is commemorated by a tomb shaped like a bird's house. Still one of the most honoured occupants of the cemetery is the student 'martyr' Jan Palach, whose tomb (just to the right of the main entrance) is usually shrouded with flowers and candles; his body was immediately placed here after his dramatic death in 1969, but then was removed in 1974 to his country village, and only brought back here in November 1990.

Immediately to the east of this cemetery is the **New Jewish Cemetery** (Židovské Hřbitovy), the entrance to which is adjacent to the Prague-Strašnice metro station: arrows here will direct you to its most visited tombstone, that of the writer Franz Kafka (the monument is a symbolical Cubist crystal designed in 1924 by Leopold Ehrmann). Slightly further east Vinohradská skirts the northern side of the **Vinohrady Cemetery**, which was founded in 1885 and has in its centre the neo-Gothic chapel of St Wenceslas. One of the greatest Czech painters of the turn of the century, Jakub Schikaneder, is buried here, as is the most influential and original Czech sculptor of the 20C, Otto Gutfreund, who drowned in 1926 and is commemorated here by a bust by his close friend Karel Dvořák. In the Functionalist crematorium to the east of the cemetery lie the ashes of the journalist and writer Egon Erwin Kisch.

■ Olšany and Vinohrady cemeteries open daily dawn to dusk. New Jewish cemetery open Apr–Aug Sun–Thur 08.00–17.00, Sept–Mar Sun–Thur 08.00–16.00.

Due south of the Olšany Cemetery is a quiet residential street lined with grand suburban villas and named bratří Čapků after the brothers Josef and Karel Čapek who spent much of their later life in the ochre-coloured building at No. 30, which was built by L. Machoň in 1923–24. Further south begins the district of **Vršovice**, where you will find, standing on the náměstí Svatopluka Čecha, the Constructivist **Church of St Wenceslas** (sv. Václav), which was built by Josef Gočár in 1929–30 and is dominated by a tall tower, now turned a dirty grey on the outside. This narrow building clings to the slope of a verdant hill, and is built on different levels that lead up to the apse, a delicate and luminous structure largely composed of stained glass. On a hill to the west of the church is the pleasant **Havlíček Park** (Havlíčkovy Sady), commanding good views of southern Prague, and featuring at its northern end the late 19C **Gröbe Villa** (now a Youth Centre), a large villa of Italian Renaissance inspiration, designed by A. Barvitius.

Žižkov

North of Vinohrady is the district of Žižkov, a traditional working-class area with a long history of revolutionary activity that once earned it the name of 'Red Prague'. It also has strong associations with poetry, being the birthplace both of the German poet Rainer Maria Rilke and of the Nobel Prize-winning poet, Jaroslav Seifert, who was born here in 1901 and was recently honoured by changing the name of the district's main street from Kalininova to Seifertova. Seifert once referred to this place where he had spent both his childhood and adolescence as 'my beautiful and adored Žižkov', though this is not a reaction which is going to be shared by most of the casual visitors here, the majority of whom come simply to climb up to the monument of Jan Žižka. The traditional approach to this monument from the centre of Prague is to walk from the Powder Gate to the eastern end of Hybernská, and then turn left on to Husitská.

Coming instead from Vinohrady's náměstí Míru, you should walk north along Italská, skirting the western side of **Rieger Park** (Riegrovy Sady), a late 19C park with fine views and, in its southwestern corner, a monument to the 19C politician František Rieger by J.V. Myslbek; at No. 4 Chopinova, on the other side of the park to Italská, is an interesting brick building by Jan Kotěra, erected in 1909–10 for the Laichter Publishing House. At the northern end of Italská you will reach Seifertova, a junction marked by the náměstí Winstona Churchilla, on which stands one of the pioneering examples of Functionalist architecture of the 1930s, the former **Pensions Institute** (now the Central Trade Unions Council). This vast structure, comprising two great rectangular blocks arranged in cross formation, was described by the architect Martin Shand as 'the white cathedral of Prague', but now is a depressing grey and, for all its originality in the context of 1930s architecture, is a foretaste of the worst architecture of the post-war period.

After crossing Seifertova and continuing north along Řehořova, you will come to Husitská: off its western end, a path begins the climb up the wooded hill to the Jan Žižka Monument, passing to the right a grey block containing the post-1918 holdings of the **Military Museum** (the earlier holdings are in the Schwarzenberg-Lobkowicz Palace; see p 151): howitzers, armoured tanks and other grim weaponry guard the entrance to the building, while inside is an exhibition covering such subjects as the Czech contribution to the Second World War, the invention of Semtex, and even the anti-chemical unit prepared for the Gulf War of 1991. **Open** Apr–Oct Tues–Sun 08.30–17.00, Nov–Mar Tues–Sat 09.30–16.30.

Some knowledge of an earlier period in Bohemia's military history is needed to appreciate fully the monument to Jan Žižka, the Hussite hero, at the top of the hill.

Jan Žižka and the National Monument

After the burning at the stake of Jan Hus in 1415, the Hussites came to be divided into two main camps, moderate and radical, the former (known usually as the Utraquists) being drawn mainly from the Bohemian nobility and the more conservative nationalists. The more popularly based radical wing of the Hussites went far further in their views than the Utraquists, maintaining that the Holy Bible was the sole authority in all matters of religious belief, and rejecting the doctrine of the existence of Purgatory, all the Sacraments with the exception of baptism and communion, and many other of the teachings of the Church. The radicals enjoyed the leadership of one of the greatest of Bohemia's military commanders, Jan Žižka, a man whose early background is little known other than that he came from a family of the lesser nobility in South Bohemia, and had held a post at the court of Queen Sophia; he and his followers, the Taborites, were to establish as their principal base a stronghold in South Bohemia which they named Tábor after the biblical hill where Christ had been transfigured.

The widespread unrest resulting from Hus's death came to a head in the summer of 1419 with Taborites from all over the country gathering at Tábor, and Utraquists storming into Prague's New Town Hall to perpetrate the first 'defenestration' (see p 35). The news of what had happened at the Town Hall had the immediate effect of making King Wenceslas so annoyed that he died of apoplexy; as he was heirless, this in turn led to the thorny problem of succession. The principal claimant to the throne was his brother Sigismund, a man widely hated in Bohemia, particularly after his treacherous behaviour towards Jan Hus at Constance (see p 102); his only supporters were the Roman Catholics, most of whom belonged to the country's German communities. In the absence of a king, Queen Sophia was appointed Regentess of the country, but shortly afterwards a Papal Bull was issued proclaiming a crusade against the heretics of Bohemia.

By June 1420, Sigismund, at the head of crusading forces drawn from almost every European country, reached the outskirts of Prague where, on July 14, he was defeated in battle by Jan Žižka, whose forces knelt upon the field of victory and intoned the Te Deum. Before fleeing to Moravia, Sigismund had himself crowned in Prague's St Vitus's Cathedral, but the ceremony was such a hurried and reduced one that his opponents considered it to be invalid. It was in any case to be a further 16 years before he would be able to take possession of his kingdom, following the crushing defeat at the Battle of Lipany near Kolín of the Taborite forces led by Prokop, who had succeded Jan Žižka after the latter had died of plague in 1424.

In 1877 the suburb of Prague where Žižka's victory against Sigismund had taken place was renamed Žižkov; and, early the next century, when patriotic monuments on a vast scale were at the height of their fashion in Bohemia, plans were made to build here a giant concrete figure of Žižka, containing a staircase leading up to an observation platform inside the warrior's head. This idea was later dropped, and in 1913 a public competition was held to find another design with which to commemorate the great hero. Many of the country's leading artists and architects participated, including several prominent 'Cubists', who were anxious to respond to the challenge of reconciling Cubist architecture with figural sculpture. 'It's a long time since I have seen such a distressing sight as this exhibition of draft projects for a Žižka monument', was how the poet František Procházka (an outspoken opponent of Cubism) judged these various efforts, among which was a sensational collaborative design by the architect Pavel Janák and the sculptor Otto Gutfreund. Two further competitions had to be held—in 1923 and 1925—before the decision was made to adopt a rather conservative scheme by the architect Jan Zázvorka and the sculptor Bohumil Kafka.

The monument, known officially as the **National Monument**, partly comprises a granite-faced building dating back to 1929–30, adorned inside with mosaics by M. Švabinský and J. Obrovský and relief carvings by K. Pokorný. This building was enlarged and adapted after the Second World War to contain the Grave of an Unknown Soldier from Dukla, together with the tombs of prominent Communists such as Klement Gottwald, Antonín Zápotocký and Ludvík Svoboda. Gottwald himself was originally embalmed Lenin-style, which involved the construction of a refrigerated morgue as well as elaborate apparatus both to control carefully the monument's temperature and to raise the mummy up and down from casket to slab. Unfortunately Gottwald's corpse, heavily pickled in alcohol even before he died, disintegrated at a rate that defeated the finest scientific attempts to preserve it; damaged further by fire in 1963, it was finally cremated. In 1990 the remains of both Gottwald and his fellow Communists were offered back to their next-of-kin (Gottwald's ashes, refused by his family, were placed in a mass grave in the Olšany Cemetery). Since then the building has been closed pending a decision about its final fate.

In front of the building rises the monument's great focal-point—Bohumil Kafka's enormous equestrian bronze of Jan Žižka, which is certainly impressive from a great distance, but is largely of interest for featuring in the Guinness Book of Records as the world's largest sculpture. The greatest reward of a walk up to the monument is the magnificent panorama of Prague to be had from here, a panorama which used to inspire the young Jaroslav Seifert, who was later to write some of the finest poetry ever dedicated to this city.

Karlín

East of the National Monument a monotonous tree-lined avenue runs the whole length of the hill's ridge, at the eastern end of which you can turn left and descend a steep path down to the railway line and across to U Invalidovny. You have now entered the district of Karlín, and will see to your right the impressive if rather dilapidated block of a great hospital (now the Invalid War Veterans' Home), which was built in 1730–37 by Kilian Ignaz Dientzenhofer; though of enormous size, what you see today represents only a corner of a projected complex of truly monumental proportions. The surrounding district, arranged on a grid plan, and named after the Empress Carolina Augusta (wife of Francis I), was created after 1817, and as such was Prague's earliest suburb.

Sokolovská stretches west from here all the way back to the Jan Šverma Park, at the entrance to the New Town. Alternatively, you could catch any bus east along this street to the náměstí Organizace spojených národů, from where two specialist detours can be made into the northeastern suburbs of the city. Bus 183 will take you from the square all the way to the **Ďáblice Cemetery** (Ďáblický hřbitov), which was laid out between 1912–14 by the Cubist architect Vlatislav Hofman, whose main achievement here was the imposing entrance gate with its flanking Cubist kiosks. Aircraft enthusiasts, and those of a military bent, might appreciate instead the **Museum of Aviation and Space** (Museum letectur a Kosmonautiky), which can be reached from the square on bus Nos 185, 280, 302 and 354. **Open** May–Oct Tues–Sun 10.00–18.00.

Situated within a military airfield on the southwestern outskirts of Kbely, the museum features over 100 civil and military planes, some of which are either unique or else unrepresented in similar museums in Western Europe. The planes, together with complementary exhibits of engines and aviation memorabilia, are displayed in a series of old hangars, while outside are tanks, rocket launchers and other military vehicles, most of which are of Soviet origin.

7 · Western Prague

Střešovice

Střešovice, which lies immediately to the west of the Hradčany, is traditionally the most luxurious of Prague's suburbs, and is a quiet area of attractive modern villas, spaciously laid out. The district had sinister connotations for Prague's Jewish community during the Second World War, for it was in one of these villas, confiscated from a wealthy Jew, that the Central Office for Jewish Emigration was situated. This office was directly subordinate to the Gestapo and was responsible for the organisation of the notorious 'transports' to the ghetto at Terezín and elsewhere: accounts of the compulsory visits to Střešovice are included in Jiří Weil's disturbing novel, *Life with a Star* (1964), which was based on the author's war-time experiences.

Examples of the sort of tram used by Weil's protagonist can be seen in the enjoyable **City Transport Museum** at Patočkova 4, which has shiningly maintained examples of every type of city tram and trolley-bus that ever ran through the streets of Prague; during the summer months it runs a tram service to and from the city centre. **Open** Apr–Oct Sat, Sun 09.00–17.00.

West of the museum extends the large area of Střešovice known as the **Ořechovka Villa Quarter**, which was planned by J. Vondrák and J. Šenkýř in 1920–23 on the model of England's 'garden suburbs'. In the course of the 1920s this quarter was greatly expanded and, between 1929 and 1931, there was built on its outer southern limits (at No. 14 Nad hradním vodojemem) by far the most distinguished of Střešovice's villas, the **Maison Muller**. This cube-like structure, with large expanses of bare masonry discreetly pierced by small, irregularly placed openings, is the work of the revolutionary Moravian-born architect Adolf Loos (assisted by Josef Fanta), and is the only one of his buildings to be seen in the Czech Republic; the interior, characterised by its every space being of different height and shape, may be opened as a museum in the near future.

Břevnov

The district of Břevnov, which extends to the south of Střešovice and to the west of the Petřín Hill, begins at its eastern end with the largest sports stadium in the world, the **Spartakiáda Stadium**. Designed by Alois Dryák in 1926 for a seating capacity of over 200,000, this ungainly complex looks for most of the time like some stranded folly of megalomaniac scale, but comes to life every five years with an internationally renowned gymnastic display known as the Spartakiáda; the next such event is planned for the millennium.

Running west from near here is the long **Bělohorská**, which passes through an area of large housing estates, including one of 600 apartments dating from the late 1930s. Further west along the street, at No. 28, is the elegant Empire-style hostelry known as **At the Chestnut** (Dům U kaštanu), where on 7 April

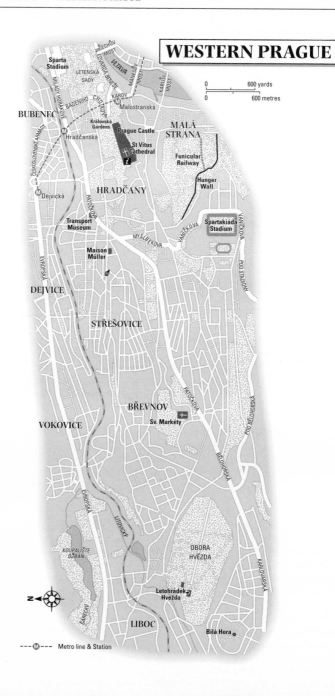

WESTERN PRAGUE

Sparta
Stadium
LETENSKÁ
SADY
VLTAVA
LECHŮV
MOST
EDUARDA BENEŠE
MÁNESŮV
MOST
KARLŮV
MOST

0   600 yards
0   600 metres

BUBENEČ
MILADY HORÁKOVÉ
BADENIHO
CHOTKOVA
KAROV
M Malostranská
Malostranská
Královská
Gardens
Prague Castle
Hradčanská
St Vitus
Cathedral
i
MALÁ
STRANA
Funicular
Railway
Hunger
Wall
ČESKOSLOVENSKÉ ARMÁDY
M Dejvická
HRADČANY
PATOČKOVA
Transport
Museum
MYSLBEKOVA
VANIČKOVA
Spartakiáda
Stadium
VANIČKOVA
POD STADIONY
Maison
Müller
EVROPSKÁ
DEJVICE
STŘEŠOVICE
PATOČKOVA
BŘEVNOV
Sv. Markety
POD BĚLOHORSKOU
VOKOVICE
BĚLOHORSKÁ
EVROPSKÁ
LITOVICKÝ
KOUPALIŠTĚ
DŽBÁN
OBORA
HVĚZDA
KARLOVARSKÁ
N
ŠÁRECKÝ
Letohrádek
Hvězda
LIBOC
Bílá Hora

--- M --- Metro line & Station

1878, a secret meeting headed by J.B. Pecka and L. Zápotocký led to the formation of the Czech Social Democratic Workers' Party, an event marked by a plaque.

Just beyond the building the street turns into a wide thoroughfare which is bordered on its northern side by a neglected corner of countryside surrounding the **Monastery and Church of St Margaret** (sv. Markéty), accessible by trams No. 8, 22 and 23, which run the whole length of Bělohorská. Though recently restored, and reclaimed by monks, this unfairly neglected place, with its isolated situation in a generally grey Prague suburb, may induce a sense of great pathos in the visitor, particularly in those who come here in the knowledge that they are visiting the oldest monastery in Bohemia and one of Prague's finer Baroque complexes. Founded for the Benedictine Order in 993 by Boleslav II and the Prague bishop, St Adalbert, the monastery and church were completely rebuilt by Christoph and Kilian Ignaz Dientzenhofer in the early 18C. The monastic buildings, with fine ceiling frescoes by C.D. Assam of 1727, are not open to the public. But the interest of the complex lies essentially in its church, which was built by Christoph Dientzenhofer between 1700 and 1715, and has a powerful and tightly composed exterior with a giant order of pilasters and columns running around its whole length, and a dynamic attic level of gables crowned by undulant pediments. The single-aisled interior is composed of a series of inter- secting transverse ovals, with giant piers projecting diagonally into the nave as in Christoph Dientzenhofer's comparably majestic Church of St Nicholas in the Little Quarter; the ceiling frescoes, by J.J. Steinfels, represent the founding of the monastery by St Adalbert. The crypt, open on Sundays only, is that of the orig- inal Romanesque building of the late 10C. Within the orchard garden behind the church is a Baroque pavilion surrounding a well where St Adalbertus is said to have met Boleslav II at the time of the monastery's foundation.

■ Guided tours Sat 10.00 and 14.00, Sun 10.30 and 14.00.

At the westernmost end of Břevnov is the limestone hill associated with one of the most famous and tragic battles in the history of Bohemia, the Battle of the White Mountain (Bílá Hora). It was here, on 8 November 1620, that the Protestant army led by Count Matthias von Thun was defeated by the Habsburg troops under Maximillian of Bavaria; Elector Frederick of the Palatinate, who had been elected King of Bohemia by the Protestants the previous year, was forced to flee, and Bohemia was not to regain its independence until after the First World War. Much of the site is taken up by an English-style **park** which was laid out in 1797 on a game reserve founded by Ferdinand I in 1530 (to reach its main gates you can continue along Bělohorská on trams No. 8 or 22, and get off at Na Vypichu).

Within the park long alleys of trees lead to the remarkable Renaissance building known as the **Star Castle** (letohrádek Hvězda). This star-shaped struc- ture of 1555–58 was built by Hans Tirol and Bonifác Wohlmut as a hunting- lodge for Ferdinand of Tyrol, and later became the residence of the latter's future wife, Philippine Welser. The exterior, restored by Pavel Janák after the Second World War, is austere and rather dilapidated, but the interior features outstanding stucco ceiling decorations of mythological scenes and grotesques by Italian artists. The building, which was turned into a powder-magazine after the 16C, now houses on its upper floors a **museum** devoted to the 19C writer of historical romances, Alois Jirásek, and to his painter contemporary, Mikoláš Aleš, who is represented here largely by his book illustrations. In the basement is a large model of the Battle of the White Mountain. **Open** Tues–Sat 09.00–16.00, Sun 10.00–17.00.

The western continuation of Bělohorská is **Karlovarská**, on which stands, at No. 6, the early 18C **Church of Our Lady of Victory** (Panny Marie Vítězné), which replaced a 17C chapel commemorating the Habsburg victory at the Battle of the White Mountain; the interior has ceiling paintings by V.V. Reiner and C.D. Assam.

8 · Northern Prague

Letná

Rising above the Vltava immediately to the northeast of the Little Quarter is the large **Letná Park** (Letenské Sady), which was laid out after 1858. Occupying an excellent vantage point at its western end, with beautiful views across the river to the Old Town, is the **Hanava Pavilion**, an exuberantly eclectic structure mingling the neo-Baroque with tentative Art Nouveau forms. Built by Otto Prieser for Prague's Jubilee Industrial Exhibition of 1891, it was admired in its time (and later by Le Corbusier) for its innovative use of cast iron—a material promoted in Bohemia by the man who commissioned the building, Prince William of Hanava, the owner of ironworks at Komárov near Hořovice. The building proved so popular with those who attended the exhibition that it was rebuilt in its present location seven years later; now brightly restored, it functions as an elegant restaurant.

Further east in the park is a giant **immobilised metronome** designed by David Černý in 1991, the same year that this notorious 'situationist artist' was arrested for painting the Soviet tank memorial in Smíchov (see p 184): this particular work has its own political resonance, standing as it does on the granite plinth that had once supported a massive statue of Stalin.

The Stalin Monument

The competition held in 1953 to erect a Stalin monument was won by a team that included Otakar Švec, who ingeniously overcame the problem of spectators having to look up at Stalin's bottom by placing behind his figure lines of Czech and Soviet workers (hence the monument's nickname of 'the queue'). Six hundred men spent 500 days erecting the colossus, which weighed in at 14,000 tons and attained a height of 30 metres. By the time it was finally completed in 1955, Švec had committed suicide, and Stalin's reputation was on the verge of collapsing. Krushchev's speech of 1956 denouncing Stalin's personality cult led the embarrassed Czech Communists to encase the monument in scaffolding which remained in place until 1962, when demolition by a series of small detonations became the only solution (a single explosion would have done away with most of

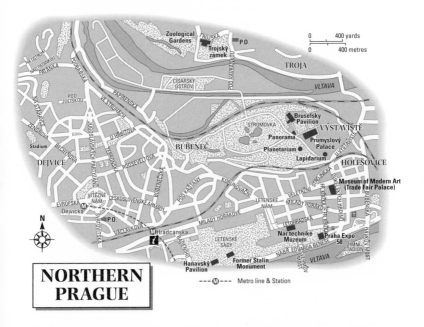

Zoological Gardens · TROJSKÁ · P.O.
Trojský zámek
TROJA
CÍSARSKÝ OSTROV
VLTAVA
NA OSTROVĚ · NAD PAZDERKOU · PATANKA
POD JULISKOU · PAPÍRENSKÁ · VZ.STRUHÁCH
U HŘBITOVA
JUGOSLÁVSKÝCH PARTYZÁNŮ
Bruselský Pavilion
STROMOVKA · VÝSTAVIŠTĚ
Panorama · Prumyslový Palace
Planetarium
BUBENEČ
Lapidarium
Stadium · ZENGROVA · BERHNLOVA · TERRONSKÁ · ROOSEVELTOVA
DEJVICE
HOLEŠOVICE
Museum of Modern Art (Trade Fair Palace)
KORUNOVAČNÍ · STROJNICKÁ · DUKELSKÝCH HRDINŮ · BUBENSKÁ
VÍTĚZNÉ NÁM. · ČESKOSLOVENSKÉ ARMÁDY · POD KAŠTANY
LETENSKÉ NÁM. · VELETRŽNÍ · MILADY HORÁKOVÉ
EVROPSKÁ · Dejvická
P.O.
VÁCLAVKOVA · BANSKOVITSKÁ · MILADY HORÁKOVÉ
LETOHRADSKÁ
Hradčanská
LETENSKÉ SADY
Nár.technické Muzeum · Praha Expo 58
HAVLÍČKŮV MOST · ZIMNÍ STADION
Hanavský Pavilion · Former Stalin Monument
NÁBŘ. EDVARDA BENEŠE
VLTAVA

N

0   400 yards
0   400 metres

NORTHERN PRAGUE

---Ⓜ--- Metro line & Station

the hill and the bridge below). In his novel *The Miracle Game* (1972), Josef Škvorecký described the monument's surviving base as looking 'like the dark side of a Mayan pyramid, with wide granite steps on either side leading to an empty platform on top'. The cellars below, used intermittently since 1962 to store potatoes and hold unofficial parties, have now been taken over by mushroom-growers.

At the opposite end of the park to the Hanava Pavilion is the similarly well-located *Praha-Expo 58 Restaurant*, which originally formed part of the Czech Pavilion for the Brussels World Fair of 1958; the indifferent quality of the food which is served here is partially compensated for by the dining-room's panoramic, semi-circular window.

Holešovice

To the west and north of the restaurant extends the district of Holešovice, which was annexed in 1869 to the village of Bubeneč, and incorporated into Prague in 1884; the place today is now experiencing new life thanks to its popularity with the city's expatriate communities, and the recent opening of its extraordinary modern art museum (see below). A large and grim Functionalist block immediately behind the *Praha-Expo 58 Restaurant* houses the **National Technical Museum** (Národní technické muzeum), which includes among its extensive collections sections devoted to astronomy, metallurgy and horology. Of particular interest to children is the guided tour of a reconstructed coal-mine in the basement; also entertaining is the section labelled in English 'the Centre for Noise Ecology', where you can play around with numerous objects for making and recording sounds. But, above all, you should visit the Hall of Transport at the back of the building, a tall space crammed to capacity with every conceivable form of transport from the early 19C onwards; the exhibits are arranged in three superimposed galleries around the hall and also in the centre of the room, where old bi-planes and even a hot-air balloon hover above a traffic-jam of old cars and trains, including the luxury train carriage in which the Emperor Franz Joseph travelled in 1891. **Open** Tues–Sun 09.00–17.00.

The Trade Fair Palace

A grid of streets lined with blackened apartment blocks of the 19C and 20C begins behind the museum. Head east on Letohradská, and at the end of this street turn left on to F. Křížka, which crosses the busy shopping street of Milady Horákové and comes to an end at the wide Veletržní, near the 1960s block of the luxury Park Hotel. Directly in front of this hotel, at 45 Dukelských hrdinů, is the enormous former Trade Fair Palace (Veletržní palac), the first Functionalist building of its scale in Europe, now stunningly adapted to house the modern holdings of the National Gallery.

History of the Trade Fair Palace

The enormous success of the Prague Jubilee Industrial Exhibition of 1891, and of its more modest 1908 sequel (the Chamber of Commerce Exhibition), highlighted the need among Czech politicians and businessmen for an annual trade fair at the heart of what had by now become the Habsburg Empire's most industrial region. However, it was not until the creation of Czechoslovakia that a Prague Trade Fair Committee was finally established. In 1924, in a competition held to design a Trade Fair Palace (for which six architects were invited to submit plans), first prize was awarded to Oldřich Tyl (a graduate of the Prague Technical University) and third prize to Josef Fuchs, a pupil of the idiosyncratic Classical architect Jože Plečník. In the end Tyl and Fuchs combined their talents to produce the project that was eventually carried out, following a second competition held in 1925. The building, erected between 1926 and 1928, was designed to hold 10,000 visitors and 4000 exhibitors: in addition to its administrative offices, corridors with 'shop bays', and Small and Great Halls (the latter reserved for heavy machinery), the palace featured an elegant restaurant, a 600-seat cinema, a post office and a telephone exchange; it was also the first building in Prague to be centrally heated from a remote source, in this case from the Holešovice Power Plant.

Among the first visitors to see the completed building was the French architect Le Corbusier, who, despite a number of criticisms, was excited to find vindicated his belief in applying Functionalism on a vast scale: 'Seeing a building quite as large as this one,' he wrote, 'quite unique in its category, I can imagine what my United Nations Palace, which exists only on paper, would look like, and what my even bigger Centrosaiuz building in Moscow is going to look like ... Seeing the Trade Fair Palace, I understood how to make large buildings, having so far built only relatively small houses on a low budget.'

Bizarrely, for a building of such bold modernity, the official opening of the palace—which took place on 21 September 1928, two weeks before Le Corbusier's visit—was marked by an exhibition of the monumental but highly reactionary canvases constituting Alfons Mucha's *Slav Epic* of 1911–28 (now in the castle of Moravský Krumlov). The celebrated Art Nouveau artist had himself proposed the idea, having probably been excited by the newspaper reports of the enormous dimensions of the Great Hall. The clash between the daringly simple, light and futuristic setting of the palace and the fussily detailed historical bombast of Mucha's paintings was none the less glossed over in the exhibition's pre-publicity, which stressed instead that with these works on the walls, 'the monumental hall of the Trade Fair Palace will be transformed into an exquisite temple dedicated to the Slavic spirit, love and enthusiasm, where the individual images will be symbolical steps in the historical journey of the Slavs toward the final victory of the Slavic race.'

The Trade Fair Palace maintained its original function until 1951, when the Prague Trade Fair was closed down and its activities transferred to Brno. Subsequently the palace was used by several state-run foreign trade companies, who treated the building with scant respect either for the architecture or for the safety of their employees. In 1974, some varnish-soaked overalls in a makeshift painting workshop self-ignited and set fire to the building. After four years of deliberating about what to do with the charred surviving structure, the stubborn persistence of an endearingly naive one-time law student, political prisoner and minor employee of the National Gallery, Vratislav Vaňousek (who was thought of by his contemporaries almost as a comic figure), finally persuaded the Czech Government to let the building be used to display the National Gallery's modern holdings. The reconstruction of the building, entrusted to the Liberec architectural firm of SIAL, was finally begun in 1985 and not completed until 1994, nine years after Vaňousek's death. The museum opened its doors to the public early in 1997.

With the opening of the **National Gallery's Collection of Modern Art** in the Trade Fair Palace, Prague has gained not only an attraction rivalling any of its older monuments, but also one of Europe's most exciting new galleries. As yet attracting a relatively small stream of tourists, this spacious and peaceful gallery is worth a visit as much for the architecture as for the collections: the building shows that Functionalism in its early stages was far from being the drab and pedestrian style that it so often became in the hands of its later imitators. The vitality, originality and exhilarating freshness of the building is exemplified above all in the pristinely white **Great Hall**, which offers an architectural thrill as intense as the Vladislav Hall in the Hradčany. This luminous sky-lit hall, situated at the eastern end of the palace, near the entrance to the actual museum (the palace's main western door leads to a part of the building still used for trade exhibitions) is surrounded by balconied galleries that, on one side, form an inwardly sloping wall of railings reminiscent of the hull of some futuristic ocean liner of *Titanic* proportions. **Open** Tues, Wed, Fri–Sun 10.00–18.00, Thur 10.00–21.00.

Although the galleries themselves are lined with lively modern sculptures, the hall itself has sensibly been left bare, allowing the visitor some uncluttered, breath-taking moments before walking through a door on the western side and entering the room containing the lifts leading up to the permanent collections on the fourth and fifth floors. Before you make the ascent be sure to look into the small, darkened space off the southern side of this ground-floor room: here you will find a modern reconstruction of a kinetic, coloured light structure designed by Zdeněk Pešánek in 1936 for a transformer station in Prague's Klárov district: this remarkable, pioneering work (activated by a series of buttons the visitor can press) gives a wonderful foretaste of the originality of so much of the Czech art you will shortly be seeing.

Modern art at the Trade Fair Palace

Inevitably, in view of how little is known about Czech art outside the Czech Republic, most foreign visitors head directly for the **second floor**, where, in a long suite of interconnected small rooms, the gallery's foreign holdings are displayed, beginning with a large and celebrated selection of French art from the Impressionists to the Cubists. Among the artists represented are Pissarro (an excellent view of Pontoise, before 1870), Renoir, Manet (a head of Proust, 1855–56), Degas (*Portrait of Lorenza Payese*), Van Gogh (*Green Rye*, 1889–90), Sisley, Cézanne (*House in Aix*, 1885–87, and a superlative portrait of the Pontoise doctor, patron and friend to the Impressionists, Joachim Gachet, 1896–97, Gauguin (a wooden relief done in Tahiti, and the famous Pont-Aven parody of Courbet, *Good-day Mr Gauguin*, 1889), Rodin (a bronze maquette of his Balzac monument), Toulouse-Lautrec (*Moulin-Rouge*, 1892), the Douanier Rousseau (this artist's only known self-portrait, 1890), Signac, Van Dongen, Matisse, Bonnard, Chagall, Utrillo and Dufy.

Many of these works were amassed by **Vincenc Kramář**, the enlightened director of the Prague National Gallery during the 1920s, who donated his collection to the gallery in 1960, a few months before his death at the age of 83. Kramář's greatest contribution to the arts in Czechoslovakia was his early championing of Cubism, buying in Paris in the first and second decades of the 20C works that would profoundly influence a whole generation of avant-garde Czech artists and architects.

Thanks to Kramář, the National Gallery has a collection unrivalled in central Europe of the works of Picasso and Braque. The **Picassos** begin with two paintings belonging to his so-called Negro Period (a *Self-Portrait* of 1907 and a *Female Head* of the same year) and continue with a large group of 'analytical Cubist' works of 1910 and 1911; there are also some 'synthetic Cubist' works of 1912 and 1913, and later purchases such as his monumental *Standing Nude* of 1921.

The paintings by **Braque** trace his career from the analytical Cubist period of 1910–11—when his works were virtually identical to Picasso's of these years—to the development of his very lyrical and painterly still-lifes of the 1920s. Among the other Cubist paintings are some early works by Derain, most notably a view of Cadaqués of 1910; Derain's later manner is represented by a sturdy and very Classical *Seated Woman* of 1921.

The rest of the foreign school holdings are particularly notable for their fine **German and Austrian works** dating mainly from the first three decades of the 20C. Among the former are three paintings by Liebermann, a self-portrait by

Corinth showing the plump and manic artist naked to the waist, Expressionist canvases by Schmidt-Rottluff and Pechstein, and a disturbing work by the undeservedly little known Max Oppenheimer, entitled *The Operation*: it shows an hysterical group of hands and scalpels. The Austrian holdings are dominated by superb paintings by Schiele, Klimt and Kokoschka. **Schiele** is represented by a small townscape of 1911 (a view of Česky Krumlov) and a haunting tall canvas of a monk and a woman; the sole painting by **Klimt** is a large decorative composition in vivid blues and purples, entitled *The Virgin* and showing an entwined group of female nudes (1913). **Kokoschka** lived in Prague in 1934–35, and there are several works by him from this period, of which pride of place must go to three large and expressively painted views of Prague from the river, constituting possibly the finest landscapes ever made of this city.

The Russians Repin, Mikhail Nesterov and A.V. Lentulov, the Italians Severini, Guttoso and Carlo Carrà, and the Spaniards Oscar Dominguez, Miro and Tápies, are among the other foreign artists whose works are owned by the National Gallery. But the artist whose work was more relevant to the development of early 20C Czech art was Edvard Munch, who is represented here by a single but highly atmospheric painting of a group of women dancing by a shore by moonlight (1900).

The foreign school holdings on the **fourth floor** are abruptly succeded by a series of rooms devoted to Czech art of the 1950s and '60s. Before seeing these, you should go up to the **third floor**, where the bulk of the gallery's Czech holdings are displayed, in a roughly chronological sequence. Confusingly for those new to Czech art and unfamiliar with most of the names, the works of a particular artist are rarely shown altogether but are instead divided up according to the perceived artistic preoccupations of specific decades—preoccupations that are sometimes categorised in the accompanying catalogue with such unhelpful titles as 'The Mythology of the Mundane' and 'Primitivism, Civilism and Spiritual Realism'.

The earliest of the Czech paintings provide a natural sequel to the atmospheric, darkly coloured works by **Schikaneder** that bring to a close the 19C collections in the St Agnes Convent. An almost Scandinavian degree of introspection is evident in the penumbral landscapes of **Antonín Hudeček**, which feature the small lake at Okoř (20km northwest of Prague off the Kralupy road), where the artist **Mařák** had a small painting school: especially haunting is the work entitled *Evening Silence* (1900), in which a woman with her back to the spactator stares down towards the fading light of the distant lake.

Another lake, the imaginary Black Lake, is an obsessive motif in the works of Hudeček's contemporary **Jan Preisler**, an artist of strong Symbolist orientation whose paintings betray the influence of Puvis de Chavannes and Gauguin. The third outstanding painter of this generation is **Antonín Slavíček**, who created landscapes and cityscapes of extraordinary emotional intensity and pictorial expressiveness, including a number of rain-swept views of Prague and its surroundings, for instance the *Mariánské náměstí* of 1906.

Munch (whose influential exhibition held in 1905 in Prague's Mánes Gallery was partly organised by Preisler) became a seminal early influence on the subsequent generation of artists, notably **Václav Špála**, **Emil Filla** and **Bohumil Kubišta**. Works such as Špála's fiery *Self-Portrait with Palette* (1908), Filla's spiritually tormented *Reader of Dostoyevsky* (1907) and Kubišta's sinisterly green

Cardplayers (1909), are pure *hommages* to the Norwegian artist. These three painters, together with **Otakar Kubín**, **Antonín Procházka** and **Josef Čapek**, later embraced no less whole-heartedly the Cubist works of Picasso and Braque: many of their Cubist paintings would be virtually indistinguishable from the art of their French peers were it not for the occasional Czech lettering and landscapes, as in, for instance, Kubišta's *Quarry in Braník* (1910–11) and Filla's *Still Life with Art Monthly* (1914).

A far more idiosyncratic painter than any of these was the deeply spiritual artist **Jan Zrzavý**, some of whose early works, such as *The Anti-Christ* (1909) display a powerfully expressive use of colour and brushstroke. At the same time he began developing a completely different style characterised by strange doll-like figures and an almost naively simple handling of paint and composition: one of the earliest such paintings was his *Valley of Sorrow* (1908), which he later described as being imbued with all his sense of 'sadness and hopelessness'.

But the most original and truly outstanding Czech painter of these years was **František Kupka**, whose works on show here reveal his development from a Fauve-like manner in, for instance, his *Actress from the Cabaret* (1909–10), to the pioneering abstract compositions of 1911 onwards, such as the fluently lyrical blue and red *Fugue in Two Colours* (1912). A sensational transitional work—and one which first reveals the influence of music on his art—is *Piano Keys–Lake* (1909), in which reflections on water are effortlessly transformed into the keys of a piano. With his creation of pure abstraction two years later, Kupka experi-

mented with what he called 'cosmic architecture', which is demonstrated here in a series of ambitious canvases begun in 1911–13 and reworked at the beginning of the 1920s, some of which resemble coloured and fractured organ pipes, such as his *Perpendicular and Transverse Areas* (1913–1923). A literal climax to his art is reached in the magnificent *Story about Pistils and Stamens, 1* (1920), which has been described as a 'depiction of a cosmic sexual act'. From the 1930s onwards, his art becomes more academic and rigorously geometric, in particular in his *Abstract Painting* (1930), which comprises a white canvas marked with one vertical and two horizontal black lines: not even Mondrian could match such minimalism.

The gallery's **early 20C Czech paintings** are interspersed with a superbly representative selection of Czech sculpture, beginning with three famous nudes by **Jan Štursa**—a standing bronze of *Eve* (1908–09), a limestone carving of strong Oriental influence entitled *Melancholy Girl* (1906) and the elongated, daringly poised *Wounded Man* of 1921. Dominating **Czech 20C sculpture** in the same way that Myslbek had presided over the preceding century was **Otto Gutfreund**, who began his career in a Cubist vein in, for instance, the bronze *Cubist Bust* (1912–13), and later went on to develop a very realistic yet highly personal style devoted to the portrayal of the everyday world. These latter works, characterised by their simple, stately forms and complete lack of sentimentality,

A work by
Otto Gutfreund

as in the bronze *Family* (1925), often made use of colour, for instance, in the terracotta *Self-portrait* (1919) and the groups *Industry* and *Commerce* (both 1923) in wood and plaster respectively. They represent a truly Czech style of sculpture and their so-called Objective Realism was to be emulated by numerous other artists such as **Karel Pokorný** in *Earth* (1925) and *Ostrava* (1936), **Josef Jiřikovský** in *Girl brushing Hair* (1923), **Jan Lauda** in *The Potter* (1923), **Karel Kotrba** in *Portrait of the painter Miloslav Holý* (1924), **Bedřich Štefan** in *Girl drinking Grenadine* (1924), **Otakar Švec** in *The Motorcyclist* (1924) and **Karel Dvořák** in *The Girl Friends* (1924).

Much of the remaining space on the **third floor** is taken up with the delicate dream-like Surrealism of painters who came to the fore in the 1920s such as **Toyen**, **Jindřich Štyrský** and **Josef Šima**. More arresting and memorable examples of the influence of Surrealism are the 1930s assemblages of **Zedeněk Rykr** and **Ladislav Zívr**: Rykr used glass boxes in which to assemble a mixture of treated paper and unorthodox (and often ephemeral) materials such as pebbles, silver paper, cotton wool, wood and silver foil (as in his Orient series of 1935); Zívr also improvised from random materials but in a more three-dimensional and morbid way, as in his *Heart Incognito* (1936), in which a heart-like object is trapped in netting above a black vase. But the prize for originality must be awarded to the kinetic light sculptures of **Zdeněk Pešánek**, whose principle work on this floor is the *Torso* that formed part of a fountain exhibited at the World Exhibition of Art and Technology in Paris in 1937: this luminous, welded blend of plastic, glass, neon and lightbulbs, is like an avant-garde response to the *Venus of Milo*. Sadly, the Second World War intervened before the artist was able, as he intended, to reassemble the whole fountain on a site in between Prague's Rudolfinum and the Vltava.

Surrealism continued to dominate the work of the avant-garde (and often censored) Czech artists of the '40s and afterwards, such as **Mikuláš Medek**. But the works on the second floor that have perhaps the greatest appeal today fall into the 'Mythology of the Mundane' category, for instance the haunting urban landscapes of Jan Smetana, such as *Last Stop* (1944), **František Gross**'s ironically titled *Garden of Eden* (1943) and, above all, the works of **Kamil Lhoták**, which are a perfect blend of realism, poetry, colouristic subtlety and arresting imagery, notably the *Officer's Mess in Paris* (1947), *Baseball Player* (1947) and *Metereological Station after a Storm*.

The Dukelských hrdinů leads north of the museum to the entrance of the **Prague Exhibition Ground** (Výstaviště Praha), which was the main site of the Jubilee Exhibition of 1891; between the wars the place was used for trade fairs before being transformed into a park named until recently after the Communist journalist killed by the Nazis, Julius Fučík. The large glass and ironwork structure which faces you on entering the park was the main hall of the Jubilee Exhibition, and was built by Bedřich Münzberger and František Prášil in 1891; the adjoining Prague Pavilion, houses the remarkable **Lapidarium of the National Museum**, featuring many of the originals of famous public statues that have been replaced *in situ* by copies as well as many other Czech sculptures from the 11C–19C; this is now open Tues–Fri 12.00–18.00, and Sat and Sun 10.00–12.30 and 13.00–18.00. Behind the main hall is a large cylindrical structure containing a vast circular canvas by J. Marold of the *Battle of Lipany of*

1434 (1898); the canvas is displayed in a darkened setting, surrounded by real earth, sticks and other objects, the whole forming a powerful illusionistic recreation of the battlefield. Elsewhere in the park, which is used regularly for folkloric events and an annual reconstruction of battles in the Thirty Years War, are a sports stadium, a swimming pool, a planetarium and the main section of the Czech Pavilion designed for the Brussels World Exhibition of 1958.

A gate on the western side of this park leads into the large and wooded **Stromovka** ('Royal Enclosure'), which was laid out as a public park in 1804 on the site of a royal hunting-ground founded by King John of Luxemburg in the early 14C.

Troja

North of Holešovice-Bubeneč, on the other side of the Vltava, is the suburban district of Troja, which was named after a large Baroque country house known generally as the **Troja Château** (Trojský zámek): the easiest access by public transport is by bus No. 112 from the Praha-Holešovice metro station. This magnificent house, brashly restored in the late 1980s and early '90s, was built in 1679–85 for Count Václav Vojtěch of Sternberg; the architect was Jean-Baptiste Mathey, who introduced a French pavilion plan with projecting wings. Its principal façade is its southern one, dominated by a monumental oval staircase profusely decorated with statues of gods and goddesses battling with Titans. The rooms on the main floor boast one of the most extensive cycles of Baroque frescoes to be seen in the Czech Republic, including, in the side rooms, some amusing allegorical ceiling paintings by Francesco and Giovanni Francesco Marchetti, and illusionistic landscapes on the walls; the enormous Grand Hall is covered all over with frescoes by Abraham Godyn set in an ambitious illusionistic framework featuring fictive architecture and tapestries, one of which is marked by the shadow cast by a Moor plunging head forwards into the room.

The building now houses the collections of 19C Czech painting belonging to the **Prague Municipal Art Gallery**. Most of the leading Czech artists of this period are represented, though largely with minor works: among these artists are Viktor Barvitius, Alois Bubák, František Ženíšek, Jakub Schikaneder, Maximilian Pirner, Max Švabinský, Jan Preisler, Luděk Marold and Mikoláš Aleš. Particularly numerous are the works of Jaroslav Čermák and Václav Brožík, the latter being the author of the gallery's two most celebrated pictures, *Master Jan Hus facing the Council of Constance* and *The Election of George of Poděbrady as King of Bohemia*. Below the building's southern façade is one of the earliest examples in Bohemia of a French formal garden, with terraces adorned with eccentric ornamental vases by Bombelli. **Open** Apr–Oct Tues–Sun 10.00–18.00.

Next to the house is the entrance to Prague's **Zoo**, which was founded in 1931, and can be recommended only to those who might enjoy the experience of riding over an aviary in a chair-lift. **Open** Apr daily 09.00–17.00; May 09.00–18.00; June–Sept 09.00–19.00; Oct–Mar 09.00–16.00.

Dejvice

The suburb of Dejvice, which lies to the north of the Hradčany and to the west of Bubeneč is served by Dejvická metro station (formerly Leninova). The large square on which this station is situated forms the axis of a radiating group of wide, long avenues, one of which, Jugoslávských partyzánů, leads north to the **Hotel International**, a towering block of the 1950s inspired by Moscow University; the gloomy, spacious and oppressively marbled interior is an atmospheric reminder of the heyday of Soviet domination of Czechoslovakia. Immediately to the north of the hotel turn left on to Pod Juliškou and walk up to Na Šťáhlavce, which curves its way to the top of the wooded hill on which stands the innovatory suburban estate known as the **Baba Villa Colony**. The idea for this estate came about as a result of the exhibition 'Nový dům' ('New House'), which was organised in Brno in 1928 by the Czech architectural group known as the Werkbund. Nineteen members of the Prague Werkbund, following a general lay-out devised by Pavel Janák, subsequently created on this hill a group of 33 houses built in close consultation with the clients, who had the freedom to chose their own architect. This 'ideal estate', spaciously arranged along the parallel streets of Na ostrohu, Na Babě and Nad Paťánkou, comprises an interesting variety of Functionalist houses, including five buildings by Josef Gočár and three by Pavel Janák himself (his own house was at No. 16 Nad Paťánkou, at the edge of the estate, and with potentially beautiful views looking east towards Troja).

9 · Days out from Prague

Almost everywhere in Bohemia and even Moravia is within a relatively short distance of Prague, making the possibilities for day excursions from the capital almost endless. Included below are the major sights that fall within the administrative region of Central Bohemia, most of which can be reached by public transport in under one and a half hours; suggestions for excursions further afield are to be found in the next section. Buses are invariably the fastest and most convenient way of getting around, but train travel is generally more relaxing and should be undertaken if only for the pleasure of the often delightfully antiquated rolling stock.

Kutná Hora and Kolín

Picturesquely situated above the northern banks of the narrow and meandering Vrchlice river, Kutná Hora is a place that had until very recently a melancholic, decayed beauty. Major restoration is now rapidly turning the town into a pedestrianised showpiece, and bringing back some of the splendour of its medieval heyday, when it was the second most important town in Bohemia.

History of Kutná Hora

The rapid development of Kutná Hora in the Middle Ages was due to the discovery here, in the late 13C, of rich silver deposits, a discovery which was soon to make the Czech monarchs among the richest in Europe. Wenceslas II invited Florentine minters to found a Royal Mint at Kutná Hora, and, by

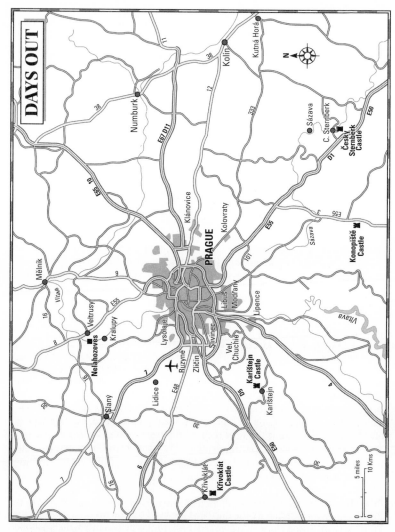

the 1380s work was begun here on one of the greatest of Bohemia's cathedrals. At the end of the century the town became the favourite residence of Wenceslas IV, but it was to suffer greatly in the course of the Hussite Wars, the retreating Hungarian troops under Sigismund of Luxemburg even setting fire to the place in 1421. Kutná Hora experienced a brief renewal of prosperity during the late 15C and early 16C, when the townspeople were able to secure for the completion of their cathedral two of the most outstanding architects of the time, Matěj Rejsek and Benedikt Ried. However, by the middle of the 16C the local silver deposits were exhausted, a crisis resulting in the cathedral being left unfinished in 1558, and the town entered a long decline which was to be consolidated by the Thirty Years War and a severe fire in 1771. Kutná Hora is today a district capital, with engineering works and a tobacco factory on its outskirts, but with an essentially unspoilt historical centre reflecting the town's many years of stagnation. Today new life is being given to the local economy both by renewed tourism and by a huge injection of cash from the American tobacco giant Philip Morris.

The highpoint of a tour to Kutná Hora is the **Cathedral of St Barbora**, which is situated in a verdant southwestern corner of the town. The cathedral represents one of the most extreme developments of the late Gothic style in Europe, and has a bizarre and exotic skyline comprising three massive tent-like forms that from a distance give the impression that some fabulous Turkish sultan has encamped here.

History of the Cathedral

The building, founded in 1388, was initially conceived on the model of a French Gothic cathedral, in emulation of Peter Parler's cathedral at nearby Kolín; by 1421, however, when work was suspended, only the eight chapels in the apse and part of the aisles had been vaulted. Work on the building was not to be resumed until 1481, first under the direction of Master Hanuš, and then, after 1489, under that of the great Matěj Rejsek, who was responsible for the vaulting of the chancel. Six years after Rejsek's death in 1506, the burghers of Kutná Hora, anxious as always to employ the most fashionable and prestigious architects of the time, called on the services of the royal architect Benedikt Ried, who had only recently completed his remarkable work for Prague Castle. The possibility that funds might run out before the massive structure originally envisaged could be finished may have encouraged Ried drastically to change the plan of the building and transform it into a three-aisled hall church, the side aisles becoming galleries, and flying buttresses being used to support sheer walls pierced with enormous, traceried windows. The vaulting of the nave was completed to his design in 1547, but just over ten years later work on the cathedral was abandoned, and the west end left as a blank wall; the present west façade is a dreary, compromise solution of the late 19C.

The fantastical character of the light and spacious interior is due largely to the extraordinary **vaulting**, comprising stiff rib patterns of exceptional complexity in the chancel and, in the nave, flowing lines of endlessly fascinating geometrical inventiveness, spreading out like tree branches from the piers before bursting out in the centre into six-petalled flowers. The furnishings of the cathedral include a pulpit of c 1560 decorated with stone reliefs of the Evangelists, 17C confessionals, and an exuberant Baroque organ. The most interesting addition to the interior are the anonymous late 15C frescoes to be found in the **Smíšek Chapel** on the southern side of the ambulatory. Jan Smíšek of Vrchoviště—a rich mine owner and the Administrator of the Royal Mines—acquired this chapel in 1485 and was buried here in 1512. The decorations on the walls, executed c 1496, include a *trompe-l'oeil* recess in which Smíšek can be seen dressed as a sacristan and preparing for a mass with the assistance of his two sons; the other scenes are the *Crucifixion, Trajan's Justice,* the *Arrival of the Queen of Sheba before Solomon,* and *Augustus with the Tiburtine Sibyl.* The figurative style of these works and their perspectival illusionism suggest a knowledge of North Italian painting of the early Renaissance.

The cathedral once stood isolated from the rest of the town, but in the late 17C the Jesuits built immediately to the north of it their largest **seminary** outside Prague. The attractive **Barborská** runs in between the long eastern façade of this building and a Baroque balustrade adorned with statues by Baugut; from here can be had one of the best views of Kutná Hora, with some of the town's finest buildings—including the distant church of St James (sv. Jakub)—standing huddled around the edge of a curving slope which is covered in gardens and falls steeply down to the Vrchlice river. Just to the north of the seminary, on the right-hand side of the street, is the **Hrádek**, a structure of 13C origin with a charming late Gothic oriel window, originally forming part of the fortifications but later adapted as the home of the Administrator of the Mines, Jan Smíšek; it now houses the town's **Mining Museum**, from where you can pick up a white coat, helmet and torch and walk through gardens down to the entrance of the medieval mines, into which you descend to a depth of 50m. **Open** Apr–Oct Tues–Sun 09.00–12.00 and 13.00–17.00.

From the First World War Memorial just to the north of the Hrádek a charming, cobbled lane called Ruthardská heads east towards the Church of St James (see below). Continuing instead north on Barborská, at the end of the street you will reach the Komenského náměstí, where you should turn left and walk up Rejskova until you come to a remarkable 12-sided **Gothic fountain** (Kašna), which was created in 1493–95 to provide the town with a supply of drinking-water uncontaminated by the mine workings: designed probably by Matěj Rejsek, this is an extensively rebuilt structure ringed with finials and blind ogee arcading. Head east of here along Husova, and take the first turning to the left, which joins up with Radnická. Directly facing you, on the northern side of the street, is the so-called **Stone House** (Kamenný dum), a late 15C structure with a much-restored gabled façade dominated by a box-shaped oriel covered all over with lively carvings; inside is a dreary local museum. Just to the east of this is the Václavské náměstí, where you should head south on Šultysova, a beautiful short street which is lined with decayed 17C and 18C buildings and leads to a Marian **plague column** of the early 18C; at the end of the street, on the left-hand side, is an excellent old beer-cellar. The exceedingly narrow Vysokokostelecká, which runs south from here, is hemmed in by narrow houses, above which rises the impressively tall Gothic tower of the **Church of St James** (sv. Jakub).

When this triple-aisled hall church was begun in the 1330s, it was conceived on a scale comparable to that of deanery churches such as the one at Plzeň, but work was brought to a halt by the Hussite Wars, leaving even the south tower unfinished; the interior, completed at a much later date, is Gothic in structure, but entirely Baroque in its furnishings, which include a high altar of *Christ and St James* by Petr Bendl.

Leaving the church by its south portal you will find immediately to your left the most important secular building in town, the former Royal Mint or **Italian Court**, which was built in 1300 for the Italian minters invited to Kutná Hora by Wenceslas II; in around 1400 the place was enlarged and remodelled as a residence for Wenceslas IV and, following the closure of the mint in 1727, was converted into a town hall, which it remained until very recently. The interior, which can be visited on a guided tour, features a ground-floor room where a selection of coins are displayed, including the most famous ones to have been minted at Kutná Hora—the Prague silver *groschens*, the last of which was made in 1547. The most important room is the early 15C **Session Hall**, which has a panelled ceiling of 1400 and two large wall-paintings of the late 19C, representing *The Election of Vladislav Jagiello* and *The Decree of Kutná Hora*—a decree passed by Wenceslas IV in 1409 whereby the rights of Czechs at Prague University were greatly improved; these late Romantic works were painted by the Spilar Brothers in collaboration with K.J. Klusáček. Another room, The Hall of Revolutionary Traditions, has a bombastic canvas of around the same date by Adolf Liebscher, depicting *Jan Žižka outside Kutná Hora*. The chapel which Wenceslas IV founded in 1400 was completely redecorated early in the 20C. **Open** Apr–Sept daily 09.00–17.00, Oct–Mar daily 10.00–16.00.

At the Havlíčkovo náměstí, which lies on the eastern side of the Italian Court, turn left to reach the large **Palackého náměstí**, the town's main square, where there are a number of fine old houses as well as a rather bleak modern hotel, the Medínek. Heading east from here on Tylova, you will pass immediately on the right-hand side, at No. 507, the 18C house where the pioneering Czech dramatist and theatre director J.K. Tyl was born in 1808; inside is a small commemorative museum to him. Continuing east on Tylova, and taking the third turning to the left, Brandlova, you will reach the late Gothic **Church of Our Lady** (Panna Maria), where the great Baroque painter Peter Brandl was buried in 1735. Return to the Palackého náměstí and head north on Na Sioně, which will take you to Jiřího z Poděbrad, where there stands a former **Ursuline Convent**, begun by K.I. Dientzenhofer on a pentagonal plan in 1734 and never finished.

One of the outlying residential districts to the east of the convent is **Sedlec**, which you can reach by a No. 1 or 4 bus. The first monument you will see as you head there from the town's ring road is the imposing church of the former **Cistercian Abbey of Sedlec**.

History of the Abbey of Sedlec
The abbey was founded in 1142, but the present church dates back to around 1300, when work was begun on a building modelled on a French cathedral, with a five-sided apse and seven radiating chapels in the chevet. This church, which was more or less complete by the 1320s, was gutted during the Hussite Wars, and was not to be rebuilt until 1702. This task was first entrusted to the German architect P.I. Bayer, but he was soon replaced by an architect at the very beginning of his career, Santini-Aichel. The new building, completed by 1706, is a masterly example of the 'Baroque-Gothic' manner peculiar to this architect, and features vaulting which is as complex as Ried's in the cathedral of St Barbora in Kutná Hora (to which it clearly owes a debt), but treated with dynamic, Baroque fluency.

At present, unfortunately, you can visit neither the church—which has been closed for many years for restoration—nor the adjoining monastic buildings (now a tobacco factory partly owned by Philip Morris), which feature a vast refectory of 1752–57, decorated with 16 enormous frescoed scenes by the Moravian painter with the appropriate name of Juda Tadeáš Supper. What you can see, however, is the nearby **ossuary** (just to the north of the church, along Zámecká), which was formed initially of the bones of 30,000 people killed in a plague of 1318; the chapel to house these was remodelled in the 18C by Santini-Aichel, and again in the 19C. In 1870 the Schwarzenberg family, who had acquired the chapel following the dissolution of the monastery in 1783, commissioned one František Rinta to arrange the skulls and bones in a decorative manner, a task which had first been undertaken in the early 16C by a half-blind monk. The results of Rinta's endeavours, which were to occupy him and members of his family for four years, are morbidly fascinating, and include chandeliers, bones hung like Christmas paper chains, and even the coat of arms of the Schwarzenberg family.

■ Open summer Tues–Sun 08.00–12.00, 13.00–17.00, winter 09.00–12.00, 13.00–16.00.

Kolín

Kolín, which has been described as 'Bohemia's Crewe', is a heavily industrialised town and one of the main railway junctions of the Czech Republic. You should come here, however, if only to see the **Deanery Church of St Bartholomew** (sv. Bartoloměje), which rises on a small hill just to the south of the main square. Begun in the late 13C, it seems to have been damaged by fire in 1349, and was partially rebuilt after 1360 by the great Peter Parler, who had been called in by the building's patron, the Abbot of Sedlec. The dark and broad nave—built around 1280, and the earliest example in Bohemia of a German Hall structure—is joined awkwardly by steps to Parler's light and elegant chancel. The large main square was rebuilt after a fire in 1734, and features on its western side a group of extraordinary gabled houses by the local Baroque architect, Josef Jedlička.

❖ **Transport**. Buses depart regularly to Kutná Hora from stand 56 at Praha-Florenc or from metro Želivského (1hr 15min). The direct trains to the town all leave from Prague's Masarykovo nádraží (1hr by the very occasional express service, and 2hrs by the normal one); if you travel from Prague's Main Station (Praha Hlavní nádraží) you have to change trains at Kolín. The main station at Kutná Hora (Kutná Hora hlavní nádraží) is near the outlying township of Sedlec; to get from here to the centre you have either to take a No. 2 or 4 bus, or else the shuttle train service to the Kutná Hora město station.

Průhonice and the Sázava valley

Průhonice, which has a famous golf course, is of interest largely for its **castle** and surrounding grounds. The castle, which dates back to the 13C, was rebuilt in a neo-Gothic style at the end of the 19C for Count Ernest Emmanuel Silva-Tarouca; it has retained, however, an old chapel with much restored 13C frescoes. Next to the chapel is an entrance to a small and enjoyable **art gallery**,

largely composed of French-inspired landscapes by Czech artists of the first half
of the 20C, including works by Antonín Slavíček, among them the delightful
Veltrusy Park (1897), Josef Ullman, Josef Hubáček, Otakar Nejedlý, Jan Slavíček,
Vilém Nowak, Otakar Kubín, Josef Kilián, Oldřich Blažíček and Václav Špála.
Especially delightful are the castle's extensive **gardens**, which were laid out at
the end of the 19C and bought by the Czech state in 1927. The gardens, which
are now administered by the Botanical Institute of the Czech Academy of
Sciences, are informal in their layout and filled with rare and exotic plants. **Open**
daily Apr–Oct.

A visit to Sázava is of more historical than architectural or artistic interest.
The former **Monastery of Sázava** is situated by the Sázava river, in the middle
of a beautiful forested area popular as a summer resort.

History of the Monastery

The monastery was founded by Prince Oldřich in around 1032, supposedly
as a result of a chance meeting in the forest with the hermit priest St
Procopius. Procopius, a Slavonic scholar, became the first abbot of the
monastery, which belonged initially to the Basilian Order, a Slavonic order
founded by Basilius the Great in the late 4C. Sázava became a great centre
of Slavonic culture, and it was here that the Slavonic liturgy was used for
the first time in Bohemia; this liturgy was to be banned after 1096 following
the expulsion of the Slavonic monks by Břetislav II. The abbey church was
rebuilt after 1315, and the whole complex greatly altered in the 17C and
18C. Shortly after its dissolution by Joseph II in 1785, the monastery was
sold at auction and converted into a private residence for Emmanuel Tiegel,
Knight of Lindenkron. Archaeological excavations carried out after 1940
have revealed fragments of the medieval monastery.

The interminably protracted guided tour around the monastery buildings is
devoted to the ground-floor rooms around the former cloisters, beginning with
displays relating to the history of the Great Moravian Empire, and including a
collection of archaeological finds from the site. The richly stuccoed early 18C
refectory is decorated with frescoes by Jan Kovář, representing the story of the
founding of the monastery. The highpoint of the tour is the chapter house,
where 14C frescoes of the *Life of the Virgin* were discovered in 1943. The upper
rooms of the monastery have a collection of locally made glass. The Gothic
church, begun in 1315, was left incomplete, and its western tower and the
arches of its nave stand today exposed in front of the present church, which
comprises an 18C remodelling of the 14C east end. The white interior has a high
altar of 1755 featuring a dynamic and elaborate sculptural surround by
Richard Prachner; the semi-circular crypt with Gothic rib vaults in brick was
restored in the 17C and again in 1950. Nearby can be seen the excavated foundations of the original 11C church.

■ Open Apr–Oct Sat, Sun 09.00–16.00, May–Sept Tues–Sun 08.00–12.00 and
13.00–17.00.

Further south along this beautiful, forested stretch of the Sázava river is the
impressive castle of **Český Šternberk**, which rises above the trees on a great

outcrop of rock. The castle was founded in around 1240, but rebuilt and strengthened in the late 15C and early 16C. Crenellations and battlements from the medieval structure can still be seen, though the present appearance of the building is due largely to further remodelling carried out in the 17C and 18C; the interior is remarkable above all for the heavy and extensive stucco decorations executed between 1660 and 1667 by the Milanese artist Carlo Brentano.

■ Open Apr, Sept, Oct Tues–Sun 09.00–12.00 and 13.00–16.00; May–Aug Tues–Sun 08.00–12.00 and 13.00–17.00.

The castle of **Konopiště** lies 2km west of the small town of Benesov, and is set high in a hilly wooded park, with Baroque statuary and strutting peacocks adorning the upper lawns. Dating back to 1300, the castle has prominent medieval features such as tall, crenellated round towers and a moat where bears were kept until very recently. The whole place was in fact completely remodelled after 1889, when it came into the possession of the ill-fated successor to the Austro-Hungarian throne, the Archduke Franz Ferdinand d'Este. Ferdinand, who was married to a member of the Bohemian Chotek family, stayed regularly at Konopiště right up to the time of his assassination in 1914, and held here in his last year secret meetings with the German Emperor Wilhelm II: Mrs Müller, from Hašek's novel *The Good Soldier Švejk*, refers to him as 'our Ferdinand ... the fat churchy one, from Konopiště'.

The heavy panelled interior of Konopiště is immensely evocative of the last days of the Habsburgs, of whom there are numerous photographs and other mementoes, including portraits of Ferdinand and his family by František Dvořák. You are shown not only Ferdinand's bedroom but also his magnificently appointed bathroom; in addition you will see a school painting by Botticelli presented to Ferdinand by the Kaiser Wilhelm, fine collections of Meissen and armoury (including an exquisitely wrought arm-piece of 1598 made for Gesualdo da Venosa by Pompeo della Cesa), and some of the earliest radiators in the Austro-Hungarian Empire. But the lasting impression of the building is of a veritable forest of antlers and other hunting trophies, of which there are an estimated 300,000.

■ Open Apr–Oct Tues–Sun 09.00–12.00; Apr and Oct Tues–Sun 13.00–15.00; May–Aug Tues–Sun 13.00–17.00.

❖ **Transport**. Weekday buses to Průhonice (15min) leave every 30 to 60mins all morning from the ČAD stand at Prague's Opatov metro station, on Line C. The other places described above are most enjoyably reached by train (from Prague's Central Station), which will take you right to the heart of the beautiful forested scenery extending immediately to the southeast of Prague. For Sázava (1hr 30min) and Český Šternbeck (2hrs) change trains at Čerčany, and alight at Sázava Černé Budy and Český Šternberk zastávka respectively. For Konopiště take the train to Benešov (1hr, via Čerčany), and walk the remaining 2kms (15mins).

If you have your own transport, you can drive north from Benešov along the E55, and leave the road after 5km to visit the village of Poříčí Nad Sázavou, where there are two Romanesque churches of the early 13C; one is the tiny cemetery Church of St Peter, while the other is the parish **Church of St Gall**, which was remodelled inside during the Baroque period but has kept its original crypt with cubic capitals. Eleven km further north along the E55 you will rejoin the D1 at Velké Popovice, a 27km drive from Prague.

Karlštejn and Křivoklát

Karlštejn is a small wine-growing village lying under the shadow of one of the largest and most fantastically shaped castles in Bohemia. **Karlštejn Castle**, which projects high above the steep and densely forested slopes behind the village, is by far the most popular sight near Prague, and attracts daily great coachloads of tourists.

History of Karlštejn Castle

The castle was built by Charles IV in the mid-14C to house the imperial crown jewels, the Bohemian royal insignia and a large collection of relics. Designed by the great French architect, Matthew of Arras, the building was begun in 1348 and completed in the remarkably short space of seven years.

The imperial jewels were removed to Prague by Sigismund of Luxemburg in 1420, shortly before the castle was besieged for seven months by the Hussites; the jewels were eventually to end up at the Hofburg in Vienna. As for the Bohemian royal insignia, these were to be returned at the outbreak of the Thirty Years War to St Vitus's Cathedral, where they can now be seen in a room above the Wenceslas Chapel. Extensively rebuilt between 1575 and 1597, the castle complex later lost its importance and was in a ruinous state when, in 1887, F. Schmidt and Josef Mocker embarked on a restoration campaign which was to be no less drastic than that of Viollet-le-Duc at Carcassonne.

Those coming to Karlštejn by car are not allowed to drive up to the castle from the village, and have to make the arduous ascent on foot, sharing the narrow, winding road with a queue of other tourists. Your spirits are at first maintained by the castle's extraordinarily romantic and picturesque profile, but begin to sag the more you realise that what you see is largely a medieval sham, which seems almost to have been devised for the tourist market. Gloomy, insensitively restored rooms await you, as well as a guided tour of numbing boredom; however, a visit to the castle is made worthwhile not only by the magnificent forest views to be had from the top, but also, and more importantly, by the outstanding 14C decorations to be found within.

After passing through two gates you will find yourself in the **Burgrave's Courtyard**, beyond which to the west steps descend to a narrow stretch of battlements containing an 80m-deep well which was built in the 14C by mining experts from Kutná Hora. You should return to the courtyard (where the castle's ticket office is to be found) to begin a tour of the main part of the castle complex, which is built up on the slope to the north of here, its highest and furthest point being the keep.

The first part of the castle which you visit is the **Imperial Palace**, where you will find displays relating to the Bohemia of Charles IV as well as a diptych by Tomaso di Modena, which is kept at present in what was once the imperial bedroom. Next you come to **The Tower of Our Lady**, which features on its second floor the Chapel of St Mary, the walls of which are covered with dark and faded murals—attributed to Nikolaus Wurmser and painted in the 1370s—representing the Apocalypse, scenes in the history of the castle's creation (including the gift from the King and Dauphin of France of two thorns from the Crown of Thorns) and Charles IV himself, who is portrayed with unflattering realism, stooped before a gilded cross. The Emperor's own, private chapel was the adjoining **St Catherine's Chapel**, where he would shut himself up for hours in deep meditation, important documents being passed to him through a hole in the west wall. This tiny chapel can literally be described as jewel-like, for Charles had the walls embellished all over with gilded plaster and a dazzling array of coloured, polished stones, leaving uncovered only some murals of saints, of slightly earlier date.

The highpoint of the castle tour should be the **Keep**, which is joined to the Tower of Our Lady by a covered, wooden gallery. Sadly, however, this has been closed for many years for restoration, and you are thus prevented at present from seeing the remarkable Chapel of the Holy Rood. This chapel, consecrated in 1360 and divided in two by a gilded iron screen, has a gilded ceiling set with glass stars and walls encrusted with no less than 2200 semi-precious stones as well as 128 painted wooden panels by one of the greatest Bohemian painters of the 14C, Master Theodoric. The relics were once to be found behind the panels, while the jewels and insignia were kept in a niche behind the altar, over which Tomaso da Modena's diptych was originally placed.

■ Open Jan–Mar and Nov–Dec daily 09.00–15.00; Apr, Oct daily 09.00–16.00; May, Jun, Sept daily 09.00–17.00; July, Aug daily 09.00–18.00.

Křivoklát Castle lies 21km further west of Karlštejn, hidden among trees above a tiny tributary of the Berounka. It is another of Bohemia's royal castles, but a less spoilt one than Karlštejn, and with a pleasantly ramshackle character.

History of Křivoklát Castle

Founded in 1109, the castle was acquired in the mid-13C as a royal residence by Přemysl Otakar II, and was later inherited by Charles IV. Charles spent little of his time here, in contrast to his son Wenceslas IV, who was a passionate huntsman and came frequently to hunt around Křivoklát; the place provided him with respite from the duties of kingship, and he even burnt down the comfortable dwellings in the castle's outer bailey so that he would not be too troubled by emissaries coming to visit him here. He strengthened the fortifications and undertook much rebuilding at Křivoklát, but the present appearance of the castle is due largely to work carried out at the end of the 15C by Vladislav Jagiello.

The Habsburg Emperor Rudolph II stayed here several times but in 1658 the Habsburgs were obliged first to pawn the castle to John Adolph of Schwarzenberg and then to sell it to the Counts of Wallenstein. After 1685 the building came into the possession of the Fürstenbergs, who were to be responsible for much rebuilding and restoration work in the 19C and early 20C, work which was partially supervised by the leading neo-Gothicist Josef Mocker.

The castle at Křivoklát comprises a picturesque and slightly run-down assemblage of structures, dominated at the narrow, eastern end by a tall, round tower. The central building is the royal palace, which features on its south façade a delicately carved oriel window, adorned with relief carvings of Vladislav Jagiello and his son Louis. The interior, which has been gutted several times by fire, is remarkable above all for the chapel attached to the eastern end of the palace. Begun in the 13C but altered in the late 15C, it has elaborate late Gothic vaulting to which have been added wooden and brightly coloured skeletal ribs supporting a pendulant boss; the stalls are of the late 15C, as is the splendidly intricate altarpiece, a structure in polychromed wood dedicated to the life of the Virgin and attributed to a Litoměřice artist. The 13C library, once one of the most important in Bohemia, has today a largely 19C appearance. Some rooms off the outer bailey house a large collection of hunting guns.

■ Open April, May, Sept and Oct Tues–Sun 09.00–17.00, June–Aug Tues–Sun 09.00–18.00, Nov–Mar Tues–Sun 09.00–16.00.

❖ **Transport**. Trains to Karlštejn depart hourly (40min) from Prague's Smíchov Station; further up the line is the small riverside town of Beroun (50mins by express train from Prague), from where you can take the less regular Rakovník-bound train (every 2 hours) to Křivoklát (a further 50mins). There is a direct train to Křivoklát from Prague's Smíchov Station on Saturday mornings; there are also regular buses going there from Prague at weekends, leaving from Dejvice metro station (about 1hr 30mins).

Lidice

Few places in Europe testify so poignantly to Nazi atrocities as Lidice, situated 20km northwest of Prague in a grim and flat coal-mining area. The present village, a characterless grid of the post-war years, lies just to the west of the extensive memorial marking the site of the previous village, a place which the Nazis had hoped to obliterate completely from all maps but which is now, ironically, one of the most visited of Czechoslovakia's war monuments.

Despite being in the middle of an ugly, built-up area, the memorial itself is spread over a pleasant green slope fringed with distant pines. At the higher end of the hill are the **Rose Garden of Friendship and Peace** and a large and austere arcaded memorial centred around an eternal flame. At the end of the eastern arcade is a **museum** containing photographs of the murdered villagers and other sad mementoes, such as identification cards pierced by bullet-holes; visitors are also shown an old documentary film which includes an ironic last sequence in which a smiling Stalin promises an end to all of Czechoslovakia's troubles. A path below the museum leads down the green slope to the mass grave of the murdered men, adjoining which is the reconstructed wall of the farm where they were shot. Further down are the foundations of the village church and school, the latter once bearing the inscription, 'School, My Happiness'.

■ Museum open Apr–Sept daily 08.00–16.00;Oct–Mar daily 08.00–17.00.

Massacre at Lidice

The destruction of the village of Lidice on 10 June 1942 was the most notorious of the many Nazi reprisals that followed the assassination of the German Protector of Czechoslovakia, R. Heydrich. Lidice appears to have been chosen for no apparent reason other than that it belonged to a coal-mining region with a strong Socialist tradition. The official Nazi explanation was that the villagers were all partisans who had supported Heydrich's assassins, though it was later to transpire that the Nazis themselves had compromised the place by hiding a large cache of weapons in a mill outside the village. On the evening of 9 June 1942, shortly after placing these weapons, members of the Gestapo and the SS surrounded Lidice, rounding up all the village men into a farmyard and taking the women and young children to the village school. In the course of the night 173 men were executed, the oldest being a man of 84, the youngest being not yet 15; 11 more were killed early the following day after returning from night-shift in the mines. The women were all sent to concentration camps, as were most of the children (the majority being eventually gassed in Poland); the more German-looking children were given German names and placed in German homes. The village was razed to the ground, buried under soil and its name obliterated. The only male villager later to return was a murderer who had been in a Prague prison, and went back to Lidice one day hoping to surprise his mother and ask her forgiveness for his crime. The story of his return home has fired the imagination of several Czech writers, most notably Bohumil Hrabal in his novel, *I Served the King of England*: 'The murderer sat down, his hands hanging over his knees like two flippers, then stood up again and stumbled through that moonlit landscape like a drunk. He stopped by what looked like a post in the ground, fell down, and embraced it. It wasn't a post at all, it was what was left of a tree trunk with the stump of a single branch on it, as though it had been used as a gallows. This, said the murderer, used to be our walnut tree, this is where our garden was, and here ... he knelt down and felt around with his hands for the crumbled foundations of the house and the farm buildings.'

The decision to rebuild the village and erect a commemorative memorial to the old Lidice was taken almost immediately after the Soviet 'liberation' of Czechoslovakia in May 1945. An architectural competition was subsequently held, the winners of which were the architects, V. Hilský, Z. Jirsák, F. Marek, R. Podzemný and A. Teuzer; the foundation stone of the new village was laid in June 1947. In the summer of 1954, the Chairman of the British committee 'Lidice Shall Live' proposed to enlarge the memorial with the creation of a 'Rose Garden of Friendship and Peace'; opened in 1955, this was created from rose seedlings sent from all over the world.

❖ **Transport**. Lidice is a short bus journey from Prague on the line from the Dejvická metro station to Kladno (30mins); buses to Kladno leave every 30 to 60 minutes, but do not take the direct one (*přímý spoj*), which does not stop at Lidice. For those travelling by car, Lidice lies 2km west of the dual carriageway of Road 7.

Nelahozeves, Veltrusy and Mělník

The quiet and attractive village of **Nelahozeves** lies 2km north of the small industrial town of Kralupy. The composer Antonín Dvořák was born there in 1841, in an early 19C house marked today by a plaque. Dvořák's father was the local butcher and, at the back of the house, there is an outdoor toilet built in what was once the slaughter house; the house itself is now a commemorative **Dvořák Museum** containing mementoes and furniture from the composer's childhood.

Crowning the hill which rises immediately to the south of the house is the village's impressive Renaissance **castle**, which was built in the 1550s, possibly by Bonifác Wohlmut, for Florian Griespek of Griespach, a wealthy Bavarian nobleman in the service of Rudolph I; the place, now back in the possession of its pre-Communist owners, the Lobkowicz family, has been extensively restored by the Boston-bred William Lobkowicz, who puts on dinners for visiting tourists. Sgraffito decorations extensively cover the exterior of the building, while inside is a large hall with elegant Renaissance fireplaces as well as painted and stuccoed scenes of Classical history and mythology.

The greater part of the enormous interior is taken up today by old master paintings and sculptures from the former Lobkowicz Picture Gallery at Roudnice. The gallery is particularly strong on Spanish works, and though the supposed Velasquez painting is obviously a school work, there are fine portraits by Juan Pantoja de la Cruz and Sánchez Coello; the other works are mainly by 16C–18C Flemish and Italian artists, including Conrad Wiertz, Frans Francken, Cornelis van der Voort, Antonio Molinari, G.M. Preti, G.P. Panini, and Canaletto (a large view of a *Carnival on the Thames*, 1748). The 19C is represented principally by a romantic evocation of a monastery by Granet, suggestive nocturnal scenes by Jakub Schikaneder, and a view of Nelahozeves in 1841 by Carl Robert Croll.

On the other side of the Vltava to Nelahozeves is one of the most beautiful country houses near Prague, **Veltrusy**, a place which inspired the setting of Dvořák's opera, *The Jacobins*. This former residence of the Chotek family was built in the 1720s on a marshy, wooded site known as 'the island'. The house, comprising four small wings radiating from a domed cylindrical hall, was inspired by the pleasure palace designs of Fischer von Erlach.

The interior was extensively remodelled after 1760 when the then owner, Rudolf Chotek, was made Austria's first Supreme Chancellor; it contains fine collections of porcelain and 18C furniture, much Rococo stuccowork, and several painted ceilings including, in the main hall, an ambitious composition described in the English brochure to the house as 'an allegory of the four periods'. The main façade of the house, featuring a great staircase adorned with statuary, overlooks a French formal garden of the early 18C.

Behind the house, however, extends a vast wooded park which was begun shortly after a great flood in 1764, and came to be one of the greatest examples of romantic landscaping in Bohemia, with numerous splendid follies, including a mock medieval mill, a Doric pavilion, a Chinese pheasantry, a Greek rotunda and a bizarre Egyptian structure erected during the wake of publicity following Napoleon's Egyptian campaign of 1816–19. The park today, more romantic than ever for being in a slightly dilapidated state, attracts numerous weekend excursionists from Prague.

Nineteen kilometres north of Veltrusy is the small town and wine-growing centre of **Mělník**, which is beautifully situated on a vine-covered hill rising above the confluence of the rivers Vltava and Labe; the vines were brought originally from Burgundy by Charles IV. The dominant landmarks are the tall steeple of the 15C–16C **Church of SS Peter and Paul** and the imposing bulk of the adjoining **castle**. The castle, which dates back to a Slavonic hill-fort of the 10C, was the occasional residence of the Bohemian queens up to 1475. The present structure—the result of rebuilding and remodelling carried out in the 16C and 17C—houses both a small **Viticultural Museum** and a well and spaciously arranged **art gallery** devoted to Czech painters of the 17C and 18C, including Willman, Kupecký, Jan Liška, Václav V. Reiner, Jan Jiří Heinsch and Karel Škréta. Also to be found here is the *Zámecká Wine Bar and Restaurant*, where you can try the local wines while enjoying a steep view over vines down to the river. **Open** Oct–Dec 10.00–16.00; May–Sept 10.00–18.00.

❖ **Transport**. Unless you have a car, the best way of seeing this attractive stretch of the Vltava north of Prague is by a combination of bus and train. Trains depart regularly from Prague's Masaryk Station to Nelahozeves (30mins; alight at Nelahozeves zastávka); one stop further on is the bridge leading over the river to the château at Veltrusy. There are hourly buses from Veltrusy to Mělník (25mins), which can also be reached directly by bus from Prague (45mins). Buses depart both from the Florenc bus station and the Holešovice metro station.

10 · Further afield

Listed below are some of the major places of interest beyond Central Bohemia that are easily accessible by public transport and can be visited (albeit hurriedly) on day excursions from Prague; they are described fully in the *Blue Guide to the Czech and Slovak Republics*, which also suggests local hotels and pensions.

Western Bohemia

Bohemia's two most popular tourist areas are Western and Southern Bohemia. The appeal of Western Bohemia is due principally to the spa towns of **Karlovy Vary** (Karlsbad) and **Mariánské Lázně** (Marienbad) with their lavish turn-of-the-century buildings so brilliantly evocative of the Côte d'Azur. They can be visited via the large industrial town of **Plzeň**, which is popular with tourists for its brewery and imposing main square and cathedral.

❖ **Transport**. Travel from Prague to Karlovy Vary is best undertaken by bus (2hrs 20mins) and to Mariánské Lázně by train (3hrs to 3hrs 30mins) via Plzeň (1hr 30mins to 2hrs from Prague). The two spa towns are linked by a regular bus service (50mins) and a slow but very beautiful train service (1hr 40mins).

Southern Bohemia

The great draws of Southern Bohemia are its little-spoilt, rolling scenery of lakes and forests, and its wonderful series of attractive medieval and Renaissance towns, including the Hussite stronghold of **Tábor**, with its impressive hill-top

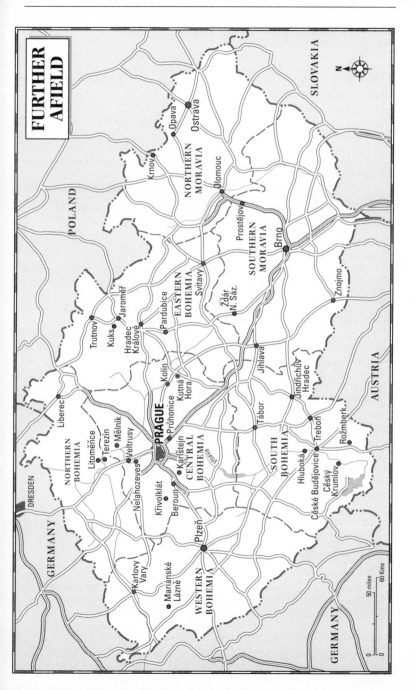

position above a lake. A good starting-pointing for the enchanting if now over-prettified '**Rose Towns**' in the southern half of the region is the large town of České Budějovice, which has one of the Czech Republic's most sensational main squares. From here you can go on to visit Český Krumlov, Třeboň, Jindřichův Hradec and Rožmberk, as well as the spectacular neo-Gothic fantasy of **Hluboká nad Vltavou**, Bohemia's most visited castle after Karlstein. The once atmospherically decayed **Český Krumlov** is now one of Europe's most congested tourist destinations.

❖ *Transport*. Tábor is on the main Prague–Vienna railway line (2hrs 15mins from Prague). The bus journey from Prague to České Budějovice takes from 2hrs 25mins to 3hrs, and the train journey from 2hrs 30mins to 4hrs 20mins. From here the towns of Český Krumlov (40mins), Třeboň (45mins), Jindřichův Hradec (1hr) and Rožmberk (1hr 30mins), and Hluboká nad Vltavou (20mins) are accessible by bus. Český Krumlov is linked directly to Prague by a thrice daily bus service (3hrs 20mins).

Northern Bohemia

An extremely popular day excursion from Prague is to the former Jewish ghetto and prison at **Terezín**, which lies in the heavily industrialised and polluted region of Northern Bohemia; you should combine a visit here with a trip to the large town of **Litoměřice**, 3km to the north, which is distinguished not only by its Baroque architecture, by Octavio Broggio, but also by one of the great jewels of Bohemian Renaissance painting, the anonymous *Litoměřice Altarpiece*.

❖ *Transport*. Travel to Terezín by bus from Prague's Florenc Station (1hr and 15mins).

Eastern Bohemia

Anyone interested in modern art and architecture should go to the town of **Hradec Králové** in Eastern Bohemia, which has a wealth of innovative architecture of the early years of the 20C and, overlooking the Baroque main square, a modern art gallery rivalled in the Czech Republic only by Prague's newly opened gallery in the Trade Fair Palace. The small town of **Kuks** is worth a long journey on account of the deeply expressive Baroque sculptures by Matthias Braun, some of which are carved into the rocks in the surrounding wood.

❖ *Transport*. Hradec Kralové is reached from Prague by bus (1hr 30mins). From there six buses a day go to Kuks (40mins).

Moravia

A further and more distant place of pilgrimage for lovers of the Baroque is the town of **Žďár nad Sázavou** in Moravia, which can easily be visited on a day trip from Prague. Though the town itself is unremarkable, the beautiful wooded surroundings contain some extraordinary chapels by Bohemia's most original architect, Santini-Aichel.

❖ *Transport*. Žďár nad Sázavou is on the main Prague–Brno railway line: there are fourteen trains a day (2hrs 30mins to 3hrs 30mins).

Index